THE AGE OF ELIZABETH IN THE AGE OF JOHNSON

In *The Age of Elizabeth in the Age of Johnson,* Jack Lynch explores eighteenth-century British conceptions of the Renaissance, and the historical, intellectual, and cultural uses to which the past was put during the period. Scholars, editors, historians, religious thinkers, linguists, and literary critics all defined themselves in relation to "the last age" or "the age of Elizabeth." Seventeenth- and eighteenth-century thinkers reworked older historical schemes to suit their own needs, turning to the age of Petrarch and Poliziano, Erasmus and Scaliger, Shakespeare, Spenser, and Queen Elizabeth to define their culture in contrast to the preceding age. They derived a powerful sense of modernity from the comparison, which proved essential to the constitution of a national character. This interdisciplinary study will be of interest to cultural as well as literary historians of the eighteenth century.

JACK LYNCH is assistant professor of English at Rutgers University. He is co-editor, with Paul J. Korshin, of *The Age of Johnson: A Scholarly Annual*. He is the author of *A Bibliography of Johnsonian Studies, 1986–1998* (2000) and *Samuel Johnson's Dictionary: Selections from the 1755 Work that Defined the English Language* (2002).

THE AGE OF ELIZABETH IN THE AGE OF JOHNSON

JACK LYNCH

CAMBRIDGE
UNIVERSITY PRESS

PUBLISHED BY THE PRESS SYNDICATE OF THE UNIVERSITY OF CAMBRIDGE
The Pitt Building, Trumpington Street, Cambridge CB2 1RP, United Kingdom

CAMBRIDGE UNIVERSITY PRESS
The Edinburgh Building, Cambridge, CB2 2RU, UK
40 West 20th Street, New York, NY 10011-4211, USA
477 Williamstown Road, Port Melbourne, VIC 3207, Australia
Ruiz de Alarcón 13, 28014 Madrid, Spain
Dock House, The Waterfront, Cape Town 8001, South Africa

http://www.cambridge.org

First published 2003

Printed in the United Kingdom at the University Press, Cambridge

Typeface Baskerville Monotype 11/12.5 pt   *System* LATEX 2ε   [TB]

A catalogue record for this book is available from the British Library

Library of Congress Cataloguing in Publication data
Lynch, Jack (John T.)
The age of Elizabeth in the age of Johnson / Jack Lynch.
p.   cm. –
Includes bibliographical references (p. 198) and index.
ISBN 0 521 81907 5
1. Great Britain – History – Elizabeth, 1558–1603 – Historiography.   2. English
literature – Early modern, 1500–1700 – History and criticism – Theory, etc.   3. Literature and
history – Great Britain – History – 18th century.   4. Historiography – Great Britain – History –
18th century.   5. Great Britain – Intellectual life – 18th century.   6. Renaissance – England –
Historiography.   7. Influence (Literary, artistic, etc.)   1. Title.
DA355. L96 2002
942.5′5′072041 – dc21   2002067364

ISBN 0 521 81907 5 hardback

Contents

Preface

Perhaps it is best to begin with what this book is not. It is not a catalogue of Renaissance sources and analogues for Johnson's works: W. B. C. Watkins produced such a list in 1936, and more than six decades later it needs little modification. Nor does it chronicle eighteenth-century responses to the major works and authors of the English Renaissance – what Johnson's contemporaries had to say about Skelton, for instance, or Marlowe – since that task is ably fulfilled by Routledge's *Critical Heritage* series and other reception histories. Neither yet does it tell the story of eighteenth-century Shakespeareanism or Miltonism, which critics such as G. F. Parker, Michael Dobson, Jean Marsden, Margreta de Grazia, and Dustin Griffin have done admirably. My work, though indebted to all of these, follows a different path, one pointed out, if not blazed, by René Wellek. In 1941, Wellek proposed "A 'History of English Literary History,'" which he believed "a legitimate and even urgent task of English scholarship" (Wellek, *The Rise of English Literary History*, p. v). In the intervening half-century, few have shared Wellek's sense of urgency; but it may now be time to synthesize the scholarship on the history of literature and of literary studies, and to try to discern significant patterns.

This book is just such an essay in the history of literary history: it is a study of the eighteenth century's conception of the era we have come to call the Renaissance. It addresses the ways in which the age of Elizabeth, Shakespeare, and Milton was conceived as a literary and cultural epoch in Great Britain. For the first time since the Italian humanists insisted on their own break with their putatively barbarous medieval past, British writers looked back on the fifteenth through the seventeenth centuries and saw not continuity but a break – they looked at their predecessors across an epochal chasm. Elizabeth's age was treated as a period both chronologically and temperamentally distant from the age of Johnson. More important, eighteenth-century thinkers, by marking the *terminus ad quem* of the previous age, marked the *terminus a quo* of their own; their sense of their own cultural identity was inseparable from the identity of their ancestors. I argue, therefore, that historiography amounts to cultural self-constitution, and focus on the uses to which this idea of "the last age" was put. At the center of the project stands Samuel Johnson, one of the most perceptive cultural historiographers of the century, through whose works flow the most important currents of contemporary thought. Johnson is our guide to the various and often competing discourses of the cultural history of the Renaissance.

This work, then, has two central concerns. The first is to argue that eighteenth-century British thinkers had a notion of what we now call the Renaissance and that, while it differs in many respects from our own essentially Burckhardtian Renaissance, it was a genuine periodic conception of the age as a whole. The second is to demonstrate the importance of historiographical language, metaphors, and methods in the culture of the eighteenth century, and thereby to show how historiography is inseparable from cultural identity. I argue, in other words, that eighteenth-century British identity is tightly bound up with what it meant to be modern.

"Modern" is, of course, a notoriously slippery term, and never has a single meaning. Many periodic schemes are operating within a culture at any time: today we measure the lifetime of the modern languages in centuries, modern art in decades, modern popular music in years, and modern computer equipment in months. Even in academic historical discourse, where one might expect greater precision, the word "modern" may legitimately mean post-classical or post-medieval, post-Industrial Revolution or post-Great War – though always post-something, since the present derives its identity from comparison with the past. None of these schemes of periodization necessarily contradicts any of the others, whether in the eighteenth century or the twenty-first. When I make claims about periodization, therefore, I am focusing on only one of the many ways eighteenth-century Britons divided history, the one I find most illuminating. There were others, as when critics like Blackmore and Ferguson drew up schemes for a universal history that subsumed dozens of centuries under a single rubric, or (conversely) when writers in the 1750s looked back on Addison and Steele in the 1710s and remarked on the great distance that separated their ages.

I have had to be very selective. Much can be said about Continental attitudes toward the past, but my attention is focused on Britain. I do not want to suggest that the Renaissance is the only context, or even the most important context, in which to understand eighteenth-century

British culture: Johnson's age defined itself in relation to antiquity and the Middle Ages, France and Spain, the Druids and the Tahitians. Its culture cannot be reduced to a mere reaction to the culture of two centuries before. The revival of learning is, however, an important context, and while I do not presume to present a comprehensive account of eighteenth-century identity, I try to pay attention to the part one age played in forming another. Even this is far too large a question for any single study to cover definitively, and much has been omitted. Bacon's place in eighteenth-century science; Castiglione's role in new notions of politeness; Reynolds's late fascination with Michelangelo; Shakespeare's influence on sensibility – all deserve inquiry, but limitations of time and space have kept them out of this book.

Nomenclature is inevitably a problem in discussing a notion that had not yet received a name. A formulation like "Johnson's Renaissance" is enticing but dangerously anachronistic: it would have made no sense to Johnson himself. As I argue in the Introduction and throughout this work, though, I believe that the eighteenth century had a nascent periodic conception, however inchoate, of the years from roughly the beginning of the fifteenth century to the middle of the seventeenth. Using strictly eighteenth-century terminology ("the restoration of polite letters") would be misleading and, after twenty or thirty appearances, positively cloying. Relying on more cautious circumlocutions, on the other hand, would be too self-conscious, and would perhaps add little precision. My approach is therefore unapologetically eclectic – sometimes uncritically borrowing terms like "the revival of learning" and even "the Dark Ages" (though always, I hope, with the understanding that the terms are not mine), sometimes using comparatively value-free terms like "the fifteenth and sixteenth centuries," but often simply using the word "Renaissance" to refer to a period that at least chronologically approximates our own idea of the word – or did, before "early modern" began to edge out "Renaissance" in English and history departments.

With other periodic terms I have been less cavalier. I have, for instance, avoided calling the eighteenth century "Neoclassical," "Augustan," or "Enlightenment." Such terms are always reductive and often deceptive, and while their histories would make for an interesting study, it is not mine. That leaves no convenient label, however, for Britain's notoriously "long" eighteenth century; by "eighteenth century" I usually mean the Restoration and eighteenth century, from roughly 1660 to 1800, and try to be explicit whenever confusion is a real threat.

ACKNOWLEDGEMENTS

In writing this book I have been blessed by the assistance of the learned and the shelter of academic bowers. It began as a doctoral dissertation at the University of Pennsylvania, where I was fortunate to have three uncommonly perceptive readers, Paul J. Korshin, Stuart Curran, and Maureen Quilligan. Rebecca Bushnell, D'Maris Coffman, Margreta de Grazia, Robert DeMaria, Jr., Nicholas Hudson, John Richetti, Lana Schwebel, Erik Simpson, and Howard Weinbrot all read parts of the typescript at various points of its development, and provided valuable advice. The catalogue of others to whom I am indebted is too long to recount, but this book would not exist without the expertise of the participants of Kevin Berland's virtual Academy, C18-L, and the flesh-and-blood members of Penn's eighteenth-century reading group. I am pleased to acknowledge their collective contributions. My colleagues at Rutgers University have been unfailingly supportive, and it has been a real pleasure to work with Linda Bree of Cambridge University Press. I would also like to thank the staffs of Van Pelt Library of the University of Pennsylvania, the Dana and Alexander Libraries of Rutgers University, the Firestone Library of Princeton University, the Bobst Library of New York University, the Butler Library of Columbia University, the New York Public Library, the British Library, and the Bodleian Library for their assistance.

Material from several chapters has appeared in print in earlier versions: "Studied Barbarity: Johnson, Spenser, and the Idea of Progress," *The Age of Johnson: A Scholarly Annual* 9 (1998): 81–108; "The Ground-Work of Stile: Johnson on the History of the Language," *Studies in Philology* 97, no. 4 (2000): 454–72; and "Betwixt Two Ages Cast: Milton, Johnson, and the English Renaissance," *Journal of the History of Ideas* 61, no. 3 (July 2000): 397–413. I am grateful for permission to reprint them here.

Final thanks go to my wife, Laura.

This book is dedicated to the memory of my father.

Note on the texts and citation

Texts are reproduced *literatim*, with the following exceptions. Obsolete typography – long *s*, running quotation marks, macrons signifying omitted letters, and so on – is made to comply with modern usage. Inverted letters and other obvious compositors' errors are silently corrected. Headwords italicized in the illustrative quotations in the *Dictionary* appear in roman, and in passages predominantly in italics, italics and roman are reversed. Black letter type used for emphasis is italicized. Except where noted, all translations are my own.

Notes provide short-title citations, with full bibliographical details in the Bibliography. In the interest of minimizing intrusive superscripts, I have often consolidated several citations into a single note, limiting them when possible to one per paragraph.

Abbreviations

Dictionary	Samuel Johnson, *A Dictionary of the English Language*, 2 vols. (London, 1755).
Letters	*The Letters of Samuel Johnson*, ed. Bruce Redford, 5 vols. (Princeton: Princeton University Press, 1992–94).
Life	James Boswell, *The Life of Samuel Johnson, LL.D.*, ed. G. B. Hill, rev. L. F. Powell, 6 vols. (Oxford: Clarendon Press, 1934–64).
Lives	Samuel Johnson, *Lives of the English Poets*, ed. G. B. Hill, 3 vols. (Oxford: Clarendon Press, 1905).
Miscellanies	*Johnsonian Miscellanies*, ed. G. B. Hill, 2 vols. (Oxford: Clarendon Press, 1897).
Rambler	Samuel Johnson, *The Rambler*, ed. Walter Jackson Bate and Albrecht B. Strauss, vols. III–V of the Yale Edition of the *Works of Samuel Johnson* (New Haven: Yale University Press, 1969).
Shakespeare	*Johnson on Shakespeare*, ed. Arthur Sherbo, vols. VII and VIII of the Yale Edition of the *Works of Samuel Johnson* (New Haven: Yale University Press, 1968).
1787 *Works*	*The Works of Samuel Johnson*, ed. Sir John Hawkins, 11 vols. (London, 1787).
1825 *Works*	*The Works of Samuel Johnson*, 11 vols. (Oxford, 1825).

Introduction

"Eighteenth-century historians," writes Karen O'Brien, "had no word for 'Renaissance,' and this concept did not form part of their schemes of historical periodisation."[1] She has a point: the word "Renaissance" first appeared in English around 1840. It is therefore only natural that Herder, Burckhardt, Pater, Hegel, and Marx should figure larger than Johnson, Warton, Gray, Gibbon, and Hume in studies of the origins of the idea of the Renaissance.

But while the eighteenth century did without some useful critical vocabulary, the lack of the term did not altogether prevent the age of Johnson from recognizing the phenomenon. Granted, the late fourteenth through the early seventeenth centuries were not christened until the nineteenth. Still, eighteenth-century critics gave serious thought to the predecessors whom their successors were to name. Their ideas can tell us much, not only about the Renaissance but about eighteenth-century Britain as well: historiography was a part of its intellectual character. The age of Johnson often defined itself in relation to the age of Elizabeth.

THE SENSE OF RELATION

History never comes pre-sliced, and eighteenth-century Britons were given no tidily wrapped Renaissance to discuss: they had to invent it first. Historians make the past comprehensible by dividing the undifferentiated continuum of real-world events into discrete periods, against which that multitude of events can be understood. As Benedetto Croce put it nearly a century ago, "To *think* history is certainly *to divide it into periods*." Marshall Brown makes the same point more grudgingly: "Periods are entities we love to hate. Yet we cannot do without them."[2]

Periodization is a fundamentally structuralist enterprise, for it means deriving identity from difference. It is the sense of relation, what Uwe Japp calls *Beziehungssinn*, that gives an era its character: an age has meaning only in relation to the ages that surround it. The Middle Ages, for instance, are "middle" not for any intrinsic reasons, but because they come between antiquity and modernity. Epochs are imposed in retrospect, and periodization is therefore never entirely disinterested or objective. The past is defined in terms of its relationship to other ages, including the present, in an attempt to extract the most useful or satisfying narrative out of that past. It is therefore inevitable that historical periods should serve the needs of the present.[3]

It is also perhaps inevitable that they should be distorting, or at least limiting. Whether or not historical objectivity can ever be attained, period boundaries are obviously subjective and arbitrary, and the imposition of names on decades, centuries, or millennia is always and self-evidently reductive. They are provisional aids to comprehension, not objective truths, and should always be regarded with circumspection. Far from being a problem, though, this reduction is the whole point of periodization: it reduces the undifferentiated flux of centuries, years, and days down to a manageable body of knowledge. Much is lost, but much, too, is gained; and that balance of gains and losses provides insights into the cultures that draw the lines.

Some of the most enduring acts of periodization come out of cultural movements that divide themselves from their immediate predecessors, dividing *us* from *them*, *now* from *then*.[4] The invocation of an ever-new sense of *now* (along with a resulting series of *then*s) amounts to a declaration of modernity. The most important such declaration, and perhaps the most important moment in the history of Western periodization, came when a group of Florentine scholars of the fourteenth and fifteenth centuries traded the classical and Christian models of six ages or four monarchies for a new model, one with three ages: ancient, middle, and modern.[5] In this transformation, the central figure is Francesco Petrarca: for him, defining modernity meant first defining a post-classical Dark Age against which to measure the brightness of modern enlightenment. He never gave a definitive account of a modern world, although by allying himself with a glorious antiquity instead of a debased "modern" age – what we call the Middle Ages – he hinted at the dawning of a new era, one that would restore the learning of the ancients.[6]

The Petrarchan legacy was inherited by succeeding centuries, as the humanists who followed him – Biondo, Villani, Ficino, Erasmus, Valla – used the new tripartite history to distinguish their enlightened age from the ignorant one that came before. They carved themselves a place in history by portraying their predecessors as barbarians, and in telling their now-familiar story of barbarity defeated by enlightenment they helped to bring about a revolution in statecraft, scholarship, the arts, science, and eventually religion. The Renaissance recognized – or at least propagandized – itself as something new, something *not medieval*. Europe had passed through a Dark Age and was at last emerging on the other side, an emergence christened by Vasari a *rinascita*, a rebirth. From its origin in the late fourteenth century, the new paradigm remained essentially intact for about three hundred years; indeed, in spite of countless challenges, it remains our dominant conception of European history, providing the terms in which even revisionists discuss periodization.

But the recognition of the Renaissance as an age, a "true period," could not be complete until later, when it ceased to be *now* and became a *then* that could be discussed from outside. Historiographical orthodoxy holds that the Renaissance became such a period only in the nineteenth century. That was indeed an important age for historiography and the philosophy of history: in the wake of the great Romantic historians came the beginnings of a scientific historiography, invested with new notions of nation, race, progress, historical destiny. And one of the greatest of the nineteenth-century historians was the most influential voice in establishing our ideas of the Renaissance. If the invention of the age is to be credited to one person, it is Jacob Burckhardt, who dominates most histories of the idea of the Renaissance.

Wallace K. Ferguson provides the best account of the development of this idea. The nineteenth-century historians, he argues, out of an inchoate cluster of paradigms, metaphors, and terms dating back to the fourteenth century, pieced together a notion of the period as a whole. In Burckhardt, the early humanists' self-conception is overlaid with nineteenth-century ideas about art, the state, and the self, and this amalgam is our inheritance. Even after a century and a half of revisionist history, Burckhardt's Renaissance is fundamentally our Renaissance, the often unconscious foundation of many of our intellectual and institutional structures: Burckhardt, in the words of two modern commentators, is still "our great original."[7] Ferguson's chapter titles are instructive, and tell this tale of Burckhardtian historiography almost by themselves. Schlegel, Winckelmann, Ruskin, and Sismondi represent "Conflicting Trends and the Beginnings of a Periodic Concept"; then comes "Burckhardt and the Formation of the Modern Concept"; followed by "The Burckhardtian Tradition"; and finally "Reaction against the Burckhardtian Tradition."

THE GOLDEN AGE

Perhaps, though, we should not rush so quickly from the fifteenth century to the nineteenth. Pausing on the age of Johnson may give us insights not only into the history of the idea of the Renaissance before Burckhardt, but also into the eighteenth century. Exploring what the eighteenth century made of the Renaissance may help us to understand what the eighteenth century made of itself.

The obstacles are considerable. Eighteenth-century Britons, to begin with, had no name for the period. "Renaissance," as we have seen, appeared only in the middle of the nineteenth century, and the noun "humanist" in 1809: our favorite shorthand terms for the age and its central intellectual movement were unavailable. We shall search in vain for any eighteenth-century expression of what the age meant as clear as this one by Michelet, on the first page of his *Renaissance* (1855): "L'aimable mot de Renaissance ne rappelle aux amis du beau que l'avènements d'un art nouveau et le libre essor de la fantaisie. Pour l'érudit, c'est la rénovation des études de l'Antiquité; pour les légistes, le jour qui commence à luire sur le discordant chaos de nos vielles coutumes."[8] The nineteenth-century historians – Burckhardt, Michelet, Pater, Symonds – disagreed over many points, but all found the Renaissance a recognizable and describable phenomenon; in them, the age coheres. Nineteenth-century audiences knew what they were talking about in a way no eighteenth-century reader could have understood. But even though eighteenth-century Britons had no name for or tidy summary of the age, they did have a sense that Europe had undergone major cultural changes beginning some time around the fifteenth century, and that their own intellectual character was tightly bound up with those changes. The want of a single term for the period was a problem solved in various and often inconsistent ways, but what matters is that eighteenth-century writers recognized the lack of such a term as a problem.

Since we will find no neat accounts of what the Renaissance meant to the eighteenth century, we have to pay close attention to the way the age of Johnson told the story of the fifteenth through the seventeenth centuries, the way it ordered its historical data and tried to make them comprehensible. The most common eighteenth-century designation for what is now called the English Renaissance was "the age of Elizabeth," a convenient way to refer to the years between 1558 and 1603. Regnal designations, however, might also be used more expansively, as Hazlitt explains: "By the Age of Elizabeth (as it relates to the History of our Literature) I would be understood to mean the time from the Reformation, to the end of Charles I. including the Writers of a certain School or style of Poetry or Prose, who flourished together or immediately succeeded one another within this period."[9] Even in this more inclusive sense, "the age of Elizabeth" wants the metaphorical richness of *rinascita*, but not all eighteenth-century designations were so prosaic. Samuel Johnson, for instance, repeatedly refers to "the Revival of Learning in Europe" and "the revival of polite literature," picking up in the metaphor of revival something at least close to Vasarian rebirth.[10] Thomas Warton provides another cache of terms: "the restitution of letters," "restoring grammatical literature," and "the revival of modern learning"[11] – the last paradoxically equating modern and ancient learning, for it was supposedly *ancient* learning that needed revival. These terms – restoration, restitution, revival – begin to suggest the character the eighteenth century attributed to the age, a character borrowed from the Quattrocento writers: the recovery of an ancient culture lost during the Middle Ages.

The new humanistic scholarship was central to many discussions of the age, but eighteenth-century descriptions were concerned with more than the recovery of ancient letters. An anonymous work from 1699 shows how wide-reaching the periodic designation could be: "There is a natural love and fondness in Englishmen for whatever was done in the reign of Queen Elizabeth; we look upon her time as our golden age; and the great men who lived in it, as our chiefest heroes of virtue, and greatest examples of wisdom, courage, integrity and learning."[12] Likewise John Bell at the end of the eighteenth century:

As the reign of Queen Elizabeth is one of the most shining parts of our history, and an age of which Englishmen are accustomed to speak with a particular pride and delight; it is remarkable for having been fruitful in eminent geniuses of very different kinds. Among the Romans, the age of Augustus is observed to have produced the finest wits; but the preceding one the greatest men: but this was a period of time distinguished for both; and, by a wonderful conjunction, we find learning and arms, wisdom and polite arts, arising to the greatest heights together.[13]

Johnson too celebrates the political and intellectual superiority of the age, and gives a description which ranges widely over the political, theological, scholarly, and cultural achievements of the Renaissance: "Many of the Roman authours were translated, and some of the Greek; the Reformation had filled the kingdom with theological learning; most of the topicks of human disquisition had found English writers; and poetry had been cultivated, not only with diligence, but success."[14] Thomas

Warton catalogues the "principles, sometimes blended, and sometimes operating singly" behind the glory of the age of Elizabeth: "The revival and vernacular versions of the classics, the importation and translation of Italian novels, the visionary reveries of refinements of false philosophy, a degree of superstition sufficient for the purposes of poetry, the adoption of the machineries of romance, and the frequency and improvements of allegoric exhibition in the popular spectacles." He observes "a restless disposition in the human mind to rouse from its lethargic state, and to break the bounds of barbarism... This mighty deliverance, in which the mouldering Gothic fabrics of false religion and false philosophy fell together, was not effectually completed till the close of the fifteenth century." At last came England's greatest age: "The age of queen Elisabeth is commonly called the golden age of English poetry."[15]

Often explicit but always at least implicit in these accounts is a faith in the Renaissance humanists' characterization of their own age as a departure from their ostensibly backward predecessors. Intellectual and cultural historians borrowed many of these ideas uncritically, often adopting their examples and metaphors without qualification. Sometimes the eighteenth-century authors even outdid their Renaissance predecessors in conceiving the Middle Ages as a vast stretch of darkness and barbarity – the hatred for the barbarous centuries is stronger in Gibbon, for instance, than in Petrarch or Erasmus, for whom Augustine and Jerome were favorite authors.

Foremost in the minds of such critics was the notion of a progression from barbarity to enlightenment, from darkness to light – one of many metaphors used to distinguish the new age from the old. "Refinement," a metaphor from metallurgy and alchemy, implies that modern purity came from burning away the imperfections of the past. "Cultivation," another common term, suggests that modern arable land lay fallow in a benighted age. These metaphors pit the utility of modernity against the inadequacy and incompleteness of what came before.

This much of the story sounds familiar; it is borrowed from the writers of the fifteenth and sixteenth centuries, and is recycled by those of the nineteenth and twentieth. But the eighteenth century's extended "age of Elizabeth" is not Burckhardt's "Renaissance," and it is not ours. It is sometimes very alien, and to appreciate it on its own terms, we must begin by abandoning much of what we have come to associate with the Renaissance. The Latin scholarship of Fracostoro and Scaliger, for example, was more important to Johnson and many of his contemporaries than the paintings of Raphael and Titian. The eighteenth-century canon had little room for Marlowe and Herbert, but lavished attention on Hooker and Camden. Robert Anderson notes that the editors of an anthology of British literature considered including Langland, Gower, Lydgate, Barclay, Skelton, Sidney, and Marlowe, but rejected them as too obscure for most readers – giving the space instead to such more familiar authors as Davies, Drayton, Hall, and Drummond.[16] And the differences lie not only in the individual texts, but also in the big picture. The state had not yet been recognized as Burckhardt's work of art; Hegel's World-Spirit was nowhere to be found; and, in spite of some comments on the passing of feudalism, the emphasis on the high-culture superstructure was far more important than Marx's economic base. We will search the eighteenth century in vain for Burckhardt's modern individual.

THE LAST AGE

However significant these differences, though, the eighteenth century's periodization of the Renaissance differs from later versions above all in its immediacy, and this is its greatest claim on our attention. For Burckhardt and Michelet, exploring the Renaissance was inevitably a more disinterested and abstract endeavor than for those who could remember the contemporaries of Davenant and Milton. For thinkers from Dryden through Johnson, the revival of learning provided one of the boundaries of their own age, their own conception of what it meant to be modern, and therefore assumed a special urgency.

By the late seventeenth century, the humanists' tripartite historical model was firmly in place, and was summarized most effectively for a learned audience by Cellarius. Paradoxically, though, at the very time that the humanist periodization was receiving its definitive expression, this idea of a single modern period began to seem inadequate. Dryden's and Pope's contemporaries, that is to say, began to question whether they belonged to the same modernity as Erasmus and Shakespeare. The three-term system of ancient, medieval, and modern needed a new term: the modern age had grown unwieldy, and had to be split in two. In that split, what we call the Renaissance was born. The humanists invented their own modernity, but it took the next age to turn it into the last age, a period with a beginning and an end.

We can see this epochal partition in Evelyn's note about *Hamlet* in a diary entry of 1661: "Now the old playe[s] begin to disgust this refined age." And at the end of the seventeenth century, Thomas Rymer refers to the time of Shakespeare as "the last age": his modernity was not Shakespeare's.[17] The late seventeenth and early eighteenth centuries, in other words, made the same sort of declaration of modernity that humanists like Petrarch and Erasmus had made centuries earlier. Just as the humanist historiographers created the Middle Ages as a by-product of their self-definition, the thinkers of the eighteenth century developed an idea of the Renaissance by drawing a line between themselves and their predecessors. Eighteenth-century Britons repeated the Renaissance's historiographical self-constitution, and the consequences for subsequent periodization were almost as significant.

But this division of ages was fraught with conflicts. Declarations of modernity are usually exultant, polemical: they amount to manifestos on the superiority of the present and the inadequacy of the immediate past, often with a celebration of the age before that, Northrop Frye's "modal grandfather."[18] This is how the Renaissance humanists portrayed the Middle Ages in favor of antiquity, how the Romantics portrayed the eighteenth century in favor of the Renaissance, and how the Modernists portrayed the Victorians in favor of several earlier periods. The creation of the boundary between the age of Shakespeare and the age of Dryden, Pope, and Johnson, however, had no such single character, nor was it static throughout the course of the century. For some, especially early in the century, it was indeed a triumphant emergence from barbarity to propriety, as the clownishness of Skelton's age gave way to the refinement of Waller's. For others, it was a wistful acknowledgment of a lost national and cultural glory, the passing of England's greatest age.

SKETCHES OF A DESIGN

To most eighteenth-century Britons the Renaissance was a literary phenomenon, if "literature" is understood in its broadest sense, and the English were naturally most concerned with the English Renaissance. But it is not always easy, or even possible, to disentangle literature from history, or Britain from the rest of Europe. Johnson's age was the first to try to achieve a synoptic view of the age of Elizabeth by addressing these questions systematically, and many of their solutions to these problems are still with us. The eighteenth century used a medley of categories both intrinsic and extrinsic to literature in looking back at English literary history, and in these early attempts to discuss the revival of learning we can see the beginnings of a "periodic conception" – an awareness of the last age *as* an age.

Alexander Pope was among the first in the eighteenth century to plan a history of English poetry, and his notes toward it, dividing history into two "æras," survive.[19] The first comprises the "School of Provence" (including "Chaucer's Visions" and Gower), the "School of Chaucer" (Lydgate, Occleve, Skelton), the "School of Petrarch" (Surrey, Wyatt, Sidney), and the "School of Dante" (Sackville). "Æra 11" is derived from "SPENCER, Col. Clout, from the School of Ariosto and Petrarch, translated from Tasso," and begins with the "School of Spencer, and From Italian Sonnets" (Phineas Fletcher, Alabaster, Samuel Daniel, Raleigh, "Milton's Juvenilia," Golding, Fairfax, Harrington), and concludes with the omnibus category of the "School of Donne" (Cowley, Davenant, Drayton, Davies, Cleveland, Crashaw, Falkland, Carew, Sandys, Fairfax). Pope's scheme, with its elaborate poetic genealogies, is complicated, but the first thing to strike modern eyes is just how far it is from our own schemes of literary history, how counterintuitive his periodization is. Pope's Renaissance is not ours.

Thomas Gray too hoped to write such a history; he received Pope's sketch, and passed along to Thomas Warton "any fragments, or sketches of a design" he had completed. The most notable thing about this sketch, however, is the correspondence of its four parts to our own period conceptions as reflected in modern literary histories, anthologies, and survey courses. Between Pope's and Gray's schemes, it seems, the more lasting and familiar outline of English literary history was born. Part one of Gray's plan, "the School of Provence," is devoted to early Middle English poetry "from the Conquest... to the reign of Edward the 3^d." His second part is what we call the high Middle Ages: "*Chaucer*... Gower, Occleve, Lydgate, Hawes, G: Douglas, Lindsay, Bellenden, Dunbar, &c." Part three, the "Second Italian School (of Ariosto, Tasso, &c:) an improvement on the first, occasion'd by the revival of letters at the end of the 15th century," corresponds almost perfectly to our modern notion of Renaissance literature, running from Surrey and Wyatt through Milton and the later Metaphysicals: it begins with "Ld Surrey, Sr T. Wyat, Bryan, Ld Vaux, &c: in the beginning of the 16th century," runs through "*Spenser*... Drayton, Fairfax, Phin: Fletcher, Golding, Phaer, &c.: this school ends in Milton," with a parallel course comprising "A *third Italian* School, full of conceit, begun in Q: Elizabeths reign, continued under James, & Charles the first by *Donne*, Crashaw, Cleveland; carried to its height by Cowley, & ending perhaps in *Sprat*." With the end of the Renaissance and the beginning of the "long" eighteenth century comes the fourth part, the "*School of France*, introduced after the Restoration. Waller,

Dryden, Addison, Prior, & Pope, wch has continued down to our own times."[20]

A similar periodization, and one with a similar regard for the Tudors, appears in Henry Headley's influential anthology, *Select Beauties* (1787). Headley's concern is not to distinguish various periods and schools from one another, but to treat Elizabethan and early Stuart literature as expressions of a coherent world view: for him, the periodization of the literature of the last age that was as yet unformed in Pope and nascent in Gray could be taken for granted. He "examine[s] the cluster of poetical names that shone, and were concentered in the space of ninety-one years from the accession of Elizabeth inclusively, to the restoration of Charles the second," and finds nothing similar among "those who have respectively flourished from that time to this, a period of an hundred and thirty-eight years."[21] He accompanies this lament on the inadequacy of the present with a table "to illustrate how large and valuable a portion of Literature is comprehended in a very narrow period":

Epic Poets.	Philosophical and Metaphysical	Dramatic.	Historical
Spencer, Milton, Davenant.	Sir J. Davis, Phin. Fletcher, Jonson, H. More.	G. Gascoyne, Shakspeare, Massinger, Beaumont and Fletcher, Shirley.	Niccols, Sackville, Daniel, Drayton. May, J. Beaumont.
Satyrical. Hall, Marston, Rowlands, Donne.	Pastoral. Warner, Drayton, Browne, Fairfax.	Amatory, and Miscellaneous. Raleigh, Drummond, Marlowe, Cowley, Carew, Corbet, King, Harington, Cartwright, Randloph, Suckling.	Translators. Fairfax, Sandys, Crashawe.

In these early sketches, we can discern the emergence of a periodic conception that corresponds more or less to our "Renaissance," and gives us some hints about what the age of Johnson made of it – and what it made of the age of Johnson.

THE AGE OF JOHNSON

I have referred casually to "the age of Johnson." This is sometimes nothing more than a convenient shorthand for the middle decades of the eighteenth century, from the thirties into the eighties, in which most of the works I discuss were written. But I also make claims for the importance of Samuel Johnson himself in the cultural historiography of "his" age. He stands at the center of his era in a way few writers do.[22]

Johnson has not come down to posterity as an authority on the Tudors, and may seem a perverse choice for a guide to eighteenth-century thought on fifteenth- and sixteenth-century cultural history. The bulk of his writing, it is true, concentrates on the period after the Civil Wars, and some have gone so far as to suggest that, apart from a few major authors, he was largely ignorant of early modern literature and history.[23] But as Walter Jackson Bate observes, "No one of his time felt more deeply drawn to the period from the Renaissance to the end of the seventeenth century," and Johnson tells the story of "Learning's triumph o'er her barb'rous foes" as convincingly as any of his contemporaries.[24] Few people of any age have known the works of the Renaissance – canonical and marginal; English, Continental, and neo-Latin – more thoroughly than Johnson. Throughout his works he refers to such learned figures as Wowerus, Cornaro, Pontanus, Caius, Camerarius, Śmiglecki, and Sabinus, to say nothing of such comparatively familiar names as Cynthio, de Thou, Buchanan, Ficino, Scaliger, Melanchthon, Buchanan, and Grotius.[25] More important, despite the Romantic reaction against so many things Johnsonian, his Shakespeare edition and his *Lives of the Poets* made him one of the most influential eighteenth-century British voices on Renaissance literature. His thoroughgoing historicism – his determination to read the literature of the Renaissance in its historical context – is among his most important critical legacies: "Those who have no power to judge of past times but by their own," he warns us, "should always doubt their conclusions."[26] As Lawrence Lipking observes, "Wherever the study of the ordering of the arts in eighteenth-century England may begin, in the end it leads to Samuel Johnson."[27]

Johnson offers none of the grand theses we find in Michelet, Burckhardt, or Pater. Unlike his contemporaries the Wartons, Collins, Hurd, and Percy, he was neither an antiquarian nor an academic literary historian, and though he planned several histories of the revival of learning, he wrote none. His formulations rarely have the kind of coherence we expect from systematic literary historians, and they must be gathered from his scattered comments. His famous description of Shakespeare describes

himself equally well: he found Shakespeare "not systematick and con-
sequential, but desultory and vagrant," and observed that "his precepts
and axioms drop casually from him."[28] As Lipking says of Johnson, "If
we seek from him...a philosophy of art, we must make it for ourselves
from scraps and fragments."[29]

The casually dropped scraps and fragments, though, are plentiful.
Among his published works we can count an edition of Shakespeare
and *Lives* not only of Cowley and Milton but also of Drake, Browne,
and Ascham. He arrived in London hoping to finish and produce his
tragedy, drawn from a source of 1603 and set in 1453; shortly after its
failure, he set to work publishing an early seventeenth-century history of
the Council of Trent. When Johnson calls Erasmus one who "will stand
for ever in the first rank of literary heroes," he suggests something about
his personal attitude toward the heroic figures of the last age. Giovanni
Giovanno Pontanno, for instance, is "a man celebrated among the early
restorers of literature"; Angelo Poliziano is "a name eminent among the
restorers of polite literature"; Justus Lipsius is "the great modern master of the Stoic philosophy."[30] Among his planned but never attempted
works are a "History of the Revival of Learning in Europe," a "History
of Criticism," and "A Hist. of the Reformation (not of England only
but) of Europe."[31] Together with hundreds of allusions in the periodical
essays and many thousands of illustrative quotations from the sixteenth
and seventeenth centuries in the *Dictionary*, they suggest the extent of his
knowledge of and interest in the English Renaissance. These scattered
comments add up not to a coherent view of the Renaissance, but to a dis-
tillation and condensation of the dominant historiographical metaphors
of the eighteenth century.

To treat Johnson as a representative of eighteenth-century attitudes,
though, is not only reductive, but potentially misleading: he is no mere
mouthpiece for the opinions and prejudices of his contemporaries. Ideas
about the age of Elizabeth came from Dryden, Addison, Pope, Gray,
Gibbon, and countless others, and Johnson echoes none of them. His
differences even from his friend Thomas Warton are considerable – to
say nothing of Hume or Hurd. Eighteenth-century notions about the
previous age were by no means uniform, and examining only Johnson
would exclude the often vigorous disputes among those asking historiographical questions. Johnson does, however, have the distinction of
being at the center of many of these debates. He not only knew but
wrote about the work of those who came before him, as in the *Lives*
of Dryden, Addison, Pope, Hughes, and Gray. He also discussed and

sometimes argued about these ideas with the most important of his contemporaries.

My method has been to contextualize Johnson broadly and deeply, using him as a way into his contemporaries' ideas. I have read mostly, although not exclusively, the canonical works of both the Renaissance and the eighteenth century, in part because the formation of a canon is itself at issue. I have included them not so much for their aesthetic value as for their usefulness in illustrating larger cultural trends. Sometimes, therefore, I compare Johnson to the century's most influential poets, historians, and scholars like Pope, Gray, Hume, Warton; at other times I draw on minor and even anonymous writers and editors. While Dick Minims rarely produces lasting or influential appraisals, their skill at parroting their betters often provides the most convenient summaries of the prevailing opinions of the age.

Most of my examples come from Johnson's professional lifetime, the late 1730s through the early 1780s, during which period I see the most significant developments. Occasionally I explore analogues and precursors as far back as Sprat and Dryden, but the sense of the last age was still nascent even in the early decades of the eighteenth century – in, for instance, Dennis, Oldmixon, and Gildon.[32] Only rarely do I venture later than the 1780s, in part because the 1790s saw in a flood of new editions, anthologies, and literary histories the first consciously revisionist interpretation of the canon of English poetry. The Renaissance canon was by then in place and taken for granted: Spenser, Shakespeare, and Milton had been declared England's greatest poets and were secure in their positions as representatives of its greatest age. The limitation of scope is also owing to the less tangible but no less real changes in sensibility, which demand to be studied on their own terms. Godwin's *St. Leon* (1799), Blake's *Milton* (1804), and Coleridge's lectures on Shakespeare (1811–12), in spite of some continuities with the criticism of Gray and Johnson, are products of a different world, one that paradoxically used the constructions of eighteenth-century writers against their creators. By the early decades of the nineteenth century, a new conception of modernity had turned the eighteenth century into a "last age," one to be contrasted with the more privileged Renaissance, in many polemic versions of Romantic literary history.[33] For this reason, I exclude most pronouncements from the later era. The general rule, however, admits a few exceptions. The new anthologies sometimes rework the canon, but they just as often echo the commonplaces of the eighteenth century: the compilers can be caught stealing entire paragraphs from Pope, Johnson, and Warton, even in the very works where they denigrate them. When early nineteenth-century writers provide convenient summaries of earlier thought, I do not hesitate to quote them.

My hope in this project, and the reason I have placed Johnson at the center of it, is twofold: to provide a broader context in which to understand Johnson's comments on the age of Elizabeth, and to subject this broader context to the more penetrating analysis which Johnson is often able to give it. This sort of contextualization makes clear where and how Johnson worked with conventional materials but, more important, it allows us to see his original insights more clearly, and it gives us his own distinctive take on the historiography of the early modern era.

I have tried in this book to follow, rather than resist, these eighteenth-century notions about the last age. Another kind of study – one more skeptical about the eighteenth century's characterizations; one more sensitive to class structures or print culture or the modern nation-state – might be illuminating. I might have given more attention to modern critics who question whether there was such a thing as a Renaissance – whether there were Dark Ages and barbarians, and whether Europe can genuinely be said to have undergone a revival of classical culture. I might even have taken a cue from those who question the very possibility of literary history. Still, it seems to me more fruitful to follow where the eighteenth-century writers lead, and to allow them their omissions and mischaracterizations – to let them tell their story before interrupting with qualifications.

Pointing out, even dwelling upon, the arbitrariness of periodization need not amount to debunking the enterprise itself, and the very contingency of periods can offer a way to understand history from unfamiliar perspectives. That we are living through a reconsideration and redefinition of the Renaissance therefore need not be a handicap, for wrestling with these questions reminds us of the cultural complexity of history. The Renaissance – whatever its character – was indisputably various and heterogeneous, big enough to include Rabelais and Bacon, Shakespeare and Muret, Erasmus and Donne, Ascham and Ficino, Grotius and Michelangelo (but perhaps not big enough to include Dante and Marvell?). It comprised movements and countermovements, as well as movements with no apparent connection to one another. It was backward-looking and prophetic, Ciceronian and Baroque, scientific and humanistic, imitative and radical, mystical and rational, Reformation and Counter Reformation. It is the age of Petrarch's lyricism, Nicolas of Cusa's Neoplatonism, Shakespeare's characterization, Machiavelli's politics.

That variety cannot be reduced to some essential unity – " 'History,' " writes Jerome McGann, "should always...be written in the plural"[34] – and the eighteenth century, in looking back on it, did not regard it monolithically. I try here to treat it with a similarly open mind, and to respect, even to highlight, its many contradictions. Shakespeare, for instance, is sometimes the paragon of the Gothic aesthetic, and sometimes the champion of the revolution that definitively defeated Gothicism. I have not tried, therefore, to present a single version of the age, a tidy narrative to call *the* eighteenth-century conception of the revival of learning. Instead, I have worked to describe multiple competing visions, for as Joseph Levine writes, "A culture can be defined by its contentions as well as its agreements."[35] I have, however, been interested in the shared language, metaphors, and paradigms for understanding the past. This means I sometimes draw on disparate figures who make strange historiographical bedfellows – Johnson is discussed together with Hume, Hurd, and other seemingly inimical writers. In spite of their differences they have much in common, and it is inadvisable to turn Johnson into an arch-Augustan and Warton into the first of the Romantics, with a declaration of never-the-twain-shall-meet. The strands traditionally called neoclassical and pre-Romantic cannot always be so easily untangled.

The central argument of this book is that what may seem at first the province of a few recondite specialists – critics, antiquarians, historians, theologians – was in fact essential to the constitution of a British character, for these specialists helped to set the terms by which the modern nation was to be measured. When eighteenth-century British thinkers began to regard the old works of their country as classics, they turned to the age of Petrarch and Poliziano. When they celebrated the triumph of modern learning over childish ignorance, they turned to the age of Shakespeare and Scaliger. When they promoted Britain's often beleaguered political stability, they turned to the age of Elizabeth. When they sought a place for the Church of England safe from Catholics, Dissenters, and Evangelicals, they turned to the age of Hooker. When they worked to define a standard for their language, they turned to the age of Erasmus and Camden. When they looked for models for poetic form and structure, they turned to the age of Spenser. And when they began to lament the sterility of their own poetic productions, they turned to the age of Milton. In short, the eighteenth century defined itself by comparison and contrast with the last age. Each chapter of this book surveys some aspect of eighteenth-century British identity – literary, scholarly, political, religious, and linguistic – and contextualizes it in the culture of the age before.

Chapter 1 explores the historiographical rupture between the Middle Ages and the Renaissance as it was first conceived in the Renaissance itself, and later adopted by eighteenth-century thinkers in their attempt to understand the "Dark Ages." The eighteenth century, like the Renaissance, resorted to terms such as "barbarous" to create a canon of classic works and to edit their texts, thereby mingling the historiographical and the aesthetic.

Chapter 2 looks at the eighteenth century's essentially historicist understanding of the revival of learning as an educational and scholarly movement, and relates the growth and development of children to the development of a culture.

Chapter 3 considers the rise and adoption of the "Tudor myth" and the glorification of the age of Elizabeth, "the favourite period of English greatness."[36] Johnson and his contemporaries traced the progress from the chaos of the Middle Ages to the pinnacle of national glory under Elizabeth, and measured the policies of Walpole and the Hanoverians against this lofty standard.

Chapter 4 studies Elizabeth's delicate *via media* between Roman superstition and Calvinist iconoclasm. When English orthodoxy later found itself seeking a similar path among threats from Catholics, Dissenters, Deists, and Evangelicals, the age of Elizabeth exerted a powerful attraction, and reinforced the English self-image as a reasonable middle ground between extremes. The doctrine of "things indifferent" especially served as a means of avoiding the disastrous doctrinal divisions of the previous century.

Chapter 5 examines the development of the English language and the English sense of nationhood. The late sixteenth and early seventeenth centuries became England's linguistic golden age, just as the Renaissance had championed Ciceronian Latin over medieval barbarism. English national identity and linguistic identity were mutually dependent and equally insular, and both looked backwards to the Elizabethan age.

The last two chapters are case-studies of the two greatest English epic poets, and of two contrasting ways of looking at Britain's cultural heritage – and its future. Chapter 6 examines the idea of cultural progress and Edmund Spenser's complicated place in eighteenth-century literary culture. Ben Jonson best exemplifies cultural progress from medieval rudeness to modern refinement, but the descent of his reputation over the course of the eighteenth century corresponds to the rise of Spenser's, whose apparently barbarous design, allegory, and versification frustrated proponents of cultural progress such as Addison. Spenser forced eighteenth-century readers to question the inevitability of a progression toward the decorum of their own practices.

Chapter 7 returns to the themes of this introduction and chapter 1: the rupture that separates an age from what came before. This chapter considers the break in the seventeenth century, when the Renaissance first became "the last age." Milton's involvement in the events of the Civil War and Interregnum required eighteenth-century literary historians to consider the grounds on which the boundaries between eras are marked. Johnson's *Life of Milton* offers a number of explanations of the relationship between history and aesthetics. Milton was instrumental in developing a historically grounded conception of literature, even as proto-Romantic bardolatry worked to turn Shakespeare into the genius who transcended history.

CHAPTER I

Struggling to emerge from barbarity: historiography and the idea of the classic

In a children's logic puzzle, an archaeologist discovers a Greek coin inscribed "413 B.C." and at once rejects it as fraudulent. The trick, of course, is that Plato's contemporaries could not date themselves "before Christ." Behind the puzzle lies a salutary reminder about periodization: few ages get to choose how the future will regard or name them. Because periods depend upon teleologies imposed in retrospect, antiquity could not conceive of itself as antique, and the Middle Ages could not view themselves as being in the middle of anything.

But the Renaissance is different. A group of Florentine scholars writing in the late fourteenth and early fifteenth centuries seem to have willed their age into being in their own polemical act of periodization – "The legend of the Renaissance," writes C. S. Lewis, "is a Renaissance legend"[1] – and their self-constitution set the terms for subsequent efforts at periodizing the epoch. By distinguishing their own age from the ostensibly barbarous one before them, and by defining themselves in relation to their past, they created both the last age and their own, both the Middle Ages and the Renaissance. Theirs is the West's first self-conscious declaration of modernity. Half a millennium later, the humanists' account still dominates our historiography, after Michelet, after Burckhardt, even after modern critics have challenged the validity of their most basic claims to accuracy and originality.

A myth so hardy deserves to be taken seriously. To understand eighteenth-century conceptions of the Renaissance, it will be useful to trace this myth back to its origin in the fourteenth and fifteenth centuries, and to follow it down through the next several hundred years. This is not to say that the myth was transmitted to the eighteenth century intact. In following it, we will have to negotiate many twists and turns; and we will inevitably project later ideas and teleologies onto the story, to some degree misrepresenting early humanistic thought by overemphasizing the elements which show up later. The sharp division between the Middle

Ages and the Renaissance, for instance, was not fully in place until the seventeenth century, and the aspects of humanism that later ages considered with the greatest attention were not always what the humanists themselves considered their essential business.[2]

Such a retrospective approach is not wholly unjustified, though, even if it risks distortion. The idea of the Renaissance was first embodied in a cluster of metaphors which have their origins in the early humanists. Later ages may have exaggerated their importance or understood them anachronistically, but these metaphors are the basis for eighteenth-century periodic conceptions, and provide the terms that Johnson's age used to tell the story of the transition from the "Gothic" age to the revival of learning. They show us what the eighteenth century believed about the Middle Ages and the Renaissance, but more important, they show us how the eighteenth century regarded itself by using the past as a point of reference. The eighteenth century based much of its cultural identity on the age that came before it, just as the early humanists defined themselves in terms of their predecessors. I begin, therefore, by tracing the Renaissance myth from its birth in the age of Petrarch to the threshold of the age of the great nineteenth-century historiographers, and by looking at the way this myth helped to produce the most important literary by-product of periodization, the classic.

NOT A LINE DESERVING PRAISE

Humanist definitions of the self began with a definition of the other: in order to situate themselves historically, the early Italian humanists conceived a historical rupture between themselves and their immediate predecessors. However valid this notion may have been – our own age has been filled with challenges to its fundamental assumptions – many thinkers of the Renaissance saw it that way, and it was increasingly accepted over the next half millennium, to receive its definitive form in Burckhardt. As one critic puts it,

Whatever later historians may have thought about the matter, the humanists themselves were convinced that the movement which they represented marked a turning point in history. They believed, rightly or wrongly, that a dismal and barbaric age had at last come to an end, that the world was making a new start, and that they themselves were the first "modern" men.[3]

This break of medieval from modern depends upon another break, said to have happened some time around the fall of Rome – an event recognized as momentous as soon as it happened, but given true epoch-making status only in the Renaissance. Exactly when this first break occurred was a matter of dispute. Sicco Polenton dates it from Juvenal's death (*c*. A.D. 140); Petrarch and Vasari, from Constantine's reign (A.D. 306–37); Favio Biondo, A.D. 412; Valla, the death of Boethius (*c*. A.D. 524). Whatever the exact date, though, the pattern is the same. On one side of the line are the cultures of Greece and Rome; on the other, a dark age, a millennium-long hiatus between classical and modern culture (characterized as a "Middle Age" as early as 1469) filled only with ignorance and barbarism.[4]

This distinction between antiquity and the Middle Ages made possible the distinction between the Middle Ages and modernity. According to humanist orthodoxy (and most subsequent historiography), a second historical rupture restored the classical culture to Europe in a *rinascimento* or *renaissance des beaux arts et des lettres*. Ficino, for instance, uses the myth of a golden age to celebrate the new era as a return to antiquity: "This age, like a golden age, has restored to light the nearly extinct liberal arts."[5] Erasmus, too, was an enthusiastic panegyrist for the new era, delighting in "saeculo huic nostro," as he writes to Pope Leo X, "this age of ours, which has good hopes of becoming an age of gold, if there ever were such a thing."[6] Such self-promotion colors most subsequent discussions of the period: centuries before the English first used the word "Renaissance," the myth of the restored golden age was in place.

This age shone the more brightly when set next to its darkened predecessor. In describing this contrast, humanist historians recapitulated and inverted a millennium-old historiographical metaphor. The Church Fathers, employing familiar biblical images, divided the dark pagan past from the bright Christian present. The humanists, on the other hand, fascinated by pre-Christian Rome, borrowed these biblical and patristic metaphors and polemically, even heretically, reversed them, labeling the Christian age benighted and the pagan centuries enlightened.[7] Characterizing the Dark Ages was fraught with dangers, for it meant celebrating pagan culture at the expense of Christianity. Few in the Renaissance had the nerve to hazard Erasmus's directness – "The death of letters was to be laid at the door of the Christian religion," he writes, and insists "there is no erudition in existence except what is secular" – and the devout Erasmus is cautious enough to put this sentiment in the mouth of a character in a dialogue.[8] But even those hesitant to draw attention to their rejection of patristic historiography were quick to employ images of light and darkness to distinguish the privileged classical past from medieval barbarism. Light and darkness underlie one of the most common metaphors for understanding the break between the Renaissance and the Middle Ages, one in which the Middle Ages are defined by *lack*. For humanist historiographers, the millennium from the fourth century to the fourteenth is an "aetas tenebrae," an age of darkness, devoid of the light of antiquity. Medieval culture was no culture; it was a mere interim with no positive identity. Since the Middle Ages are characterized by privation, we might call this the "privative" metaphor or model.

This conception apparently has its origin in Francesco Petrarca.[9] It is safe to call the Middle Ages his invention: he was the first to draw a line between the ancient world and its barbarous modern successor. Modernity suffers by comparison with antiquity because it wants learning: he thereby denies barbarism any positive identity. This privative historiographical conception is perfectly in character for Petrarch, who makes similar distinctions in areas far from historiography – in ethical theory, for instance, he distinguishes the privative vice of ignorance from a more positive vice such as drunkenness: "Ignorance might be the consequence of laziness or inborn slowness; drunkenness is a vice of the will and the perverted mind."[10] Figuring darkness as the absence of light and evil as the absence of good, and denying positive existence to either, is a habit borrowed from his patristic hero, Augustine. The *locus classicus* of the Augustinian conception of evil appears in the *Confessions*: "All corrupted things are deprived of some good. If they were to be deprived of all good, they would not exist at all . . . All things that exist are good, and the evil I was considering is not a substance, for if it were a substance, it would be good."[11] Petrarch's life's work was dispelling this darkness by distributing knowledge, defeating modern ignorance by disseminating ancient texts.

Others picked up this privative conception of the Middle Ages. Some shared his pessimistic evaluation of modernity: Poggio, for instance, uses the ruins of Rome as an analogue for the ruin of learning. In a dialogue of 1430, Antonio Lusco tells him: "Poggio, how far are these Capitoline ruins from those of which our Virgil sang: 'Now golden, once bristling and overgrown with thorns.' It's better to transpose the verse: 'Once golden, now rough with thorns and overgrown with briars.'"[12] Lorenzo Valla, on the other hand, develops Petrarch's notions of privative medieval barbarism while celebrating the new restoration of classical learning: "As wretched as those earlier times were, when no learned man was found, so much more is our age to be praised, in which (if we exert ourselves a little more) I am confident that the Roman language will soon grow stronger than the city, and with it all disciplines will be restored."[13] True Latin, lost during a millennium devoid of learned men, awaits restoration. Valla was ready to do his part to restore the ancient culture, to fill the medieval cultural void.

Such metaphors long outlived the Quattrocento, and flourished in England as well as in Italy, growing less ambivalent and more pointed as the years went by. Ben Jonson, for example, remarks of the Middle Ages that "All good poetry was flown, / And art banished," with "Not a poet in an age / Worth crowning. / Not a work deserving bays, / Not a line deserving praise," and William Camden likewise notes of England "that learning after long banishment, was recalled in the time of King *Henry* the eight."[14] Such privative metaphors survive to this day, and even now dominate our nomenclature: whether the ages are characterized as Dark or Middle, they are a vast wasteland marked by lack; whether we call the succeeding age a Renaissance or the less judgmental "early modern," we tacitly admit the humanists' role in supplanting old darkness with new light. C. S. Lewis takes the humanists to task, but he is right to take them seriously, and to recognize just how radical their accusation was: "And what can *media* imply except that a thousand years of theology, metaphysics, jurisprudence, courtesy, poetry, and architecture are to be regarded as a mere gap, or chasm, or *entre-acte*?"[15]

BASE IDEAS MUST BE TORN OUT

What else can it imply? Lewis's question is disingenuous. However pervasive the privative metaphor, it provides only half the picture. In the privative model, the barbarians are marked only by lack: had they been given the classics, with their self-evident value, they would immediately have attained enlightenment. Merely ignorant barbarians pose little threat. Some, however, saw a more insidious variety of barbarism. The Middle Ages are for them not merely a harmless breach in history, but a positive evil – not a want of learning, but a perversion of it; not a lack of culture, but a poisoning of it. We might therefore distinguish this model from the privative one by calling it, for want of a better adjective, "corruptive."

Against Petrarch, then, we can put Erasmus – though not the originator, still the best early exemplar of the corruptive model. The very title of his most important work on ignorance, the *Antibarbarorum liber* (1520), reveals his sympathies: scourging the barbarians is the order of the day. It is easy to treat the work as ahistorical, aimed at whatever barbarians and dunces happen to be on hand. We might, however, make the case that the barbarians should be understood as historically specific enemies by contextualizing it in Erasmus's other works. "The historical view accompanying Erasmus' antibarbarian struggle," writes one critic, "is quite simple":

True civilization is identified with antiquity, and barbarism is identified with the ages which followed antiquity... Erasmus clearly adopts the view of history developed in the Italian Renaissance, with a tripartite division of history into a positively valued antiquity, negatively valued Middle Ages, and a present which recuperates the positive achievements of the ancients... History has to be cleansed of its barbarous, medieval stains.[16]

The central persona of the *Antibarbari*, Batt, has a disgust for the barbarians that goes far beyond pity for their ignorance: "He was as much an enemy of the barbarians as they were hostile to letters; in fact meeting with them often made him vomit or go hot with rage." Batt distinguishes the relatively harmless member of "the army of yokels" from an author who "writes commentaries on the best authors, shedding darkness on them, not light, not adorning but corrupting... They have managed to confuse, corrupt, and overturn everything." These more dangerous barbarians have a destructive power, and are "born for the sole purpose of unteaching everything which concerns Good Letters."[17] Against the natural unteaching abilities of the barbarians, Erasmus envisioned his own pedagogy as a kind of quarantine or antidote – the student must "be fortified as by certain efficacious drugs against the poisoned opinions of the common people" – and if some infections slip through, "the first effort must be to rid him of them little by little, to weed out the seeds of trouble." In the margin is the note: "First of All, Base Ideas Must Be Torn Out."[18]

Others ring changes on this basic metaphor for understanding barbarism as corruption. Linacre's motto, *ad fontes*, sums up the corruptive model: to the sources, unsullied by impurity. Some looked not only at ancient texts but at the modern languages as well, as barbaric corruption and pollution are the source of the anxiety over poetic "purity" in the vulgar tongues. Joachim du Bellay blames medieval French writing for its corruption: "Ces vielles poësies Francoyses... corrumpent le goust de nostre Langue." Ascham asserts his distaste for the superfluity and corruption in Hall's *Chronicle*, suggesting that "a wise learned man... in cutting away wordes and sentences... shold leaue to mens vse, a storie... twise as good as it was." Milton too relies on the corruptive model of medieval historiography, as on *Of Reformation*'s first page: "the foule and sudden corruption, and then after many a tedious age, the long-deferr'd, but much more wonderfull and happy reformation of the *Church* in these latter dayes."[19] Harping on corrupted purity was a favorite rhetorical tactic in the Protestant Reformation, in which Catholic impurities were to be eradicated from true apostolic Christianity, and Milton develops the motif in characterizing the "threefold corruption" of the medieval bishops: "1. The best times were spreadingly infected. 2. The best men of those times fouly tainted. 3. The best writings of those men dangerously adulterated." Like Erasmus's barbarians "shedding darkness" and "unteaching," Milton's bishops have a power to negate, and can be countered only by the Reformation of the Church, "after so many dark Ages, wherein the huge overshadowing traine of *Error* had almost swept all the Starres out of the Firmament of the *Church*."[20]

HISTORY UNFINISHED, HISTORY DEFACED

This division of historical conceptions into privative and corruptive may seem a perversely Scholastic distinction to impose on sworn anti-Scholastics. There are, however, consequences of real significance, for it helps to illuminate the relationship between historiography and self-definition. The question is this: given enlightened antiquity and a barbarous Middle Age, which is the odd one out? Few moderns doubted the superiority of the ancient classics, but did they represent humanity's true nature from which the Middle Ages were an aberration, or was it the other way around? The question is not a disinterested antiquarian inquiry, but a means of characterizing one's own age. To the privative school, culture seems precarious: ancient and Renaissance culture are exceptional because of the presence of something lacking in the intervening centuries. For the contamination school, on the other hand, enlightenment is the norm: the Middle Ages were barbarous and monstrous because they were infected, and when the infection was rooted out, society returned to its natural state. Vasari, the first to use the term *rinascita*, is also one of the first to explore the larger consequences of this distinction. He develops the privative model: "As the men of the age were not accustomed to see any excellence or greater perfection than the things thus produced [in the Middle Ages], they greatly admired them, and considered them to be the type of perfection, barbarous as they were." Only ignorance prevents the barbarians from recognizing the self-evident value of classical culture. He suggests that this privative model implies that the enlightened state of modernity and antiquity, then, is not natural:

If ever it happens, which God forbid, that the arts should once more fall to a like ruin and disorder, through the negligence of man, the malignity of the age, or the decree of Heaven, which does not appear to wish that the things of this world should remain stationary, these labours of mine ... may maintain the arts in life, or, at any rate, encourage the better spirits to provide them with every assistance.[21]

For an advocate of the corruptive metaphor, however, enlightened culture is normative, and can be lost only when occluded. "The essence of Truth is plainnesse, and brightness," says Milton; "the darknes and crookednesse is our own ... If we will but purge with sovrain eyesalve that intellectual ray which *God* hath planted in us, then we would beleeve the Scriptures protesting their own plainnes, and perspicuity."[22]

These two sides of the historiographical coin – medieval history as variously deprived and depraved – dominate most subsequent discussions of the Middle Ages and the Renaissance. To associate names with these two paradigms is ultimately indefensible, since no significant writer sides entirely with one at the expense of the other. In the most interesting thinkers we can see both the interplay of the two metaphors and the interplay of their larger cultural consequences. Even Erasmus, despite his passion for the so-called corruptive party, recognizes the legitimacy of the other view: both metaphors appear in his letter to Leo X, for instance, when he talks about the recovery of "learning of the best sort, hitherto partly neglected and partly corrupted."[23]

The same dichotomy appears at the other end of the sixteenth century. By the time we reach Francis Bacon, whose concerns are far from (and often contrary to) those of the Quattrocento humanists, both metaphors are firmly in place. For all his disparagement of undue veneration of the classical past, Bacon gives us essentially the same two views of the Middle Ages. His call for the new discipline of intellectual history leads him to begin with this first broad mapping of the territory:

In times no less than in regions there are wastes and deserts. For only three revolutions and periods of learning can properly be reckoned; one among the Greeks, the second among the Romans, and the last among us ... The intervening ages of the world, in respect of any rich or flourishing growth of the sciences, were unprosperous. For neither the Arabians nor the Schoolmen need be mentioned; who in the intermediate times rather crushed the sciences with a multitude of treatises, than increased their weight.[24]

The first few sentences are pure privation: the Middle Ages are "wastes and deserts." But in the last sentence the traditional Scholastic villains appear as corrupters. Bacon in fact distinguishes *three* models of history,

"Memorials, Perfect histories, and Antiquities." Memorials, he says, "are history unfinished, or the first or rough draughts of history"; "Antiquities are history defaced, or some remnants of history which have casually escaped the shipwrack of time." His call for "perfect histories" comes only after an attack on the two historiographical models from the barbarous centuries. "History unfinished" is marked by mere ignorance – "in these kinds of unperfect histories...any deficience...is but their nature." "History defaced," on the other hand, is a matter of active rather than privative barbarism: "As for the corruptions and moths of history...the use of them deserveth to be banished...as those that have fretted and corroded the sound bodies of many excellent histories, and wrought them into base and unprofitable dregs."[25] He catalogues the threats in *The Advancement of Learning* (1605), a kind of prologue to the greatest seventeenth-century excoriation of the vulgar errors of the Dark Ages, Browne's *Pseudodoxia Epidemica* (1646).

These two traditions survive together well into the nineteenth century. They coexist in Michelet, for instance, who at one point refers to "L'état bizarre et monstreux, prodigieusement artificiel, qui fut celui du Moyen Age," and only a few pages later holds that "La révolution du seizième siècle...rencontra une mort incroyable, un néant, et partit de rien." This is no contradiction, for Michelet sees them in a temporal relationship: "Anti-nature succeeds banished nature, whence springs spontaneously the two-faced monster of false knowledge and perverse ignorance."[26] Not all of Michelet's predecessors or successors had such a tidy theory to account for the relationship of these two ideas, but from the fifteenth century to the twenty-first, they dominate discussions of the medieval and modern worlds.

THE WILD TORRENT OF A BARB'ROUS AGE

Some modern scholars have been profoundly skeptical about the humanists' take on their predecessors, arguing, for example, that Carolingian and twelfth-century French culture rival anything in the putatively enlightened age that followed. Defenders of the Middle Ages have usefully reminded us that the humanists were far from disinterested, and that the picture they drew was sometimes grossly distorted. As Pat Rogers has argued, "A self-consciously 'refined' culture needs to naturalize its prejudices, and the ideological function of 'middle ages' is to give essentially normative terms the force of neutral historical markers."[27] In fact these humanist characterizations of their predecessors amount to little more than public relations, even propaganda: in reducing a millennium of European culture to a uniform "barbarism," they did no justice to Augustine, Aquinas, or Dante. But propaganda, especially successful propaganda, has its own value, and the humanist writers relied on it to carve themselves a niche in history. They asserted the superiority of modernity, albeit a modernity dependent on antiquity.

The eighteenth century, in seeking to understand the age we now call the Renaissance, began by accepting this understanding of the Middle Ages almost uncritically. The humanists defined their own age as that which was not barbarous, neither deprived nor corrupt by comparison with their predecessors, and the age of Johnson bought this self-characterization wholesale. Late in the seventeenth century, for instance, Dryden borrows the privative metaphor to excuse Chaucer's faults by pointing out that "He lived in the infancy of our poetry, and . . . nothing is brought to perfection at the first." Perfection – in its radical sense, completion – necessarily implies a prior incompleteness. Thus Dryden's project of "translating" Chaucer for modern understandings involves filling the cultural lacunae left by Chaucer's barbarous age, and "add[ing] somewhat of my own where I thought my author was deficient, and had not given his thoughts their true lustre, for want of words in the beginning of our language." Thomas Warton uses darkness to characterize medieval culture and light to characterize its successor: "Even from the time of the irruptions of the northern barbarians, some glimmerings of the antient erudition still remained." Compare the "glimmerings" in Henry Headley: "The star of Science no sooner appeared in the British hemisphere, than, struck with the luxury of its beams, the minds of men were suddenly aroused and awakened to the most animated exertions . . . the dark and long-impending clouds of barbarism were dispelled." Upton likewise writes that Ascham, "appearing early amongst our first Restorers both of Learning and sound Religion, by the Light he held forth, was instrumental in dispelling the darkness of former Ages, that so unhappily had overspread the land."[28] Petrarch's metaphor flourished.

Alexander Pope, on the other hand, invokes Erasmus in his party-line Erasmian account of the Middle Ages and Renaissance:

> *Learning* and *Rome* alike in Empire grew,
> And *Arts* still *follow'd* where her *Eagles flew*;
> From the same Foes, at last, both felt their Doom,
> And the same Age saw *Learning* fall, and *Rome* . . .
> A *second* Deluge Learning thus o'er-run,
> And the *Monks* finished what the *Goths* begun.

> At length, *Erasmus*, that *great, injur'd* Name,
> (The *Glory* of the Priesthood, and the *Shame!*)
> *Stemm'd* the *wild Torrent* of a *barb'rous Age*,
> And drove those *Holy Vandals* off the Stage.[29]

The association of the fall of culture with the sack of Rome, the attacks on Scholasticism (wittily conflating monks and Goths), and the figuring of the Dark Ages as overrun by savages – all are sixteenth-century commonplaces, albeit couched in an unmistakably eighteenth-century idiom. And Pope was not alone in recovering Erasmus's disgust for "Holy Vandals." John Oldmixon picks up on the religious corruption when he speaks of "the several *Reformers* that attempted to purge Religion of the Filth contracted in the Course of many Corrupted Ages."[30]

Just as the two paradigms of privation and corruption were intermingled in the early modern authors, they coexist in the eighteenth century, even at the risk of inconsistency. William Winstanley, for instance, looks back to the fourteenth century to find the beginning of the English golden age, and praises Chaucer's "earnest desire to enrich and beautifie our *English* Tongue, which in those days was very rude and barren." "Barren" here connotes an emptiness waiting for cultivation, a clear statement of the privative critique of medieval culture. But he also finds Gower "the first refiner of our *English* Tongue," switching from an agricultural to a metallurgical or alchemical metaphor to point out the cultural and linguistic impurities that must be burnt out. Gibbon sees Christian barbarians as "immersed in ignorance," but "their vulgar tongues were marked with the rudeness and poverty of the manners." Thomas Warton, the first to publish a comprehensive history of English literature, also uses the two metaphors willy-nilly, even in the same sentence: "Italy, during the darkest periods of monastic ignorance, had always maintained a greater degree of refinement and knowledge than any other European country" – darkness and refinement make for a curiously mixed metaphor, explicable only in the context of this long tradition of characterizing the Middle Ages. So too with privative exile and corruptive vandals in William Collins's account of the beginning and end of the Dark Ages: "As Arts expir'd, resistless Dulness rose; / *Goths, Priests*, or *Vandals*, – all were Learning's Foes. / Till *Julius* first recall'd each exil'd Maid…"[31]

These are the metaphors Samuel Johnson inherited, passed down from Petrarch and Erasmus through Dryden and Pope. His account of sixteenth-century England echoes the traditional humanistic argument about an emergence from barbaric darkness:

The English nation, in the time of Shakespeare, was yet struggling to emerge from barbarity. The philology of Italy had been transplanted hither in the reign of Henry the Eighth; and the learned languages had been successfully cultivated by Lilly, Linacer, and More...But literature was yet confined to professed scholars, or to men and women of high rank. The publick was gross and dark.[32]

The language here, as in many early humanistic accounts of the Dark Ages, is predominantly privative: the passage ends with darkness, from which the new age is still struggling to emerge. But the corruptive model also shows up in his verse history of the English stage, which opens with a striking couplet:

> When Learning's triumph o'er her barb'rous foes
> First rear'd the stage, immortal SHAKESPEAR rose.[33]

Humanist learning trumps medieval barbarism, and a new age dawns.

TEXTS FREE FROM ADULTERATION

Nothing better illustrates the interplay of the privative and corruptive models than the dispersal of texts. One of the great scholarly projects of the fifteenth century, given new impetus by the invention of movable type, was the reproduction of the texts of the ancient world. Petrarch, a leading participant in this effort, sought to bring these texts to light, to fill the medieval intellectual void with classical matter. But not long after he and his contemporaries began publishing long-forgotten works, many humanists were anxious about the state of the texts they were releasing. And no one was more anxious about textual corruption than Angelo Poliziano, who waged his historiographical war in the field of textual criticism. Rather than optimistically and uncritically piling text upon text, Poliziano took pains to reject what was barbarous even *within* the ancient texts. Petrarch and other figures in the revival of learning of course recognized that the old texts had been badly transmitted through the Dark Ages, but Poliziano thought they arrived positively soiled. Removing that pollution became for him an obsession.

Petrarch and Poliziano form an instructive pair, for their respective approaches to classical texts illuminate complementary conceptions of the rebirth of classical letters. The distinction between the two is clearest in a comparison of their greatest works: the Petrarchan *De ignorantia* on the one hand, emphasizing what is missing, and Poliziano's *Castigationes* on the other, emphasizing what must be censured. We might call them

Renaissance as restoration *versus* Renaissance as eradication. Petrarch's project was the recovery and multiplication of texts; Poliziano's was the excision and reduction of exemplars. This much is evident in the latter's development of genealogical philology, in which he established the grounds on which textual witnesses should be disregarded as sullied – the *eliminatio codicum descriptorum*. Anthony Grafton explains his proto-Lachmannian stemmatic method:

Given three sources *A*, *B*, and *C*, all of which agreed on a given point; if *B* and *C* depended entirely on *A* for their information, should they be considered to add any weight to *A*'s testimony? Poliziano insisted that they should not...

For him, the object is no longer...simply to amass evidence, but to discriminate, to reduce the number of witnesses that the scholar need take into account.[34]

As the *translatio studii* took humanism north and west, this model of textual transmission came along. It is no coincidence that this passage comes from Grafton's book on Joseph Scaliger, who works in Poliziano's "corruptive" tradition, as Grafton's metaphors of infection reveal. Finding the text of Festus "extremely corrupt," Scaliger realized "desperate remedies were needed," and was "both willing and able to burn and cut...If his desperate scalpel sometimes sank too deep, much of his surgery was curative as well as brilliant."[35] Corruption, burning, cutting, scalpels – the language everywhere suggests a desire to excise what is impure. A similar concern shows up in Milton, who finds Catholicism corrupt to the core, and who approaches Popery as if it were a disease. The terms he uses to attack Catholic doctrine repay attention: "Who knows not how many surreptitious works are ingraff'd into the legitimate writings of the Fathers, and of those Books that passe for authentick who knows what hath bin tamper'd withall, what hath bin raz'd out, what hath bin inserted?"[36] He finds corruption not only in men, not only in minds, but in books. Theological legitimacy rests on textual legitimacy, a central concern of the early humanists.

The age of Johnson, then, inherited a set of methods and metaphors from the humanists, but with one fundamental difference: the texts in question were not only ancient and Latin, but also modern and vernacular. The change amounted to a revolution in eighteenth-century taste. "If the '[Elizabethan] Revival' is to be traced to any one factor," writes Earl Wasserman, "it is to the transference of the method employed in editing classical texts to the editing of the English classics."[37] The eighteenth century realized, in other words, that the works of the age of Elizabeth would benefit from classical treatment. Rymer's 1709 edition of Shakespeare is important in this connection: it marks a significant break from the handling of Shakespeare's text in the seventeenth century, when a series of anonymous compilers produced the four folios. Seventeenth-century editions of Shakespeare were not published entirely without care, but they show none of the *reverence* accorded to the texts by Rymer, Pope, Theobald, and their successors. Eighteenth-century textual critics fought with one another, often fiercely, and proposed many incompatible standards by which to determine the true text of Shakespeare. For all their diversity, though, they were jointly committed to recovering Shakespeare's words and rooting out interpolations.

As we have seen in Valla, in Poliziano, and in Milton, historiographical speculation readily manifests itself in linguistic and textual criticism. And Johnson, one of the most important editors of his century, was sensitive to the historiographical implications of his work. In shepherding works from the age of Elizabeth into the age of Johnson, he reproduces the work of the humanists of three or four centuries earlier. The two historiographical models come along, sometimes, even, in the same sentence: "Not a single passage in the whole work has appeared to me corrupt, which I have not attempted to restore; or obscure, which I have not endeavoured to illustrate."[38]

No writer prompted more eighteenth-century editorial labors than Shakespeare, for it was a commonplace that his texts were in exceptionally bad shape, and had suffered more than any others in their transmission. Lewis Theobald laments in 1726 that "we have scarce any Book in the *English* Tongue more fertile of Errors, than the Plays of SHAKESPEARE," a complaint Thomas Hanmer echoes in 1744: "The works of this Author... were more injured and abused than perhaps any that ever pass'd the Press." Zachary Grey agrees in 1754: "No *dramatic poet*, either antient or modern, has had the hard fate of our author; or contains still more mistakes, than the plays of the most celebrated *Shakespeare*." Warburton has the same gripe: Shakespeare's works "at length... struggled into Light; but so disguised and travested, that no classic Author, after having run ten secular Stages thro' the blind Cloisters of Monks and Canons, ever came out in half so maimed and mangled a Condition."[39] Notice that the seventeenth century is being compared to the Dark Ages: the humanist vilification of actual monks has become metaphorical, and the two models of medieval history are used to describe textual transmission through a figurative dark age. Johnson elaborates. Shakespeare's works were vitiated by the blunders of the penman, or changed by the affectation of the player; perhaps enlarged to introduce a jest, or mutilated to shorten the representation . . . thrust into the world surreptitiously and hastily, they suffered another depravation from the ignorance and negligence of the printers . . . It is not easy for invention to bring together so many causes concurring to vitiate a text. No other authour ever gave up his works to fortune and time with so little care . . . and in no other age was the art of printing in such unskilful hands.[40]

The intrusion of Renaissance historiographical metaphors into eighteenth-century editorial theory is no accident. Johnson saw his textual criticism as fulfilling a Renaissance legacy: he places himself at the end of an exalted tradition when he writes, "Conjectural criticism has been of great use in the learned world; nor is it my intention to depreciate a study, that has exercised so many mighty minds, from the revival of learning to our own age," and follows this passage with allusions to Scaliger and Lipsius.[41] He has Scaliger in mind when he proposes an emendation to *A Midsummer Night's Dream*: "Scaliger transposed the lines of Virgil's *Gallus*. Why may not the same experiment be ventured upon Shakespeare." He knew not only Petrarch's work but also its place in literary history, as when he described Petrarch's poetic gift in the *Life of Cowley*: "Petrarch, who, in an age rude and uncultivated, by his tuneful homage to his Laura, refined the manners of the lettered world, and filled Europe with love and poetry." Poliziano, too, was a personal hero: on his arrival in London Johnson planned an edition of the Latin works of "Politian, a name eminent among the restorers of polite literature."[42] Thus he writes in his Shakespeare edition, "These corruptions I have often silently rectified; for the history of our language, and the true force of our words, can only be preserved, by keeping the text of authours free from adulteration."[43] The echoes of Poliziano and Scaliger are apparent: Shakespeare's text suffers from infection, which it is the editor's job to expunge. Johnson is significantly the first to apply Poliziano's stemmatic method to modern authors, and the first to reject derivative witnesses of an English work, as in his comments on Theobald's edition:

In his enumeration of editions, he mentions the first two folios as high, and the third folio as of middle authority; but the truth is, that the first is equivalent to all others, and that the rest only deviate from it by the printer's negligence. Whoever has any of the folios has all, excepting those diversities which mere reiteration of editions will produce. I collated them all at the beginning, but afterwards used only the first.[44]

The similarities to Poliziano's *eliminatio codicum descriptorum* are unmistakable. Johnson's critical practice, as Malone and Steevens noticed, often fell short of the standard he set for himself, and he unhappily followed the eighteenth-century practice of using the *textus receptus* as copytext rather than an early folio or quarto. But his regard for editorial theory, and his twin concerns for textual privation and corruption, show that he was the first Englishman to internalize the humanistic lessons in the editing of vernacular classics.

THE DIGNITY OF AN ANCIENT

Vernacular classics are exactly what were at stake. The eighteenth century was the first age consciously to develop a canon of English classics. This move was possible only after the age of Shakespeare became "the last age," for classics are not only great works, but *old* works. Frank Kermode argues that immediacy and contemporaneity are essential elements of a classic – "The doctrine of classic as model or criterion entails... the assumption that the ancient can be more or less immediately relevant and available, in a sense contemporaneous with the modern" – but he might also have made the opposite case, for a classic is the point of contact between the new and the old, in which proximity and distance mingle. The eighteenth century had achieved just enough distance from the age of Shakespeare to treat his works as modern classics. After a hundred years, writes Johnson, "the term commonly fixed as the test of literary merit," Shakespeare "may now begin to assume the dignity of an ancient, and claim the privilege of established fame and prescriptive veneration."[45]

In according Shakespeare the dignity of an ancient, eighteenth-century critics perhaps inevitably followed sixteenth-century examples, for the early humanists were the most self-conscious collectors and propagators of old classics. Nor should it be surprising that they used the twin metaphors of privation and corruption to create the canon of the great works of antiquity, favoring those of the first century B.C. Works by Lucretius and Tacitus were newly celebrated for bringing classical light to a dark modernity, while many Barthollist legal scholars and Scholastic philosophers were jettisoned as worthless. The deserving texts had to be passed down through a deprived age, and kept free of medieval contaminations. The familiar categories of privation and corruption were useful to the critics assembling the new canons.

Eighteenth-century critics, too, found them useful for thinking not only about the classics of antiquity, but also about the newly conceived modern and vernacular classics. It is perhaps no coincidence that the "modern classic" rises in English literature at the same time that the *querelle des anciens et des modernes* was entering its decline. The literature of the English Renaissance began to be treated as the product of another age, which demanded the sort of historically informed interpretation that the Renaissance writers accorded to the works of antiquity. Patrick Hume's 321 pages of *Annotations* to *Paradise Lost* (1695) mark the first serious attempt to give a modern vernacular work a classical treatment. "All the obscure parts [are] render'd in phrases more familiar," writes Hume, and "the old and obsolete words" are "explain'd and made easie to the English reader" – the commentary betrays no sense that Milton's poem was then only twenty-eight years old.[46] From it flowed a torrent of editions of English works on classical models. George Sewell, in his Preface to the unauthorized seventh volume of Pope's Shakespeare, is clear about the necessity of treating the works of the age of Elizabeth as modern classics: "What then has been done by the really Learned to the dead Languages...we in Justice owe to our own great Writers, both in Prose and Poetry. They are in some degree our *Classics*." Robert Anderson, writing seven decades later, notes that Shakespeare's works were published "with an accumulation of emendatory criticism and philological learning, unparalleled in the illustration of any of the classical writers of antiquity." And although Richard Bentley went too far in his *Paradise Lost* (1732), suggesting notoriously inappropriate conjectural emendations to a recent printed work, he demonstrates convincingly that Renaissance works were now English classics. "The key question," says Kristine Haugen, "is not how a hopeless pedant like Bentley could believe he had the right to edit *Paradise Lost*, but rather why a celebrated classical scholar like Bentley should have decided to edit *Paradise Lost*."[47]

Like the early humanists, eighteenth-century critics applied the ideas of privation and corruption both historically and aesthetically, using the two categories to reinforce one another. These metaphors, working in tandem, provided the dynamic by which classics were formed – and the creation of classics means the creation of a canon. The eighteenth century set about the business in the same way as their humanist predecessors: some works were celebrated, some reviled, and many ignored.

The first step is to recognize a lack that the modern classic can fill. John Upton thus uses a privative metaphor in describing his reason for reprinting Ascham's *Scholemaster*: "When I first undertook the bringing of this Treasure into Light, more valuable than the Gold of *Ophir*, it had lain above an Age little known unto the World." Robert Anderson takes pride in being the first to shepherd some Tudor and early Stuart works into the

English canon, a canon openly compared to the classical one. Drayton's works "are now for the first time received into a collection of classical English poetry"; Carew's *Coelum Britannicum* "is now, with his poems, for the first time, admitted into a collection of classical English poetry" – the sentiment is repeated, in nearly the same words, for Samuel Daniel, William Browne, Giles Fletcher, Ben Jonson, and William Davenant.[48] This sort of inclusion presupposes a lack.

But canons are not so inclusive as to be ecumenical, and the delight in filling cultural vacuity is always paired with vigilance in excluding undesirables. Not all the works of the English Renaissance, in other words, made it into the eighteenth-century canon. They were excluded on grounds similar to those used by the humanists: they were rejected as barbarous. It is perhaps surprising to see the texts of the golden ages of the sixteenth and seventeenth centuries censured as examples of barbarity, but (as we shall see) many extended the revival of learning in England well into the seventeenth century, not granting even Shakespeare's contemporaries a full measure of enlightenment. David Hume even suggests that had Milton "lived in a later age, and learned to polish some rudeness in his verses," he would have "enjoyed better fortune." Thomas Warton, too, notes that in Milton's day, "our poetry was not yet purged from its Gothic combinations; nor had legitimate notions of discrimination and propriety so far prevailed, as sufficiently to influence the growing improvements of English composition."[49] This consideration paradoxically casts much of the age of Elizabeth in the same terms the early humanists used to describe the Goths: Elizabethans and even Jacobeans are accused of ignorance, rudeness, superstition, and worse. The humanists' weapons were turned against their creators as the barbarous was assiduously weeded out of the new canon.

We may see this sort of canon creation best in a few examples of eighteenth-century handling of earlier poetry. The inclusion mentioned above is everywhere evident, as eighteenth-century critics published a growing stream of important works from the age of Elizabeth in new editions and florilegia. Inclusiveness, however, is balanced by rejection of things that did not measure up. The first example is infamous. Johnson's dismissal of the sonnet in the *Dictionary* as "not very suitable to the English language" is memorable for its bluntness and, of course, its seeming perversity. But a brief glance at poems written and anthologized in the eighteenth century reveals that his judgment was not idiosyncratic: the continuation of his definition, "and has not been used by any man of eminence since *Milton*," is entirely accurate. Apart from scattered minor efforts by Thomas Edwards, Thomas Warton, and Thomas Gray, the first important eighteenth-century collection of sonnets was published by Charlotte Smith in the year of Johnson's death.[50] Wordsworth's hortation, "Scorn not the Sonnet," is an attempt to restore to canonical status the poetic tradition which ran from Petrarch, through Tasso, Camões, Spenser, and Shakespeare, up to Milton, but which was thoroughly moribund in the age of the frowning "Critic" to whom he addresses his poem.

Johnson is one of the most influential eighteenth-century commentators on Metaphysical poetry; in addition to popularizing the term, he traced the school from Marino, through Donne, and to Suckling, Waller, Denham, Cowley, and Cleveland.[51] These poets had little chance of passing Johnson's critical muster, however, given his discussion of their poetic style: "Language suffers violence by harsh or by daring figures, by transposition, by unusual acceptations of words, and by any licence, which would be avoided by a writer of prose." His criticism is well known: "The fault of Cowley, and perhaps of all the writers of the metaphysical race, is that of pursuing his thoughts to their last ramifications, by which he loses the grandeur of generality, for of the greatest things the parts are little; what is little can be but pretty."[52] Such undignified prettiness is characteristic of many eighteenth-century attitudes toward the poetry of the Middle Ages. Arthur Murphy is right to notice that eighteenth-century criticism of the Metaphysical poets, especially Johnson's, uses the same terms of opprobrium the humanists applied to their rivals: "In Johnson's review of Cowley's works," he writes, "false wit is detected in all its shapes, and the Gothic taste for glittering conceits, and far-fetched allusions, is exploded, never, it is hoped, to revive again." Cooper can render Donne admirable only by classing him with the satirists rather than the lyricists; in the early decades of the century, in fact, his prose was more widely known than his lyric verse. The situation changed only late in the century: in 1792, for instance, Anderson could note that "Donne is better known as a poet, than as a divine." But even at that late date, Anderson could recycle this criticism of the Metaphysical style: "All [Donne's] contemporaries are lavish in his praise. Prejudiced, perhaps, by the style of writing which was then fashionable, they seem to have rated his performances beyond their just value."[53] The implication is clear: Metaphysical conceits were "fashionable," but we have now arrived at a more just and permanent estimation of their value.

It should be obvious that canons are not disinterested catalogues of great works, but collections that speak to and for the cultures that form them, telling us as much about the age in which they are codified as about the age in which they were written. What is perhaps less obvious is that the literary canon is the product of a complex set of attitudes toward the past, and emerges from historiographical conceptions of what it means to be modern. The classic and the contemporary are always in an implicit dialogue, and when Johnson helps to build the eighteenth-century canon, he does so on a distinction between enlightened and benighted. He uses the privative and corruptive metaphors for the very reasons the humanists themselves initially developed them: it is an act of self-constitution. Johnson, like Petrarch and Poliziano, places himself and his age into a historical narrative. His is an age that follows Shakespeare's emergence from barbarity, and is therefore aligned with modern enlightenment rather than Gothic darkness.

CHAPTER 2

Learning's triumph: historicism and the spirit of the age

Having characterized a barbarous Middle Age and an enlightened modernity, eighteenth-century critics set about charting the progress of European culture from one to the other. Johnson offers one powerful explanation of this progress when he writes that "Nations, like individuals, have their infancy."[1] The metaphor – the nation as an individual growing from infancy, through childhood, and into adulthood – was one of the most beloved analogues of Johnson's contemporaries, for whom cultural phylogeny recapitulated individual ontogeny. Likening society to the growing child was an old, even ancient, metaphor; it has been traced back to the first or second century, when Lucius Annaeus Florus "divided Roman history into four periods corresponding to infancy, adolescence, adulthood, and old age."[2] It flourished as never before, though, in the eighteenth century, when "the revival of learning" was figured as the adolescence that separates the ignorant childhood of the Dark Ages from the enlightened adulthood of modernity.[3]

THE GOBLINS OF WITCHCRAFT

This notion of intellectual infancy allowed cultural historians to understand and to evaluate their medieval past: the Middle Ages could be disparaged as merely infantile, or valued for glimmerings of future promise, but not accepted in its own terms. Late seventeenth- and early eighteenth-century critics vigorously and repeatedly dismissed the trappings of medieval culture as the playthings of children. Dryden, for instance, charges the early English poets with immaturity; Chaucer, he says, "lived in the infancy of our poetry, and...nothing is brought to perfection at the first. We must be children before we grow men."[4]

Nowhere was this growth clearer than in attitudes toward the supernatural. With maturity comes an abandonment of childish superstitions: we lose our fear of the dark. The eighteenth century congratulated itself

38

on this accession to enlightened adulthood by demonstrating that the cultural children of the last age had not yet entirely shaken their medieval (and Catholic) belief in fairytales and monsters under the bed. Sprat's association of the supernatural and the medieval is revealing: "These *Fantastical Forms* were reviv'd and possess'd *Christendom*, in the very height of the *Schoolemens* time: An infinit number of *Fairies* haunted every house; all Churches were fill'd with *Apparitions*." England's childish age was just waning during the age of Elizabeth, when the medieval fascination had not yet entirely passed. "The Reformation," Johnson observes, "did not immediately arrive at its meridian, and tho' day was gradually encreasing upon us, the goblins of witchcraft still continued to hover in the twilight." These goblins haunted the literature of England's adolescence, even Shakespeare – especially Shakespeare. Thomas Warton argues that Shakespeare belonged to a primitive age, with rude trappings ill suited to the more refined eighteenth century: "The Shakespeare of a more instructed and polished age, would not have given us a magician darkening the sun and noon, the sabbath of witches, and the cauldron of incantation." Johnson makes the connection with childhood unequivocal: "A poet who should now make the whole action of his tragedy depend upon enchantment," he writes, "would be banished from the theatre to the nursery."[5]

As Shakespeare is the author who best demonstrates the point, *Macbeth* is the most illustrative of his works. The supernatural elements in such comedies as *A Midsummer Night's Dream* bothered few eighteenth-century readers, who were prepared to admit mischievous fairies and magical herbs when they served comic ends. (As Fielding writes in *Tom Jones*, "The only supernatural Agents which can in any Manner be allowed to us Moderns are Ghosts...Nor would I advise the Introduction of them... by those Authors...to whom a Horse-Laugh in the Reader, would be any great Prejudice or Mortification."[6]) Nor were the nocturnal visitations in *Richard III* or *Julius Caesar* a cause for much concern: especially after mid-century, the preternatural was an accepted device for producing the fear requisite to a sublime psychology. *Macbeth*, on the other hand, depends for its action on the prescience of the witches. A long note on Shakespeare's attitude toward these witches, therefore, opens Johnson's first published piece of literary criticism, his *Observations on Macbeth*. "The reality of witchcraft or enchantment," he writes,

has in all ages and countries been credited by the common people, and in most by the learned themselves. These phantoms have indeed appeared more frequently, in proportion as the darkness of ignorance has been more gross; but it cannot be shown, that the brightest gleams of knowledge have at any time been sufficient to drive them out of the world. The time in which this kind of credulity was at its height, seems to have been that of the holy war.[7]

The implicit charge of gross Shakespearean ignorance betrays the discomfort Johnson and his contemporaries felt in accounting for these embarrassing blemishes in the national poet, and exemplifies the kinds of readings to which they resorted in their attempts to preserve his reputation. Their solution: historicist criticism.

THE GENIUS OF HIS AGE

Johnson is rarely given his due as a historicist critic; many commentators, confused by his emphasis on "generality" and "universality," assume this precludes any attention to Shakespeare's historical situation. Johnson, they say, is concerned only with timeless verities, not with the specific historical conditions under which authors lived. And yet this opinion so little reflects Johnson's practice that it seems attributable either to an ignorance of Johnson or to a willful misreading of his works. Robert Stock, responding to such critics, quotes from the first page of the Preface to Shakespeare – "Every man's performance, to be rightly estimated, must be compared with the state of the age in which he lived" – and adds, "It would be difficult to state the problem more concisely." Such emphasis on an author's historical moment informs nearly all of Johnson's works, from his earliest to his latest critical publications. "In order to make a true estimate of the abilities and merit of a writer," he writes in his *Observations on Macbeth* (1745), "it is always necessary to examine the genius of his age, and the opinions of his contemporaries"; almost four decades later, he writes in the *Life of Dryden* (1779), "To judge rightly of an author we must transport ourselves to his time." Lawrence Lipking writes that Johnson "loathed" historicism – but if Johnson be not a historicist critic, where is historicism to be found?[8]

Johnson's ability to transport himself to the past was limited, to be sure, by his ability and willingness to carry out meticulous research, at least compared to his more professional successors. Eighteenth-century historicism was admittedly unsophisticated in its distinction of various ages, with its relatively homogeneous treatment of the Middle Ages and even much of the sixteenth and seventeenth centuries as an undifferentiated "Gothic" era. An imagined difference in historical ages was often used by the unsophisticated to explain away every oddity the eighteenth century found difficult to address directly: historicism was sometimes simply an excuse. But these are the limitations and abuses of a method which, at its best, was one of the most notable elements in eighteenth-century British criticism generally, and Johnson's in particular. It is, moreover, part of the legacy of Renaissance scholarship, which first developed the themes and techniques which have informed our reading ever since. Johnson inherited from the early humanist critics three related convictions: first, that historical periods are distinct from one another and have their own characters; second, that works of literature reflect this character; and third, that these works can be understood only with reference to it. He shared these convictions with many critics of his day. "The spirit of the age," writes Hume, "affects all the arts," and Elizabeth Montagu reminds us that reading earlier authors is impossible "if we do not remember the different circumstances under which these writers were composed."[9] Thomas Warton makes as clear a statement of the importance of historical criticism as we are likely to find anywhere:

In reading the works of a poet who lived in a remote age, it is necessary that we should look back upon the customs and manners which prevailed in that age. We should endeavour to place ourselves in the writer's situation and circumstances. Hence we shall become better enabled to discover, how his turn of thinking, and manner of composing, were influenced by familiar appearances and established objects, which are utterly different from those with which we are at present surrounded.[10]

This sort of criticism gives us an insight into how the eighteenth century imagined the relationship between culture and history. Shakespeare made sense only against the background of the sixteenth century: "works" and "manners" are inseparable.

Relating Shakespeare to his age had canonical consequences. No other writer of the sixteenth or seventeenth century came close to inspiring such interest, and eighteenth-century bardolatry drew a distinction not only in degree but in kind between Shakespeare and all his contemporaries. Most of them were in fact forgotten by the general public, neither printed nor acted during the century.[11] Among playwrights, only Jonson and Beaumont and Fletcher could be called popular, and although Dryden noted that his age preferred them to Shakespeare, by the end of the eighteenth century they were thoroughly eclipsed.

Paradoxically, though, the popular predominance of Shakespeare over contemporary writers led not to their increased obscurity, but to their virtual rediscovery in the eighteenth and early nineteenth centuries. Understanding Shakespeare demanded an understanding of his age, and therefore the study of other sixteenth-century literature was ancillary to the study of Shakespeare. In this spirit, Johnson describes his objective in his edition of Shakespeare: "The editor...hopes, that, by comparing the works of Shakespeare with those of the writers who lived at the same time, immediately preceded, or immediately followed him, he shall be able to ascertain his ambiguities." He therefore credits Charlotte Lennox for "her Plan which comprised...translations, and extracts from such Writers as he appears to have made use of." Johnson's collaborator, Steevens, argued that "From a diligent perusal of the comedies of contemporary authors, I am persuaded that the meaning of many expressions in SHAKESPEARE might be retrieved." Peter Whalley likewise notes that "In reading the Plays of *Shakespeare*, I could not help comparing some Passages, with familiar ones in the other Drammatic Writers of the same and subsequent Age. I found they mutually borrowed, and reflected Light upon each other." Always the scholarly movement is from Shakespeare to his contemporaries and immediate predecessors, in the hope that they will shed their reflected light back on Shakespeare.[12]

Glossing secular texts by finding parallels in other texts of the same historical moment was a characteristic practice of the humanist grammarians, but before the eighteenth century it had not been systematically applied to vernacular works. In Johnson's age, however, the hunt for modern sources and analogues got under way. Among the most conspicuous examples of this phenomenon are the volumes devoted to recovering and examining Shakespeare's sources. Thomas Percy devotes an entire book of his *Reliques* to "such ballads as are quoted by SHAKESPEARE, or contribute in any way to illustrate his writings." Thomas Hawkins's *Origin of the English Drama* appeared in 1773, reprinting plays from *Everyman* at the beginning of the sixteenth century through *The Wily Beguiled* at the beginning of the seventeenth. The headnotes stress not their intrinsic merit, but their usefulness in illuminating Shakespeare and in tracing for the reader the teleological "rise and gradual improvement of our Drama before his time." Even clearer in its intention is a pair of volumes published on the same plan in 1779, *Six Old Plays, on which Shakspeare Founded His Measure for Measure, Comedy of Errors, Taming of the Shrew, King John, K. Henry IV. and K. Henry V., King Lear*. "Their claim to be preserved," says the Advertisement, "is built on their having suggested such plans as [Shakespeare's] superior genius and judgment enabled him to improve." Among the most impressive works in this tradition is Edward Capell's *School of Shakespeare; or, Authentic Extracts from Divers English Books, that Were in Print in that Author's Time*. In collecting hundreds of passages from sixteenth-century authors, major and minor, as potential parallels and sources for Shakespeare's plays, he produced the rudiments of a dictionary of Elizabethan usage, even a period-specific encyclopedia on the customs of Shakespeare's contemporaries.[13]

Historicism and the attention accorded to comparatively minor authors played an important part in the professionalization of editing, for it raised the scholarly stakes. Though historical criticism came to influence almost every reading of older texts, it was the textual scholars who owed the most to the new methods. Early in the century, Swift and Pope could ridicule editors who wasted time pedantically sorting through the literary rubbish of the last age: as Pope put it in the *Essay on Criticism*, "*Not* to know some Trifles, is a Praise." But their approach did not survive their century: a new kind of annotator of vernacular classics was being born, and belletristic Temples and Popes were gradually edged out by diligent Bentleys and Theobalds. "Theobald was the first of this class of editors," says Hawkins; "For the purpose of publishing Shakespeare, he ... asserts, that he had read no fewer than eight hundred old English plays, besides histories and novels to a great amount." Theobald's figure may be inflated, but by the time we reach Malone's 1821 variorum, tremendous scholarly application is an indispensable critical credential. Scholarship after Malone, notes Trevor Ross, became "a specialized forensic science whose degree of requisite erudition was beyond the reach of most common readers." Thomas Warton sums up the new scholarly ethos: "Pope laughs at Theobald.... [But] If Shakespeare is worth reading, he is worth explaining."[14]

The new methods did more than rescuing commentators from Scriblerian ignominy: they helped to codify a canon of second-tier authors. The need to understand the national poet turned critics' attention to his contemporaries, and reinforced their notion of Shakespeare's day as a distinct age. The new canon grew up around Shakespeare, the gravitational center of a new literary solar system, and eighteenth-century critics catalogued his satellites with the same zeal that Halley and Herschel gave to the literal heavens. The development of a canon of modern vernacular classics amounted to a literary Newtonian revolution.

The use of minor authors to illuminate their betters could be continued down the hierarchy of writers, shedding light on an ever-expanding field. Spenser, for instance, could be used to illuminate Shakespeare;

and Johnson in turn praises Thomas Warton for using still lesser
contemporaries to understand Spenser:

You have shown to all who shall hereafter attempt the study of our ancient
authours the way to success, by directing them to the perusal of the books which
these authours had read . . . The Reason why the authours which are yet read
of the sixteenth Century are so little understood is that they are read alone, and
no help is borrowed from those who lived with them or before them.[15]

Having worked its way from Shakespeare down to the meanest of our
ancient authors, the progression of scholarly interest went further still,
and crossed the line between literature and the real world. We have
already seen that the eighteenth century recognized the need to read
Renaissance works historically, but the particular form this historicism
took – comparing literature to "customs," rather than strictly to other
literature – was by no means inevitable. The association of art and life
probably began when, in the hopes of explicating difficult passages and
curious actions in the national poet, critics looked beyond Renaissance
texts to Renaissance customs: a move permitted, encouraged, and perhaps even required by the emphasis on mimesis in so much Renaissance literary theory. Books were not enough. The assumption was that
the sixteenth-century text would make more sense when compared not
only with other sixteenth-century texts, but with actual sixteenth-century
practice, which was assumed to differ from what came before and after
it. The seven hundred pages of Zachary Grey's Shakespearean exegesis
in *Critical, Historical, and Explanatory Notes on Shakespeare* (1754) exemplify
this trend as they range over the chronicle history of Holinshed and Hall;
the drama of Jonson, Kyd, and Shirley; the poetry of Skelton, Drayton,
Quarles, and Henryson; the scholarship of Erasmus, Reuchlin, Raleigh,
James I, Knolles, Melanchthon, and Minshew; and dozens of other contemporary works, as well as more recent publications such as Echard's
History of England, Baker's *History of the Inquisition*, and even Ray's *Collection
of English Proverbs*. The entire world, from the highest culture to the lowest,
could be used to illustrate Shakespeare's meaning.

ERRORS OF THE TIMES

Although this historicizing practice may have begun in explication, its
most potent use was justification. The sixteenth century, after all, meant
intellectual childhood or adolescence, and this was a problem. Everyone knew Shakespeare's works were filled with preposterous elements

unworthy of serious consideration by grown-ups, but Shakespeare himself could not be relegated to the nursery quite so easily. By the eighteenth century, substantial British cultural capital had been invested in him. Few could admit that his puerile fascination with ghosts and goblins was essential to his works: that was to give in to the malicious carping of Voltaire and other Continental critics. Although some textual critics and dramatic adaptors sought a way out through "correcting" old texts to remove the most palpable absurdities – Pope's demotion of troublesome Shakespearean passages to the foot of the page and Bentley's proposed emendations to Milton's *Paradise Lost* are the most infamous examples – the more common approach, and the one Johnson adopts in his *Observations* and elsewhere, was to *defend* Shakespeare's judgment by blaming his intellectual immaturity on his entire age. Thence arose the effort to point the finger of blame for his artistic faults not at Shakespeare himself, but at his audience: in George Sewell's words, "Yet, you great Judges, sometimes wink at Crimes, / Most were not his, but Errors of the Times." Although Shakespeare is responsible for many things "which a modern audience would not easily endure," says Johnson, we must "make some allowance for his ignorance" – and, more to the point, the ignorance of his entire age.[16]

The obverse of this blame is that texts could be not only explicated but also exculpated with reference to their age. Against the background of such a vitiated age, Shakespeare appears not backwards but remarkably enlightened, as George Sewell marvels in his "Essay on the Art, Rise, and Progress of the Stage": "I must always think our Author a Miracle, for the Age he liv'd in."[17] And in a curious bit of critical legerdemain, the same habit of extending criticism from literature to real life can give the whole age some of the glory, if not the refinement, of its greatest authors. A backward age was redeemed by its writers, who in turn made the age glorious.

"A people newly awakened to literary curiosity," writes Johnson, "being yet unacquainted with the true state of things, knows not how to judge of that which is proposed as its resemblance. Whatever is remote from common appearances is always welcome to vulgar, as to childish credulity." The intellectual childhood is not Shakespeare's, but an entire age's. Examples are plentiful, for Johnson often resorts to such explanations in his edition. He adduces Camden's *Account of Ireland* to show that some superstitious practices are "founded upon a practice really observed by the uncivilised natives of that society." He finds Gloucester's blinding in *Lear* unbearable, "Yet let it be remembered that our authour well knew what would please the audience for which he wrote." Shakespeare's own judgment is sound, and his excesses are explained away as an awareness of his audience and market savvy. So Johnson rationalizes "the seeming improbability of Lear's conduct" by observing "that he is represented according to histories at that time vulgarly received as true." He summarizes all this in his Dedication to *Shakespear Illustrated*: "This disposition of the age concurred so happily with the imagination of Shakespeare that he had no desire to reform it, and indeed to this he was indebted for the licentious variety, by which he has made his plays more entertaining than those of any other author."[18] Others take the same tack, as when Grey attributes Shakespeare's "*jingles, puns*, and *quibbles*" (those favorite *bêtes noires* of eighteenth-century critics) to "the false taste of the times in which he lived."[19] Whalley attributes much of Shakespeare's "unjustifiable Wildness" to "the Taste and Humour of the Times," and "allow[s] their Appetites to have been much depraved."[20]

It is no surprise to see fourteenth-century writers treated this way, as when Elizabeth Cooper writes that "In the Rudeness of [Langland's] Lines, we plainly discover the Rudeness of the Age he wrote in." It is only slightly less accountable in the works of the early English Renaissance, as when she is pleased to find "more Merit" in Barclay's *Ship of Fools* "than, I think, could be expected from so barren, and unpolite an Age." But it is perhaps unexpected to see even the seventeenth century blamed for its Gothic darkness, as when William Duff complains that Shakespeare's age was "certainly not the æra of correct and refined taste." Such accounts make sense, though, if we recall the assumption that Elizabethan England was just entering its adolescence, and, though it had achieved vigor, it had not yet acquired mature judgment. Shakespeare "lived in an age when the books of chivalry were yet popular," says Johnson, "and when therefore the minds of his auditors were not accustomed to balance probabilities, or to examine nicely the proportion between causes and effects."[21]

Magic, as suggested above, was the most important blemish that needed to be explained away with reference to the age, and in discussions of magic we can see this historicist justification in action. Johnson's defense of Shakespeare's use of enchantment – "the existence of which was, I am afraid, believed very seriously" – is typical: "A survey of the notions that prevailed at the time when this play was written, will prove that Shakespeare...only turned the system that was then universally admitted to his advantage," for "He that wrote for such an audience was under the necessity of looking round for strange events and fabulous transactions." Johnson searches for other possibilities as well, including dramatic characterization – "Shakespeare put these forced and unnatural metaphors into the mouth of Macbeth as a mark of artifice and dissimulation" – and political shrewdness – "The system of *Daemonologie* was immediately adopted by all who desired either to gain preferment or not to lose it."[22]

DISPELLING THE EMPIRE OF SUPERSTITION

"Of these trifles enough." Beginning in the sixteenth century, "When Learning's triumph o'er her barb'rous Foes / First rear'd the stage,"[23] England entered its cultural adolescence and traded its trifles for truth, its fear of the dark for a measure of enlightenment. The giants and dragons were banished by the revival of learning. Johnson, the Wartons, and others, as I shall argue in chapter 7, considered this later instruction and polish a mixed blessing; for now, it is enough to point out that the bogeymen of the Middle Ages were put to rest at the restoration of polite letters.

The reasons for the rebirth of classical learning were complex, and eighteenth-century critics and historians considered a number of explanations for this onset of maturity. One suggests that "the imperfect Discoveries which had been lately made in the new World" played a part.[24] Thomas Warton notes that Germany's "mechanical genius" was responsible for "an admirable invention, which was of the most singular utility in facilitating the diffusion of the antient writers over every part of Europe: I mean the art of printing," and observes that "the recent introduction into England of the art of typography...greatly contributed to multiply English composition."[25]

For Protestants, however, the single most important cause of the revival of learning was the decline of the institution that enforced the darkness of the Middle Ages: the Catholic Church. The Reformation will be discussed in greater length in chapter 4, but we must now observe how large a role Protestantism played in the revival of learning. It was the priests who strove to keep the laity in the dark: "In the barbarous ages, Sir," Johnson told Boswell, "priests and people were equally deceived; but afterwards there were gross corruptions introduced by the clergy." The infantile monsters, in other words, often came from Rome, and the gross corruptions belonged to the same childish age as the ghosts and goblins of witchcraft. Warton's remark on "the corruptions and impostures of popery" is thoroughly conventional.[26]

The rise of Protestantism was often seen as a lifting of ecclesiastical restrictions on what the Middle Ages were allowed to read. "The passion for LETTERS was extreme," remarks Hurd, in part because of the passing of "the artifices that had been used to keep men from them." Horace Walpole suggests that literacy and rationality were mutually reinforcing, as increased literacy resulted in the decline of popery: "Letters were then [*c.* 1500] in their most flourishing state in Italy, and contributed to dispel the empire of superstition, at that time so forcibly attacked by the reformers."[27]

The matching rise of secular learning and decline of traditional piety is a familiar part of nineteenth-century and later accounts of the Renaissance; the term "humanism" is still routinely paired with "secular." Eighteenth-century Anglicans were doubtless more sensitive than we to the piety of such Christian humanists as Erasmus and More, but many of them do note a trend in which secular classical learning becomes more important than religion. The Protestants' intellectual heroes knew about the superstitious impostures of the Church as early as the eleventh century. Peter de Blois becomes for Thomas Warton a herald of the new age when he "quotes Quintilian, Cicero, Livy, Sallust, Seneca, Virgil, Quintus Curtius, Ovid, Statius, Suetonius, Juvenal, and Horace, more frequently and familiarly than the fathers." Warton praises Thomas à Becket's twelfth-century "private ideas concerning the bigottries and superstitious absurdities of his religion." John Gunthorpe secured for the English universities a number of Italian manuscripts which "were of much more real value, than the sumptuous silver image of the virgin Mary, weighing one hundred and forty-three ounces." This celebration of the triumph of secular learning over religious superstition reaches its apogee when David Hume, who praises Leo X as "one of the most illustrious princes that ever sat on the papal throne," justifies his part in the early Counter Reformation: "Leo, from the penetration of his genius, and his familiarity with ancient literature, was fully acquainted with the ridicule and falsity of the doctrines, which, as supreme pontiff, he was obliged by his interest to promote."[28] Rank hypocrisy, it seems, is more forgivable in an esteemed pope than the thought that he may have taken Romish superstition seriously.

THE ACADEMICAL LIFE

The whole maturing process was helped along by a regimen of education: during the reign of Henry VIII, adolescent England was sent to school under the tuition of an Italian master. As England entered its adolescence under Continental tutelage, it began to acquire its own mature character, and the awakening to polite learning was reflected in every aspect of Renaissance culture.

England's sixteenth-century educational revolution was promoted by the serendipitous occurrence of a fifteenth-century political revolution. "An event," Thomas Warton writes, "almost fortuitous and unexpected, gave a direction to that spirit of curiosity and discovery... About the year 1453, the dispersion of the Greeks... totally changed the state of letters in Europe." The letters were, of course, classical, and therefore superior to the "unprofitable definitions and unnecessary distinctions" of the "unintelligible elucidations of Scotus and Aquinas." Medieval learning, says Warton, was "clogged with pedantry, and depressed by the narrow notions of the times. Their writings shew, that they knew not how to imitate the beauties of the antient classics." The new learning then dispersed "the scholastic cloud which inveloped our universities."[29] Warton's account of the revival of learning presents a representative eighteenth-century canon of "illustrious" English scholars:

In the reign of Henry VII. classical literature began to be received and studied in England; and the writings of the antients were cultivated with true taste and erudition, by Sir Thomas More, Colet, Ascham, Leland, Cheke, and other illustrious rivals in polished composition. Erasmus was entertained and patronised by the king and nobility; and the greek language, that inestimable reposistory of genuine elegence and sublimity, was taught and admired.[30]

The *rinascita* was for classically educated writers the single most important cultural development of the last age. The importance of these backward looks toward antiquity is evident in some of the terms, nearly all beginning with the *re-* prefix: the revival of learning, the restoration of letters, the restitution of grammatical literature, and so on. A common Renaissance motto was "renovatio, restitutio, restuaratio."[31] The new billed itself as a return to the old.

The fall of Constantinople marked an important turning point in eighteenth-century conceptions of European history. Before that, the West was benighted, and what learning survived was in the East. But with the fall of the Byzantine Empire, learning was driven back to western Europe, as Hume explains: "In 1453 Constantinople was taken by the Turks; and the Greeks, among whom some remains of learning were still preserved... imported, together with their admirable language, a tincture of their science and of their refined taste in poetry and eloquence."[32]

The fall is equally epochal in Cellarius, who uses it as the point of division between his medieval and modern histories, and in Gibbon, who closes his *Decline and Fall* with it.

There were, to be sure, qualifications. Petrarch was widely admired as a harbinger of the new learning from well before 1453, and "Efforts were made in our English universities for the revival of critical studies," writes Warton, "much sooner than is commonly imagined" – as early as 1439. "It should be remembered, that some learned Grecians…frequented Italy, and taught their language there, before the taking of Constantinople."[33] (In fact Grosseteste was studying Greek at Oxford as early as the twelfth century, as Johnson knew, and Pilato taught it in Florence by 1360.) Neat myths, though, are often more satisfying than narratives riddled with precursors and qualifications. No other event better indicated the transition from medieval ignorance to modern learning than the fall of Constantinople. When Johnson therefore refers to "The first race of scholars, in the fifteenth century,"[34] he means the years after 1453. His clearest statement comes in the *Life of Ascham*: "The destruction of the Constantinopolitan empire had driven the Greeks, with their language, into the interiour parts of Europe…Learning was, at that time, prosecuted with that eagerness and perseverance, which, in this age of indifference and dissipation, it is not easy to conceive. To teach or to learn was, at once, the business and the pleasure of the academical life."[35] He suggests its larger cultural importance by using it as the backdrop of his only drama, *Irene*, where he gives an account of the *translatio studii*:

> The mighty *Tuscan* courts the banish'd Arts
> To kind *Italia*'s hospitable Shades;
> There shall soft Leisure wing th' excursive Soul,
> And Peace propitious smile on fond Desire;
> There shall despotick Eloquence resume
> Her ancient Empire o'er the yielding Heart;
> There Poetry shall tune her sacred Voice,
> And wake from Ignorance the Western World.[36]

This is not only fortuitous and unexpected, but a curious paradox: the encroachment of heathen barbarians resulted in the new enlightenment of Europe. The fifteenth-century Vandals followed in the footsteps of their fifth-century predecessors, but with the opposite results. Luckily for the West, in their grab for land, the barbarians were content to let learning escape unharmed. Warton notes with relief that Bajazet II was willing to part with Greek manuscripts, so long as he was able to keep Greek cities.[37] Greece suffered a fall, but for the West it was a fortunate one.

The masters of Greek learning settled predominantly in Italy, where the revival of learning began in earnest: as one critic writes, fifteenth-century Italy "could boast a Set of Learned Men, and a Vein of Learning little inferior to that of the *Augustan* age."[38] And though it began in Italy, the new learning was international in scope. Warton praises the scholars of Germany (Rodolphus Langius, Reuchlin, Maximilian I), Spain (Antonio de Lebrixa, Cardinal Ximenes), and "Even Hungary, a country by no means uniformly advanced with other parts of Europe in the common arts of civilisation" (Mattheo Corvini, Cardinal Bozmanni).[39]

Maturity finally arrived in England in a great infusion of Continental culture:

The philology of Italy had been transplanted hither in the reign of Henry the Eighth; and the learned languages had been successfully cultivated by Lilly, Linacer, and More; by Pole, Cheke, and Gardiner; and afterwards by Smith, Clerk, Haddon, and Ascham. Greek was now taught to boys in the principal schools; and those who united elegance with learning, read, with great diligence, the Italian and Spanish poets.[40]

The dependence of native English culture upon the fertilizing influence of Continental culture is a commonplace. Anderson makes the point in his *Life of Surrey*: "After the death of Chaucer, no considerable improvements were made in English poetry, till about the beginning of the sixteenth century. At that point, our intercourse with Italy, not only introduced the study of classical literature into England, but gave a new turn to our vernacular poetry." Warton observes that shortly "Before the year 1490, many of our countrymen appear to have turned their thoughts to the revival of the study of the classics... chiefly in consequence of their communications with Italy." Gray too is aware of the effect of Continental literature on that of England's adolescence; his plan for a history of English poetry begins its second part with "*Chaucer* who first introduced the manner of the Provençaux by the Italians into our country," and in its third traces "The lyric poetry of [Tasso's] & the former age introduced from Italy by Ld Surrey, Sr T. Wyat, Bryan, Ld Vaux, &c: in the beginning of the 16th century." Even those who did not travel to the Continent still had access to Continental learning: "Another capital source of the poetry peculiar to this period," as Warton explains, "consisted in the numerous translations of Italian tales into English."[41]

THE FIRST RANK OF LITERARY HEROES

This is the refined scholarly air Johnson breathed throughout his life. If the almost mythical story is to be believed, Johnson's first taste of learning came from one of the first figures of the revival of letters, and his own development from child to man was precipitated by his exposure to the narrative of cultural maturity. Boswell tells the story, with its suggestions of Eden and a fortunate fall:

Having imagined that his brother had hid some apples behind a large folio upon an upper shelf in his father's shop, he climbed up to search for them. There were no apples; but the large folio proved to be Petrarch, whom he had seen mentioned, in some preface, as one of the restorers of learning. His curiosity having been thus excited, he sat down with avidity, and read a great part of the book.[42]

It was a taste that stayed with him his entire life. Shortly after his arrival in London, he proposed an edition of Poliziano, and soon collaborated on the compilation of the massive catalogue of the Harleian Library; near his death, John Nichols reports, "He seriously entertained the thought of translating *Thuanus*."[43] Perhaps no period in world history had so strong a hold on Johnson's imagination as Europe's struggle to emerge from barbarity.

For most of Johnson's contemporaries, even the most educated, scholarship like Petrarch's and Poliziano's warranted only antiquarian interest. The great early modern tradition of international scholarship in Latin was moribund by the eighteenth century. But it had not quite died, and for Johnson, at least, its attraction was neither antiquarian nor superficial: the old scholars had a powerful influence on his entire intellectual life. Robert DeMaria has provided the most extensive account of this part of Johnson's character, though he was hardly the first to see him in this light. A century ago, Sir Leslie Stephen suggested that Johnson "felt a closer affinity to these old scholars [such as Sir Thomas Browne]... than to the brilliant but comparatively superficial writers of Queen Anne's time. He was, one may say, a scholar of the old type." Percy Hazen Houston, a quarter century later, noted that "With the great humanists who followed in the wake of the revival of learning Johnson found himself in thoroughly congenial company."[44]

We can take the measure of Johnson's fascination with the revival of learning by looking at some of the learned figures he refers to. He was pleasantly surprised to discover that an acquaintance knew the work of a sixteenth-century grammarian: "Mr. Langton happening to mention his having read a good deal in Clenardus's Greek Grammar, 'Why, Sir, (said he,) who is there in this town who knows any thing of Clenardus but you and I?'" In quick surveys of the history of the pastoral he refers to Sannazaro's *Piscatory Eclogues*, Badius's commentary on Mantuan's poems, and the pastorals of Poliziano, Tasso, and Guarini. A mention of Stoicism calls to mind "Lipsius, the great modern master of the Stoic philosophy." He finds Vida "a man of considerable skill in the politicks of literature," and praises him for displaying "felicity of his numbers... at the revival of learning." A discussion of old age recollects a remark "by old Cornaro" – Luigi Cornaro's *Vita Sobria* (1558) – and a meditation on death brings to mind "Pontanus, a man celebrated among the early restorers of literature."[45]

Pontanno shows up in another of Johnson's comments, in perhaps the most famous of his *Rambler* essays, on modern fiction: "I remember a remark made by Scaliger upon Pontanus, that all his writings are filled with the same images." But the more important figure here is J. J. Scaliger, of whom he writes, "He was a man of such estimation among his companions that the casual censures or praises which he dropped in conversation were considered... as worthy of preservation," and praises his "enormous, wonderful, and gigantick memory. Scaliger reports of himself, that, in his youth, he could repeat above an hundred verses, having once read them." He thought of Scaliger when he revised his *Dictionary* and when he was at work on his Shakespeare edition.[46]

Johnson calls Scaliger's greatest pupil, Hugo Grotius, "that name so justly celebrated."[47] An extended study of Johnson's debt to him will likely repay the effort, as suggested by not only the number but the importance of the references to Grotius in Johnson's works. He was one of the first religious authors Johnson tried to read, before his Latin was equal to the task, and *De jure belli ac pacis* was in Johnson's library at his death. Johnson in fact considered him the only person in history with whom he would change places (rejecting Boswell's choice, Shakespeare), and in 1777 he actively solicited financial support for an impoverished descendant of Grotius.[48] His influence on Chambers's Vinerian lectures is evident and pervasive; and some of Johnson's opinions not only on warfare but on political subordination, colonization, and slavery may owe something to the discussion in *De jure belli ac pacis*.[49]

Although Johnson's knowledge of neo-Latin scholarship was vast, not all his intellectual heroes were as recondite as Clenardus or as challenging as Grotius. Others were celebrated widely and enthusiastically. Erasmus, for instance, attracted the attention of more than scholars and antiquarians. Pope praises him in *An Essay on Criticism* and even considered writing his biography, although the task was left for John Jortin. Between 1709 and 1787, *The Praise of Folly* appeared in English translation nine times and in Latin three times. Other works by Erasmus were more popular still: at least sixty Latin, English, or bilingual editions of the *Colloquies*, a popular school text, appeared in Britain between 1725 and 1800. (Johnson included "Erasmus, with an English translation" as a text appropriate for the first year in his "Scheme for the Classes of a Grammar School.") Bowles noted Johnson's "Great regard for Erasmus," and in *Rambler* 108, Johnson praises Erasmus as one who "will stand for ever in the first rank of literary heroes."[50] Johnson may well have identified with the devout intellectual who rose from humble origins, wrote copiously but hastily throughout his career, and was unable to secure lasting patronage because he had more of the scholar than the courtier in his make-up. It is even possible (though difficult to prove) that Johnson's well-known pacifist sentiments (expressed, for instance, in *Thoughts on Falkland's Islands*) were derived from, or influenced by, humanist anti-war tracts such as Erasmus's *Querela pacis*.[51]

Erasmus's friend Thomas More was an equally important presence in Johnson's intellectual life. Just as Erasmus may have influenced Johnson's positions on contemporary events such as the dispute over the Falkland Islands, More provided a source for some of Johnson's political sentiments: he turned to *Utopia* in *Rambler* 114 to support his case for "invigorating the laws by relaxation, and extirpating wickedness by lenity."[52] In this he was entirely characteristic of his age. "The learned and ingenious Sir *Thomas More*"[53] was widely celebrated in the eighteenth century. Swift's Gulliver, in invoking the spirits of the dead in Glubbdubdrib, places More among an impressive constellation of heroes: More, Brutus, "his Ancestor *Junius, Socrates, Epaminondas*, [and] *Cato* the Younger" make up "A *Sextumvirate* to which all the Ages of the World cannot add a Seventh."[54] Publication history shows More's popularity was widespread: English editions of *Utopia* appeared eight times between 1737 and 1795, along with two Latin editions.

Ascham was another favorite: Johnson not only wrote his life, but apparently edited his works.[55] He was pleased to play tourist in Ascham's birthplace, writing from Newcastle to Mrs. Thrale, "We dined at York, and went on to Northallerton, a place of which I know nothing but that it afforded us a lodging on Monday night, and about two hundred and seventy years ago, gave birth to Roger Ascham." His praise elsewhere is more substantial: he calls Ascham "the chief ornament of a celebrated college," who "not only instructed scholars in literature, but formed *Elizabeth* to empire," and makes him, with Haddon, "the pride of Elizabeth's reign." He notes that *The Scholemaster* "contains the best advice that was ever given for the study of languages," and insists that "His philological learning would have gained him honour in any country; and among us, it may justly call for that reverence which all nations owe to those who first rouse them from ignorance, and kindle among them the light of literature."[56] For these reasons, Ascham is quoted by name 122 times in the first edition of the *Dictionary*.

We can see the influence of Ascham's *Scholemaster* in Johnson's scattered writings on education. Skeptical of the popular report that "in the art of education [Milton] performed wonders," he reminds his readers "that nobody can be taught faster than he can learn," which catches the spirit of Ascham's insistence that the tutor suit his lessons to the capacity of the student. Ascham's aversion to corporal punishment, moreover, is evident in Johnson's concern "that Milton was one of the last students in either university that suffered the publick indignity of corporal correction." Johnson quotes from Ascham's diatribe against beating in the *Dictionary*: "He was beaten out of all love of learning by a fond schoolmaster." Although Johnson maintained the right of a teacher to resort to thrashing, he "retained a strong aversion for the memory of [his old master] Hunter...who, he said once, was a brutal fellow," noting at another time, "He was not severe, Sir. A master ought to be severe. Sir, he was cruel."[57]

Figures of the late Renaissance continued to fascinate Johnson. Boswell records Maxwell's observation that "Burton's 'Anatomy of Melancholy'...was the only book that ever took him out of bed two hours sooner than he wished to rise," along with Johnson's own evaluation of the work: "Burton's 'Anatomy of Melancholy' is a valuable work. It is, perhaps, overloaded with quotation. But there is great spirit and great power in what Burton says, when he writes from his own mind." Burton also provides one of Johnson's most famous *sententiae*, delivered as a warning to Boswell: "The great direction which Burton has left to men disordered like you, is this, *Be not solitary; be not idle*: which I would thus modify; – If you are idle, be not solitary; if you are solitary, be not idle."[58] Thomas Browne too was a lifelong favorite of Johnson, who wrote his *Life* and edited his *Christian Morals*.[59] Browne's most obvious influence on Johnson was his style: the "Anglo-Latian diction" that led Johnson into his frequent examples of "*Brownism*."[60] But the influence was deeper still. Johnson writes that "Some of the most pleasing performances have been produced by learning and genius, exercised upon subjects of little importance ... [for] the fanciful sports of great minds are never without some advantage to knowledge," and uses Browne as an example of "how uncommon attainments have been gained, and what influence learning had on its possesours, or virtue on its teachers." Johnson insists that his esteem will remain high "while learning shall have any reverence among men; for there is no science in which he does not discover some skill; and scarce any kind of knowledge, profane or sacred, abstruse or elegant, which he does not appear to have cultivated with success."[61]

This gallery of heroes amounts to more than a collection of Johnson's favorite thinkers. They are important not only individually, but in the aggregate: they are the embodiment of an age, an age distinguished from its benighted and superstitious predecessor by its intellectual energy. The revival of learning was for Johnson and his contemporaries the motive spring which drove Europe from one age to another, and its effect is evident in every product of the culture – not only in scholarly editions, lexicons, and treatises, but in Shakespeare's plays, and even in the conditions of real life during Elizabeth's reign, all of which were explained with reference to the great scholarly achievements of the age. The entire sixteenth century could be seen as the struggle between childish superstition and mature learning, and as Johnson's age told the story, the latter emerged victorious.

CHAPTER 3

Call Britannia's glories back to view: Tudor history and Hanoverian historians

As a complement to and consequence of the European revival of learning came the reign of Elizabeth – in Johnson's words, "the favourite period of English greatness."[1] This greatness brims over in his first major poem, *London* (1738), one of the eighteenth century's most famous evocations of a Tudor monarch:

> On Thames's banks, in silent thought we stood,
> Where Greenwich smiles upon the silver flood:
> Struck with the seat that gave Eliza birth,
> We kneel, and kiss the consecrated earth;
> In pleasing dreams the blissful age renew,
> And call Britannia's glories back to view;
> Behold her cross triumphant on the main,
> The guard of commerce, and the dread of Spain.[2]

Although this idolatrous admiration of the 1580s is enough to make us forget for a moment the poem's satirical function in the 1730s, Johnson's history lesson is anything but disinterested. By recalling Tudor glories and contrasting Walpole's Spanish policy with Elizabeth's, Johnson uses Tudor history as a standard by which to measure the present. Similar invocations of the Tudor dynasty abound in the eighteenth century. Elizabeth and her age were discussed and celebrated by writers of every political persuasion: in the hands of a political insider, the idealized past was a useful tool for propagandizing the reigning monarch; in the hands of the satirist, it was a cudgel with which to beat the debased present.

The historiographical stakes were high, because whoever directed the interpretation of the sixteenth century could help to direct the interpretation of the seventeenth and eighteenth centuries as well: history and modern politics were inseparable. All the warring political factions therefore sought to enlist history on their side by tracing the rise of England from medieval chaos to Renaissance order – or, to put it another way, from Richard III to Elizabeth – and inviting readers to continue tracing the path from Elizabeth to the Stuarts, the Hanoverians, or Walpole. To recover the full meaning of these political invocations of the Renaissance, we must follow the eighteenth-century historians in their progression from the distant past to the present, for Britain's present made sense only in the context of its past.

THE MAJESTY OF HISTORY

It may not strike us as a promising subject. Eighteenth-century British historiography sometimes seems naïve in comparison with that of the Continent or of the nineteenth century, and many studies of the history of historiography pass over it in silence.[3] The eighteenth century had two admirable practitioners in Hume and Gibbon, but even they predate the more sophisticated German philosophies of history; and Britain had no Vico, no Herder, no Göttingen School. A great revolution in historiographical theory still lay in the future. But another great revolution in historiographical theory lay in the past: eighteenth-century British historians inherited much from their Renaissance precursors. Most of the methods and assumptions that guided eighteenth-century historians had their origins in the fifteenth and sixteenth centuries.

The most important Renaissance contribution to the writing of history was the recognition of the past's simultaneous distance from and usefulness to the present. The previous chapter took up the role of historicist literary criticism, but the eighteenth century's historicism was more wide-reaching than that: historical events, like literary works, had to be understood in their historical context. This leads us to one of the central paradoxes of eighteenth-century historiography, the attempt to reconcile two contrary convictions: first, that ages have their own characters, and can be understood only historically; second, that human nature is at its core unchangeable and universal, and that the past therefore remains relevant.

The Renaissance contribution to historiography, as has often been noted, is what we call the historical sense, the past's difference from the present.[4] This sense freed early modern historians from the universal, providential history that occupied their predecessors. Providence was never entirely driven out of studies of history, even in the age of Hume and Gibbon; it underlies the histories of Burnet, for example, and Robertson. But the new history gave new attention to the historical moment. Whereas medieval historians took providence for granted and recounted facts only to flesh out the picture, eighteenth-century historians took the facts for granted and used them to argue about providence. In the new climate it was no longer enough to explain events in the world as mere secular manifestations of a timeless eschatological scheme.

Historicism is not relativism: it is, in Friedrich Meinecke's words, "the substitution of a process of *individualising* observation for a *generalising* view of human forces in history."[5] Although it opens the door to relativism, few in eighteenth-century Britain ran the risk of abandoning *all* belief in universals. Joseph Levine touches on this in his comments on Gibbon's historical sense: "Modern historicism seems to develop in two stages. First there is the recognition... that all human activities are historical: that is to say, conditioned by time and place. Then there is a further stage... when it is alleged that all human values and even human nature itself are also conditioned by the circumstances of history."[6] Gibbon, he argues – and we can extend it to his British contemporaries – lived between the two stages. He was an inheritor of the first insight, with an exceptionally acute sense of the difference of past ages. Of the later relativism, however, Levine writes, "This stage Gibbon never reached, nor does it appear that anyone else did either in the eighteenth century."[7] There was as yet no widespread belief that various periods resisted comparison, for a fundamentally uniform human nature underlay all its historically determined expressions. Johnson, for example, declares that "human nature is always the same, and every age will afford us instances of public censures influenced by events." In *Adventurer* 95 he argues that "the interests and passions, the virtues and vices of mankind, have been diversified in different times, only by unessential and casual varieties."[8] This uniformity of human nature was one of his favorite themes, but not his alone. Anna Letitia Barbauld might have Johnson's "China to Peru" in mind when she notes that "man is still man in Turkey and in Lapland."[9] Hume's course is similar: "It is universally acknowledged," he says, that "there is a great uniformity among the actions of men, in all nations and ages, and that human nature remains still the same, in its principles and operations... Mankind are so much the same, in all times and places, that history informs us of nothing new or strange in this particular."[10] Reconciling universalism with historicism seems difficult: if humanity is always and everywhere the same, how can a historical period be distinctive? How can the age of Elizabeth be any different from the Middle Ages or the age of the Hanoverians? In short, how can a great age be particularly useful to the present?

The great humanist historians – Guicciardini, Machiavelli, Biondo, More – proudly contrasted their own theories and methods with those of the medieval chronicles and universal histories, and blamed their predecessors for their inattention to the moral usefulness of history. Most medieval historians would have been surprised to be called to answer such a charge, since the relevance of facts warranted no explanation. For them, history was above all a moral calling, all about discerning and revealing the divine order operating through a pre-ordained time bounded by creation and Apocalypse. None saw the chronicles as their most important business; they were only signposts to demonstrate the workings of providence. But as the providential and eschatological assumptions that underlay their historiography increasingly gave way to interest in the secular motivations and conditions of events in the world, the medieval moral order came to seem alien, and finally lost its explanatory power altogether.

The eighteenth century inherited the humanists' insistence on the moral utility of their own history and a corresponding disdain for the chronicles of the Middle Ages. Thomas Sprat expresses his distaste for chronicle history written by "our *Moncks*: onely Registring in an undigested manner, some few naked Breviaries of their Wars, and Leagues, and Acts."[11] Sir William Temple was equally quick to reject English historians before More as mere chroniclers; only those who wrote after 1500 were worthy of inclusion in the pastiche history of England he conceived and supervised through its early stages.[12] One of the most scathing eighteenth-century attacks on medieval chronicle history comes in the fifth of Bolingbroke's *Letters on the Study and Use of History* (1735): in attacking the "monkish annalists" for their collections of disconnected facts, he calls for true historians to "separate the pure ore from the dross" and to stamp it into coins that enrich mankind. Otherwise we have only "antiquaries," "journalists," or "annalists," but not historians. The business of history is "instructing posterity by the example of former ages."[13]

What many eighteenth-century readers sought in their histories was what they found lacking in medieval chronicles: unity and moral utility. And contemporary historians were eager to claim they could provide them. Smollett, for example, says he wants to create not a disjointed chronicle, but "a well connected detail of historical events."[14] Readers, moreover, often stressed the importance of Renaissance history to their own political situation, as disconnected annals gave way to unified histories that connected the past to the present. "By reading good History," said De Thou's anonymous translator in 1729, "we furnish ourselves with Arguments for defending our Allegiance to his present Majesty."[15] Others had similarly high-minded – if not always similarly loyalist – aspirations for their histories: the goal was to make the past serve the present.

In this spirit, Johnson criticizes most English histories for being "of no other use than chronological memorials, which necessity may sometimes require to be consulted, but which fright away curiosity, and disgust delicacy." Comments like that have earned him the reputation of being hostile to history itself. Johnson's enemy, however, is not history but chronicle history. His verdict on Raleigh makes this clear: Raleigh, though diligent and elegant, "has endeavoured ... to select facts, rather than adorn them; and has produced an historical dissertation, but seldom risen to the majesty of history."[16] For the chroniclers, Johnson complains, "History was a series of actions, with no other than chronological succession, independent on each other, and without any tendency to introduce or regulate the conclusion."[17] They treated history in the same inept way the Scholastics treated moral questions, and morality was for Johnson the most important motivation for any intellectual labor:

The knowledge of external nature ... [is] not the great or frequent business of the human mind ... The first requisite is the religious and moral knowledge of right and wrong; the next is an acquaintance with the history of mankind, and with those examples which may be said to embody truth and prove by events the reasonableness of opinions.[18]

Johnson, it must be admitted, made these accusations with little first-hand knowledge of the early historians. There is minimal evidence of his reading in medieval histories, and even later chronicle histories were not well known to him. Whereas there are many references to Holinshed and Hall in Grey's *Critical, Historical, and Explanatory Notes on Shakespeare* (1754) and the histories of Hume and Smollett, Johnson cites Holinshed's *Chronicles* rarely – only a few times in the notes to his Shakespeare edition, and at least one of those at secondhand.[19] In this he is not unusual: extensive knowledge of Holinshed, Hall, Polydore Vergil, and others was limited almost exclusively to professional scholars and historians.

But it did not require extensive experience of the chronicles to recognize their distance from the kind of history he most admired. The fragmentary medieval histories are symptomatic of an entire culture not unified, not of true universal concern. This is supported by the seemingly contradictory belief that, although humanity is fundamentally uniform, certain great historical periods are better than others at approaching this universality. Through this logical sleight of hand – some eras are more equal than others – eighteenth-century historians could hold up the Renaissance as the era in which European culture most nearly approached universality, and the Middle Ages as that in which disconnected particulars kept humanity from aspiring to its true nature.

LONG YEARS OF HAVOCK

This logical leap from the disconnectedness of medieval *histories* to the disconnectedness of medieval *history* was by no means obvious, but it was a leap many eighteenth-century historians made. In nearly all their accounts of England's Middle Ages, early history itself was inchoate – a long succession of devastating wars, political treachery, and murderous and murdered princes without discernible moral order. A few moments of national glory shone, such as the reign of Henry V; but his victories were temporary, and he was succeeded by Henry VI, who (as Rapin laments) "lost all that the King his Father had gained."[20] When Thomas Gray refers to the "Long Years of havock" before and during the "Ruinous civil wars of York and Lancaster," he echoes many traditional accounts of the Wars of the Roses. His Miltonic language aptly expresses medieval chaos:

> Give ample room, and verge enough
> The characters of hell to trace
>
> . . .
>
> ... Severn shall re-eccho with affright
> The shrieks of death, thro' Berkley's roofs that ring,
> Shrieks of an agonizing King!
> She-Wolf of France, with unrelenting fangs,
> That tear'st the bowels of thy mangled Mate,
> From thee be born, who o'er thy country hangs
> The scourge of Heav'n.[21]

Such descriptions are common throughout the eighteenth century, even among Gothic enthusiasts – few of whom paid much attention to the actual events of the age that fired their imagination.[22] Eighteenth-century Britons rarely learned of the barbarous ages through the works of historians. However successful the histories were – after a slow start, Hume's enjoyed tremendous popularity,[23] as did Rapin's and Smollett's – they were not the most important conduit of medieval and early Renaissance history into the eighteenth century. William Collins reveals the more important channel when he praises Shakespeare for giving the most satisfying history of Britain:

Yet He alone to ev'ry Scene could give
Th' Historian's Truth, and bid the Manners live.
Wak'd at his Call I view, with glad Surprize,
Majestic Forms of mighty Monarchs rise.
There *Henry*'s Trumpets spread their loud Alarms....[24]

Shakespeare's ten English histories held a surprising place in the eighteenth-century canon, as these figures from the English Short Title Catalogue show. Although *1 Henry VI* appeared in only six separate editions in eighteenth-century Britain, *King John* appeared in seventeen separate editions and one adaptation. *Henry VIII*, among the least read of the plays today, appeared in some seventeen separate editions and two adaptations – among the Shakespearean history plays, second only to the twenty-one editions and three adaptations of *1 Henry IV*. The fourteen separate editions of Shakespeare's *Richard III*, when combined with the twenty-four editions of Cibber's adaptation, make it more often published than *Love's Labour's Lost* (seven editions and two adaptations), *Coriolanus* (eight editions and four adaptations), *Much Ado About Nothing* (nineteen editions and three adaptations), and even *King Lear* (twenty-three editions and seven adaptations).

Shakespeare's histories were praised in the age of Johnson for abandoning the disconnected particulars of the barbarous annals, and giving to chronology the moral shape of history. The unlearned Shakespeare was famous, of course, for disregarding the dramatic unities. At the same time, however, he introduced a deep-lying unity of action to the historical plot in its progression from the Middle Ages to the age of Elizabeth. The reworking of the particular facts of the chronicles amounted to a translation of mere antiquarianism into a morally and politically convincing narrative, and thus Shakespeare and his contemporaries forsook the "local and temporary customs," the "changeable scenes of artificial life,"[25] for the permanence and universality of the new age. Shakespeare transmuted the annals into a pageant, a progress from medieval darkness to Tudor light.

Johnson certainly sees Shakespeare's ten British histories not as mere chronology but as an organic whole, if that Romantic adjective has any meaning in 1765. "Shakespeare," he observes, "has apparently designed a regular connection of these dramatick histories from Richard the Second to Henry the Fifth."[26] This sequence, this dramatic *liaison des histoires*, continued not only through the reign of Henry V, but straight up to Shakespeare's own day, and illuminated his present. For the whole sequence of the plays, excluding only *King John*, traced the results of Henry IV's usurpation of Richard II's throne through succeeding reigns, culminating in the birth of Elizabeth.

One of the most important periods along the way was the reign of Richard III, who provided material for one of Shakespeare's most popular plays. Many have criticized the play for its exaggerated blackening of Richard's character, but eighteenth-century readers had little sympathy for the last of the Yorkists – the last medieval king and the darkest figure of the Dark Ages. Richard's vilification was begun by Thomas More and developed most famously by Shakespeare; it continued and even intensified during the eighteenth century. Joseph Grove, writing in 1742, calls Richard "a Monster of Lust and Cruelty." "As to the Defects of his Mind," writes Rapin, "it would be a hard Matter to find in History a Prince bad enough to match him." Lindsay echoes Rapin – "It will be difficult to find in History a Prince of so ill a Character" – and lays out the long catalogue of charges against him: "his Regicide, Usurpation, and repeated Murders; his Slanders raised to the Dishonour of his own Mother, Brothers, and their Issue; his Project for an incestuous Marriage, and the other diabolical Artifices used by him to accomplish his Designs." Gray's Gothicism is singularly fitting for describing the arch-Gothic villain: "The bristled Boar in infant-gore / Wallows beneath the thorny shade."[27] More's propaganda, as filtered through Shakespeare, was successful: Richard III was in eighteenth-century historical mythology the most medieval of kings, the epitome of all the faults of the Middle Ages.

At least one historian recognized that Richard's dastardly character was a function of the glorious age that succeeded him: "The Historians who wrote in the Reign of *Henry* VII. and *Henry* VIII.," writes Rapin, "have aggravated the Heinousness of his Actions to such a Degree, that one cannot help observing in their Writings a very strong Desire to please the Monarchs then on the Throne." He was therefore curious about Sir George Buc's anti-Tudor *History of the Life and Reign of Richard III* (1646), referring to Buc as the "one Historian...who has made it his Business to vindicate this Prince." But he decided ultimately that "as he has set no Bounds to his Vindication, and has endeavoured to make him entirely innocent, he has not had the Fortune to gain much Credit," and notes that "there is no modern Author that has thought fit to take him for a Guide."[28]

The one noteworthy exception was Horace Walpole, whose exculpatory *Historic Doubts* (1768) shows Buc's influence. But even Walpole half-ironically dismisses his work as a "mere matter of curiosity and speculation," and admits it is not so much a defense of Richard as an indictment of the sloppiness of earlier historians: he aims not at a "vindication," but a demonstration "that though he may have been as execrable as we are told he was, we have little or no reason to believe so." And even as he proffers a tentative defense of Richard III, he attacks "the barbarous monkish ages," and clearly sides with More's Renaissance rather than Richard's Middle Ages in complaining of "a new deluge of error" which broke when "Christian monks and saints laid truth waste."[29]

MODERN HISTORY COMMENCES

Against the exaggerated chaos of the late Middle Ages and the fallout from the Wars of the Roses, the accession of the Tudors seemed to be the emergence of order out of disarray, the dawn of an extended age of English peace and prosperity. Such an account glosses over too many facts to make good history – it ignores the wars under Edward VI and Mary Tudor, the fates of Lady Jane Grey and Mary Queen of Scots, and the brutality and capriciousness of even the most celebrated Tudors. But it served the eighteenth century well as a national myth.

Johnson's contemporaries emphasized the comparative stability that arrived with Henry VII. "In the end of the fifteenth and beginning of the sixteenth centuries," writes Adam Smith, "the greater part of Europe was approaching towards a more settled form of government than it had enjoyed for several ages before." He contrasts medieval chaos – "the disorderly state of England under the Plantagenets" – with "the vigorous administration of the Tudors."[30] Others go further than vigorous governmental administration, proclaiming the opening of a new golden age. "A general revolution," writes Hume, "was made in human affairs throughout this part of the world; and men gradually attained that situation, with regard to commerce, arts, sciences, government, police, and cultivation, in which they have ever since persevered. Here therefore commences the useful, as well as the more agreeable part of modern annals."[31] He develops this theme in a letter to Millar with a series of rapid-fire comments on the reign of Henry VII: "Modern history commences. America was discovered: Commerce extended: The Arts cultivated: Printing invented: Religion reform'd: And all the Governments of Europe almost chang'd."[32]

"The useful...part of modern annals," "modern history commences": with the Tudors we have arrived at the beginning of genuinely useful history. Many eighteenth-century Britons echo this theme. Bolingbroke, for example, is explicit: in a letter entitled "From What

Period Modern History Is Particularly Useful to the Service of Our Country," he develops the notion of "an epocha or an era, a point of time at which you stop, or from which you reckon forward," the beginning of true and valuable history, and argues that "The end of the fifteenth century seems to be just such a period as I have been describing, for those who live in the eighteenth century." "To be entirely ignorant about the ages that precede this era," he admits, "would be shameful... But to be learned about them is a ridiculous affectation in any man who means to be useful to the present age."[33] Hume makes a similar point on history before Bosworth Field: "Whoever carries his anxious researches into preceding periods is moved by a curiosity, liberal indeed and commendable"[34] – though Hume does not provide the "but," there can be no doubt that it is implied. "Preceding periods" are the province of *mere* curiosity, however commendable. Tudor history, on the other hand, is the indispensable history of the present.

The founder of the Tudor dynasty was best known through Bacon's *History of Henry VII* (1622), a work widely admired for its emphasis on the moral utility of modern history. Johnson in particular, who grew up only twenty miles from Bosworth and taught at Market Bosworth in 1732, would have had many local reminders of Henry's victory, and he gives 353 attributed quotations from Bacon's *Henry VII* in the first edition of the *Dictionary*. But Henry VII was not a particularly remarkable monarch in his own right, neither a monster like his predecessor nor a paragon of virtue like his granddaughter. As Johnson describes him, he was "A man who put an end to the civil war of the two houses, but not otherwise remarkable for virtue."[35]

From him, however, power devolved to his son, whom the eighteenth century found far more interesting. Two of Henry VIII's most important contributions to England's history were his early patronage and encouragement of humanist scholars, explored in chapter 2, and his break from Rome, part of the subject of chapter 4. But it was his character that drew the most commentary, depictions of which show all the ambivalence we should expect. His youthful promise figures large in nearly every account: a learned prince had ascended the throne, and by encouraging Colet, More, and Erasmus, he helped the English nation to make contact with the exciting intellectual developments on the Continent.

But the promise was not fulfilled: though Lindsay calls him "a great Lover and Patron of Learning," he laments that "as he was in his Youth, a very promising Prince, both as to Person, Capacity, and Improvements; so his Reign was almost a continued Series of Cruelty, Avarice and even

Sacrilege."[36] Even his learning availed him little. "Instead of learning that philosophy which opens the mind, and extends the qualities of the heart," complains Smollett, "he was confined to the study of gloomy and scholastic disquisitions, which served to cramp the ideas, and pervert the faculties of reason, qualifying him for the disputant of a cloister, rather than the law-giver of a people."[37] And so his early promise degenerated into capricious tyranny. For some historians, especially Whigs, his was a cautionary tale about the extravagant abuses a tyrant might make of his prerogative. For others, even his tyranny served as a reminder of the extent of the royal prerogative as far back as the early sixteenth century, an implicit critique of the Parliamentarians of the seventeenth. Hume's closing note on Henry is representative: "It is difficult to give a just summary of this prince's qualities: He was so different from himself in different parts of his reign, that...his history is his best character and description."[38] This "difference from himself" lies at the center of nearly every account of Henry VIII: it emphasizes the change in ages from medieval to modern by making Henry the victim of divided allegiances, partly medieval, partly modern.

After Henry, the English throne passed to Edward VI and then to Mary Tudor. To judge from the strictly civil parts of eighteenth-century histories of the Tudors, one would be hard-pressed to know Edward and Mary even existed: their reigns, when they are mentioned at all, are figured as part of the great tug-of-war between religious factions, and are therefore discussed in the next chapter. Various reasons might be suggested for their minor place in eighteenth-century civil histories: Edward's regency, for instance. But the most important is that their reigns are dwarfed in importance by that of their successor, Elizabeth, whom every eighteenth-century historian was eager to address.

THE FAVOURITE PERIOD OF ENGLISH GREATNESS

English history reached its zenith with Elizabeth's reign: so say all the orthodox accounts. In fact what we now call the English Renaissance was, for the eighteenth century, the "age of Elizabeth," a term coined in 1611, and given ever-increasing currency over the next two hundred years.[39] The most visible monument to her eighteenth-century reputation is the mass of documents from her reign published in that period. Birch's *Memoirs of the Reign of Queen Elizabeth* (1754), for instance, stretches to some 650,000 words, and covers only the second half of Elizabeth's reign. It opens with a conventional catalogue of her achievements: "The reign of queen ELIZABETH is less distinguish'd by its length, than by the vigour and success of her government amidst many almost unexampled difficulties both at home and abroad, and by the variety of important events, which happened during the course of it. For what facts could be more considerable, than the establishment of the reformation of religion...?"[40] Even Birch's *Memoirs*, though, look small beside the ten million words in Rymer's *Foedera* (1704–35), a twenty-volume collection of laws and treaties stretching from the twelfth century to Rymer's own day, which devotes particular attention to the Tudor period. Burnet devotes over a thousand pages of his *History of the Reformation* (1681–1753) to appendices containing "A Collection of Records and Original Papers" from the age. Sir Robert Naunton's *Fragmenta Regalia* of 1641 was often reprinted in the eighteenth century, and its most important eighteenth-century descendant, Nichols's *Progresses and Public Processions* (1788–1821) in three large volumes, painstakingly collects every available document related to Elizabeth's public functions – maps, plans, crests, genealogies, invoices, celebratory poems, pamphlets, illustrations of jewelry and fans, specimens of handwriting.

Such primary documents could speak for themselves, but eighteenth-century historians added their own voices to the chorus. All that was said about the Tudor dynasty in general was repeated (and more loudly) about Elizabeth in particular, in whom the battle of Bosworth Field, the revival of learning, and the establishment of religion came together. Such celebrations began in Elizabeth's day, continued into the seventeenth century, and were echoed and amplified in the eighteenth. Hume, for instance, writes of "the auspicious commencement of this reign [which] prognosticated that felicity and glory, which, during its whole course, so uniformly attended it," and Rapin writes that "her Name is still of *Blessed Memory* with the *English*, now when *Flattery* cannot be supposed to have any share in the Veneration they have for her."[41]

Admiration for Queen Elizabeth stretched across the political spectrum. Bishop Gilbert Burnet, for example, praises her as "the Wonder of all Posterity," and finds it "wonderful indeed, that a Virgin Queen could rule such a Kingdom, for above 44 Years, with such constant success, in so great tranquillity at Home, with a vast encrease of Wealth, and with such Glory abroad." Johnson's praise is similarly glowing: "The present system of English politics may properly be said to have taken rise in the reign of Queen Elizabeth." As we have seen, he calls "the reign of Elizabeth, the favourite period of English greatness."[42] Tories and Whigs seem to forget their feuds and join to praise Elizabeth. Still, they saw in it different lessons, and represented it differently. Fulsome praise for Elizabeth could amount to an implicit critique of her less able successors, including both Stuarts and Cromwells. It is perhaps no great exaggeration to say that nearly every English history published in the eighteenth century, whether nominally concerned with the Saxon Witan or the Treaty of Utrecht, was ultimately a history of the seventeenth century. The eighteenth century studied the sixteenth to make sense of the seventeenth.

Debates over the ancient constitution and the history of royal prerogative, which came to a head in the Stuart years, gave shape to many discussions of Tudor and even earlier history, as Whig and Tory historians fought their ideological and political battles in the pages of their histories. Most modern historians are more skeptical and less adulatory toward Elizabeth's administration, but for eighteenth-century historians, the Tudor dynasty generally and Elizabeth's reign in particular was the period in which the English government most closely approximated its natural character and balance of power. As Swift puts it, "Since the *Norman* Conquest, the Balance of Power in *England* has often varied and sometimes been wholly overturned...About the middle of Queen *Elizabeth*'s Reign, I take the Power between the Nobles and the Commons to have been in more equal Balance, than it was ever before or since." George Lyttelton agrees: in Elizabeth's reign, "this Government came to an equall Balance, which is the true Perfection of it." Hume draws out the moral: "In order to understand the ancient constitution of England, there is not a period which deserves more to be studied than the reign of Elizabeth."[43]

Most admitted that Elizabeth had achieved the best balance in English history, but historians of rival political factions represented this balance differently. Whiggish historiography, for instance, depended on the existence of a strong Commons from time out of mind, against which the Stuarts could be seen as usurpers of ancient privileges and the prerogative claimed by James I and Charles I as an unprecedented aberration. For them, Elizabethan "balance" meant cooperation with the Commons. Hume, on the other hand, stresses the unprecedented monarchical prerogative under Elizabeth: "Scarcely any sovereign before Elizabeth, and none after her, carried higher...the authority of the crown." Ditto D'Avenant: "The Commons were Obedient, Her Authority was awful to the Lords."[44]

THE INFLUENCE OF A WOMAN

Although it was the most vexed question, however, the balance of power was not the eighteenth century's sole interest in Elizabeth. Much of the praise of Elizabeth's reign was directed at Elizabeth herself, in her personal, rather than regnal, character. "If we explain nostalgia for the Elizabethan age purely from a socio-economic perspective," writes Christine Gerrard, "we ignore what lay at its centre – the figure of the queen herself."[45] Hume's character of Elizabeth captures the prevailing opinions of his day: "Open in her address, gracious and affable in all public appearances, she rejoiced in the concourse of her subjects, entered into all their pleasures and amusements, and…acquired a popularity beyond what any of her predecessors or successors could ever attain."[46]

Her great popularity is all the more remarkable considering her sex. In Lyttelton's *Persian Letters* (1735), Selim tells Mirzah, "Thou wilt be surpriz'd to hear, that the Period when the *English* Nation enjoy'd the greatest Happiness, was under the Influence of a *Woman*." For Elizabeth was a woman, but a manly one, blessed with "a Mind above her Sex."[47] Hume suggests something of this when he proposes to consider Elizabeth not as a woman, but "merely as a rational being," and when he notes that "her masculine spirit" was responsible for rejecting an alliance with Spain. So too Lindsay's *Brief History* (1748): Elizabeth at the Armada "shewed herself with an Air of Masculine Courage." Thomas Warton likewise depicts her as masculine: "Queens must be ridiculous when they would appear as women. The softer attractions of sex vanish on the throne. Elisabeth fought all occasions of being extolled for her beauty… As she conquered all nations with her arms, it matters not what were the triumphs of her eyes."[48] Elizabeth combined the two characters, woman and prince, by being one of the greatest learned women in England's history – a fitting role for the queen who presided over England's revival of learning. As Boswell notes, Johnson said "She had learning enough to have given dignity to a bishop."[49] And her learning was put to good use, for it enabled her to patronize and preside over England's greatest poets. Warton has this in mind when he writes, "The age of queen Elisabeth is commonly called the golden age of English poetry," as does Hurd when he refers to "The manifest superiority of this class of writers [poets] in ELIZABETH's reign."[50]

But enthusiasm for Elizabeth, though widespread, was not unqualified, and her critics, too, were ever mindful that she was a woman. Hurd, among the more vocal critics, reminds us of the sometimes overeager elision of public and private character. He places Addison in an imagined dialogue with Arbuthnot, for whom he explains away the predominant pro-Elizabeth sentiments: "Those two great events of her time, THE ESTABLISHMENT OF THE REFORMATION, and THE TRIUMPH OVER THE POWER OF SPAIN, cast an uncommon lustre on the reign of ELIZABETH. Posterity, dazzled with these obvious successes, went into an excessive admiration of her personal virtues." Another of his personae lays out the objections to Elizabeth: "Her very minions seemed raised for no other purpose, than the exercise of her ill-humour. They were encouraged, by her smile, to presume on the royal countenance, and then beaten down again in punishment of that presumption."[51]

Such attacks were unusual, but not unheard of. Even Johnson wrote a late historical review against the "fashionable" defamation of the Stuarts in favor of Elizabeth.[52] Among those willing to oppose the popular tide, many qualms about Elizabeth are attributable to her treatment of Mary Stuart.[53] A survey of the history of Mary Queen of Scots – "*Elizabeth*'s great Blemish," says Rapin – was a favorite set piece with historians, among whom the number of Scots (Hume, Robertson, Smollett) is noteworthy. Smollett, for instance, writes, "Such was the untimely fate of Mary Stuart, a princess unmatched in beauty, and unequalled in misfortune." His regard for Mary Stuart allows him to give Elizabeth only a lukewarm character: "Notwithstanding all her great qualities," he says, "we cannot deny that she was vain, proud, imperious, and in some cases cruel." "Elizabeth," he writes elsewhere, "was a woman as well as a politician. She not only dreaded Mary as the rival of her dignity, but also envied her superior qualifications." Eighteenth-century historians were always acutely conscious of the sex of both Mary and Elizabeth in this affair, the most significant confrontation between two women in British history. Hume, for instance, comments on their "womanish rivalship," and Hurd pauses in his celebration of Elizabeth's age to rehearse the objections against her: "But, to say the very truth, the slavish temper of the time was favourable to such exertions of female caprice and tyranny."[54]

SEMPER EADEM

This blemish, however significant, was not enough to dim the lustre of Elizabeth's reputation, and other monarchs were routinely measured against her standard. As Rapin says, the "State of Felicity" of Elizabeth's reign "is the *Touch-Stone* by which all those are to be tried whom God has set over Nations and Kingdoms."[55] Addison, therefore, has George I's policies in mind when he delivers this history lesson:

Queen *Elizabeth* ... had always the Trade of Her Kingdom very much at Heart, and we may observe the Effects of it through the whole Course of her Reign, in the Love and Obedience of her People, as well as in the Defeats and Disappointments of her Enemies. It is with great Pleasure that we see our present Soveraign applying his thoughts so successfully to the Advancement of our Traffick.[56]

The message is clear: "our present Soveraign" will earn "the Love and Obedience of [his] People" only by measuring up to Elizabeth. Addison warns England away from "Fickleness of Behaviour in publick Measures, [which] cannot but be attended with very fatal Effects to our Country" – effects including, apparently, "the Perpetuating of Strife and Faction among a divided People." He offers as a counterexample "Queen *Elizabeth*, who makes the greatest Figure among our *English* Soveraigns, [and] was most eminently remarkable for that Steadiness and Uniformity which ran through all her Actions during that long and glorious Reign. She kept up to her chosen Motto [*semper eadem*] in every part of her Life."[57] In Elizabeth's "Steadiness and Uniformity" we see everything the eighteenth century missed in the Middle Ages and in Henry VIII's "difference from himself."

The Elizabethan myth flourished, perhaps as never before or since, when Anne occupied the throne and tried to occupy Elizabeth's place in history. In some respects, the analogy was so faulty as to be ridiculous: Anne was an inept administrator; far from being a Virgin Queen, she was uncommonly fecund, although none of her children lived to maturity.[58] But other points of comparison were, or could be made to seem, more favorable. Her accession followed a half century of civil war marked by both secular and religious strife, and the prospect of achieving a lasting settlement similar to Elizabeth's was a pleasing one.

The greatest political desideratum of the early eighteenth century – the one thing needful – was a unified *settlement*, and Elizabeth served as kind of metonymy for settlement itself. The exact parallels varied from application to application, but nearly everyone in the eighteenth century longed for a respite from the religious and political turmoil of the preceding decades, and they looked to the comparative order of the middle sixteenth century. In *The Patriot King* (1738), for instance, Bolingbroke invokes Elizabeth in an appeal for Opposition party unity.[59] Faction is likewise the enemy in Delarivier Manley's *Modest Enquiry* (1714):

if we do not follow Elizabeth's example in Anne's age, she warns, "Would they not look upon us as the most ungrateful, factious, fickle Race of Mortals under the Sun?" The attacks on faction pour out: she turns her scorn on those who spread rumors of the queen's death in "those vile and detestable Places which are Dedicated to Faction and Disorder," and celebrates Anne's victory over "their factions and ungovernable Temper." She notes that "The Circumstances of Qu. *Elizabeth* much resemble those of Her present Majesty," and adds that "there were many Factions at that time, both of *Papists* and *Puritans*, to neither of which she gave much Quarter... yet She carried the Respect and Duty of her Subjects with her, even to the Grave."[60]

Anne not only welcomed such comparisons with Elizabeth; she made them herself. "It was her Majesty's Pleasure," Abel Boyer notes, "that whenever there was occasion to Embroider, Depict, Grave, Carve or Paint her Majesty's Arms, these words, SEMPER EADEM, should be use'd for a *Motto*; it being the same that had been us'd by her Predecessor Queen *Elizabeth*, of glorious Memory." A modern historian elaborates on the parallels Anne herself drew: she was the first monarch since Elizabeth born of two English parents; "Her robe, red velvet lined with ermine and edged in gold, was modelled on a portrait of Queen Elizabeth I"; she donated £100,000 from her personal fortune to public purposes in "a true imitation of Q. Elizabeth's maxims."[61]

The most important celebrators of Anne as a postfiguration of Elizabeth were poets with an interest in the success of her reign, mostly Tories like Ambrose Philips, who resort to this sort of unctuous praise: "While ANNA reigns. O ever may she reign! / And bring on Earth a Golden Age again."[62] Such poets drew on the legend of a poetic golden age resulting from a political golden age. Gay, in the "Proeme" to *The Shepherd's Week* (written in imitation of E.K.'s "Dedicatory Epistle" to *The Shepherd's Calender*), avows he "know[s] no Age so justly to be instiled *Golden*, as this of *our Soveraign Lady Queen* ANNE."[63] Prior makes the same comparison: "Bright ELIZA rul'd BRITANNIA's State, / Widely distributing Her high Commands; / And boldly Wise, and fortunately Great, / Freed the glad Nations from Tyrannick Bands." He goes further, allowing Anne to surpass her predecessor: "Greatest ANNA" exercises British arms that "pursue / Paths of Renown, and climb Ascents of Fame, / Which nor AUGUSTUS, nor ELIZA knew."[64] An even more fulsome comparison appears in Pope's *Windsor-Forest* (1713), where the invocation of the nearly divine Elizabeth is preceded by a recollection of the Civil Wars:

A dreadful Series of Intestine Wars,
Inglorious Triumphs, and dishonest Scars.
At last great *ANNA* said – Let Discord cease!
She said, the World obey'd, and all was *Peace!*[65]

Reuben Brower has these lines in mind when he notes that "*Windsor Forest* is the poem of a generation that had lively memories of a revolutionary period and that after long if glorious wars was becoming almost obsessively attached to peace,"[66] and although his concern is the analogy with Rome's greatest age, the lines apply at least as well to England's. In his prophecy that "Kings shall sue, and suppliant States be seen / Once more to bend before a *British* QUEEN" (*Windsor-Forest*, lines 383–84), Pope calls for the "Sacred *Peace*" and "long-expected Days" (line 355) of a new Elizabethan era.[67]

HER CROSS TRIUMPHANT

This chapter began with a quotation from Johnson's *London*, to which we can now return. Few readers of *London* have fully appreciated the implications of the poem because of a confusion over its satirical target: for most critics, it is little more than an attack on urban corruption and a celebration of rural retirement. This is a fair description of its source, Juvenal's third satire: Juvenal congratulates his friend for leaving Rome's corruptions for Cumae. Johnson's target in *London*, however, is not entirely urban, and his ideal is not at all rural. Attacks on the city constitute only about half of the poem, and such passages follow the Juvenalian original most closely: the falling houses, flaming palace, and midnight murderers are imitated directly from the source. Such concerns are real, but comparatively perfunctory.[68]

Thales asks, "Where can starving merit find a home?" (line 191); the question is worth answering. Juvenal's answer is unequivocal: Cumae. But Johnson's invocation of pastoral bliss, whether in Wales or Scotland, is unconvincing: he may invoke the Country Party, but not the country. Thales' wish for "Some pleasing bank where verdant osiers play" (line 45) is an empty one, the sort of conceit and diction that Johnson attacked repeatedly and vehemently throughout his career. It gets even worse when Thales imagines the scene of his rural retirement, no longer a "secret cell" (line 49) but "some elegant retreat, / Some hireling senator's deserted seat" (lines 212–13), and therefore still dependent on the money of vicious urban politicians:

> There prune thy walks, support thy drooping flow'rs,
> Direct thy rivulets, and twine thy bow'rs;
>   . . .
> There ev'ry bush with nature's musick rings,
> There ev'ry breeze bears health upon its wings;
> On all thy hours security shall smile,
> And bless thine evening walk and morning toil.
>
>   (lines 216–23)

With the exaggerated pastoral and georgic clichés bordering on the ludicrous, there is little reason to believe Johnson took it any more seriously in 1738 than he did in his later attacks on hollow pastoralism ("easy, vulgar, and therefore disgusting"). He even drops a hint that rural retirement is not all it is made out to be: in "Hibernia's land," Thales' friend begins, "all whom hunger spares, with age decay" (line 12) – marginally better than the city, perhaps, but widespread starvation is hardly Elysian. "Has heaven reserv'd," Thales asks, "in pity to the poor, / No pathless waste, or undiscover'd shore; / No secret island in the boundless main?" (lines 170–72). No answer is forthcoming. For all the city's problems, Johnson is unable to suggest a better place.

Perhaps, then, place does not provide the real opposition that structures the poem. Many of the vices Thales attacks are not urban but (ostensibly) modern vices: female atheists, supple Gauls, flattering grooms; "lost in thoughtless ease, and empty show, / Behold the warrior dwindled to a beau" (lines 103–04). It is, after all, "this . . . age," not this city, that "Admires [French] wond'rous talents for the stage" (lines 132–33). In short, the opposition of *here* and *there* is less significant than that of *now* and *then*, especially the *now* of Walpole and the *then* of Elizabeth.[69]

The alternative to this debased modernity is no more easily reached than the undiscovered shore, but it is more convincing than Johnson's half-hearted pastoralism. It is England's glorious past, an age before England was Gallicized and London made a French metropolis – to wit, before 1660. Thales invokes several such periods as correctives to modern decadence: "Alfred's golden reign" (line 248), "Illustrious Edward" (line 99), "Henry's victories" (line 120). But the most important *then* of the poem appears in the opening verses, where the unnamed speaker stands with Thales "On Thames's banks" at Greenwich, waiting for the wherry which will take him away:

> Struck with the seat that gave Eliza birth,
> We kneel, and kiss the consecrated earth;

In pleasing dreams the blissful age renew,
And call Britannia's glories back to view;
Behold her cross triumphant on the main,
The guard of commerce, and the dread of Spain.[70]

Elizabeth's reign – "the blissful age" – is the best alternative to the satirized modern London, and the most suitable corrective to modern vice.

Note that this use of the sixteenth century is not wholly in keeping with other eighteenth-century invocations. We have already seen some of the political uses of the age of Elizabeth, but the "dread of Spain" reminds us that the 1730s require special consideration. Anne's contemporaries thought of Elizabeth's age as a time of peace; under Walpole, especially in the 1730s as Opposition writers were agitating for a Spanish confrontation, Elizabeth's age was remarkable as an age of successful war. So an anonymous agitator calls for action against Spain in 1729 by invoking Elizabeth, "ever Victorious, the Scourge of *Tyrants*, the *Patroness of Liberty*, the *Sanctuary* of the *Oppressed*, and *Deliverer of Nations*."[71] "Patriotic genuflections at Elizabeth's shrine," writes Christine Gerrard, "pervade the political writings of the 1730s," and the Patriot Opposition used Elizabeth's victory as a means of attacking Walpole's pacific foreign policy.[72]

The defining moment of English national glory was the defeat of the Armada in 1588, which was widely celebrated throughout the eighteenth century, especially when England was at war with Spain. In fact the Spanish wars encouraged many to use history simply as an encoded way of talking about the present. Lillo, for example, makes only the most perfunctory effort to set *The London Merchant* in Elizabeth's reign, because the references to "the king of Spain," "his vast armado," and "our peerless Elizabeth (more than in name the mother of her people)" invoke not 1588, but 1731. Visual depictions of the Armada were popular: tapestries depicting the battle hung in the House of Lords; engravings of these tapestries appeared in Edward Young's *Imperium Pelagi* (1730) and John Pine's *Tapestry Hangings* (1739), and "in 1742 William King used them to furnish the imaginary walls of his *Templum Libertatis*."[73] Hume lavishes a dozen pages on the Armada, and although he characteristically points out that both fleets would look unimpressive by modern standards, he describes the sea-fight in positively heroic terms: against the "ostentatious" Spaniards' "*Invincible Armada*," "such a fleet and embarkation as had never before had its equal in Europe," England sent a "force [which] seemed very unequal to resist so powerful an enemy," and yet emerged victorious, largely owing to "the vigour and prudence of the Queen's conduct." Smollett resorts to anti-Spanish irony to express the same thing: "Elizabeth having learned the particulars of the formidable armament [the Armada]... took the necessary precautions for giving the Spaniards a warm welcome."[74] Always this military victory was attributed to Elizabeth's superb statecraft.

Johnson's invocation of "Britannia's glories," then, is an attack on Walpole with the full force of British national mythology to back it up. What better way to highlight the bankruptcy of Walpole's statecraft than by contrasting it with "the favourite period of English greatness"? Johnson's own ambivalence about Elizabeth aside, he recognized the emotional force of the Tudor dynasty, for even the most adroit politician cannot win a battle against national mythology. The sixteenth century was the apex of England's cultural and political achievement, an era in which the balance of power was most finely adjusted and in which the nation and its subjects most nearly approached their true, universal nature. Johnson's invocation of this age shows that he learned the lesson of the Renaissance historians in making the past morally useful to the present. Britannia's glories must be repeatedly called back to view if England is ever to regain the blissful age.

CHAPTER 4

The rage of Reformation: religious controversy and political stability

In ecclesiastical no less than in civil polity, the eighteenth century looked back to the age of Elizabeth for a model. Christianity has made many glances backward, always in the hope of inspiring or regulating modern practice by the true sources of the faith. Most such movements have turned to Scripture or the early Fathers; both, for instance, played major parts in Lutheran and Calvinist theology. Where eighteenth-century Britons differed from most other looks backward was in their emphasis not on early apostolic Christianity, nor on Origen, Chrysostom, and Tertullian, but on the English Church of the sixteenth century.

It is impossible to understand, even to describe, the history of the seventeenth and eighteenth centuries without reference to the establishment of the English Church in the sixteenth century. The Reformation had a greater immediacy then than now; in many ways it was still in progress in England through 1689 – even, in attenuated form, as late as 1746, when the last serious Catholic aspirant to the English throne was defeated. Only then was the business begun by Henry VIII definitively settled and the Church of England secure. And no sooner were the old threats addressed than new threats to orthodoxy arose: Britons not only had to seek the precarious middle between Puritanism and Catholicism, but to account also for Methodists, Deists, Unitarians, and freethinkers of every stripe. Religious radicalism always seemed to loom just over the horizon. Throughout the century, therefore, theologians and controversialists turned their attention from the chaos of the seventeenth and eighteenth centuries back to the Tudor dynasty, hoping to find solutions to the problems of church government.

One typical look back is among the most formidable works of eighteenth-century religious scholarship, Strype's *Annals of the Reformation* (1709), a six-hundred-page folio on just the first twelve years of Elizabeth's reign. The dedication to Thomas Tenison, Archbishop of Canterbury, argues that modern churchmen have much to learn from the "History of the blessed Success of the Methods then taken, to free this Land from *Papal* Usurpations and Superstitions, and to establish True Religion among us." Strype advises Tenison "to read here how Your Renowned Predecessor, *MATTHEW* [Parker], Queen *Elizabeth*'s first Archbishop of Canterbury, counsilled, acted, interposed in this Illustrious Work." His goal is to make his contemporaries "understand what our Original Constitution is." Gilbert Burnet similarly dedicates the last volume of his *History of the Reformation* (1681–1753) to George II, "who, we trust, is designed by God, to Compleat the *Reformation* it self."[1] The present is inseparable from the past. The eighteenth century's religious identity, with its peculiar blend of Latitudinarianism and Erastianism, owed much to its conceptions of the origins of the English Church.

THE DOCTORS OF THE ROMISH CHURCH

England is a Protestant nation, and the *sine qua non* of Protestantism is its opposition to Roman Catholicism. And when eighteenth-century Protestants wanted to make a case against contemporary Catholicism, they knew of no better way than telling stories about the bad old days. We saw in chapter 2 that the Catholic Church was often attacked for enforcing medieval superstitions and ignorance, thereby retarding the revival of learning. Johnson, for instance, criticizes "the goblins of witchcraft [which] still continued to hover in the twilight," and attributes these goblins to Catholicism's enforced ignorance: "The doctors of the *Romish* Church...have snatched the Bible out of the hands of the people, and confined the liberty of perusing it to those whom literature has previously qualified."[2] Compare Gilbert Stuart's attack of 1780 on Catholic superstitions:

Popery, as a species of religion, when examined by the principles of reason, appears to mock the judgment and capacity of men...The ingenuity of human wit, exerted to contrive what is most extravagant, can, with difficulty, conceive inventions more absurd or romantic than the merits of pilgrimage and penance, the confession and absolution of sins, purgatory, the invocation of saints, and the adoration of images.[3]

The defining moment in the history of the *ecclesia anglicana* was therefore "the reformation, one of the greatest events in history," when England shook off her "shameful bondage." Popish superstitions were the first to go. David Hume gleefully catalogues various frauds that were debunked in the dissolution of the monasteries, mentioning especially "a miraculous crucifix": "The lips, and eyes, and head of the image moved on the approach of its votaries. Hilsey, bishop of Rochester, broke the crucifix at St. Paul's cross, and showed the whole people the springs and wheels by which it had been secretly moved."[4] Like the bishop, Hume revels in showing the man behind the curtain and exposing Papist shams.

The cast of Catholic villains was matched by a new set of heroes: the English reformers were celebrated into the eighteenth century. Cranmer, for instance, was for Hume "a man remarkable . . . for his learning, and still more, for the candour and disinterestedness of his temper." Strype finds Matthew Parker notable "for his Learning, Wisdom, Generosity and Piety." The editors of the *Biographia Britannica* praise Lancelot Andrewes, in an effusive burst, for "his great zeal and piety, his charity and compassion, his fidelity and integrity, his gratitude and thankfulness, his munificence and bounty, his hospitality, his humanity and affability, his modesty, his diligent application to study, and his talent as a preacher and a writer."[5]

Not everyone, though, could be neatly labeled hero or villain. Thomas More, for example, was a problem. His learning and integrity in the face of tyranny were eagerly claimed by later Britons as sterling examples of English honor: he is for Tobias Smollett "universally esteemed for his integrity," and Zachary Grey finds him "remarkable for doing of justice in the execution of his office." But his panegyrists had to deal with the embarrassment of his being on the wrong side theologically, an unreformed Papist to the end – "Steady More," writes James Thomson, "Who, with a generous though mistaken zeal, / Withstood a brutal tyrant's useful rage." Hume calls More "at once an object deserving our compassion, and an instance of the usual progress of man's sentiments during that age." He closes his account of More's execution this way: "Nothing was wanting to the glory of this end, except a better cause, more free from weakness and superstition. But as the man followed his principles and sense of duty, however misguided, his constancy and integrity are not less objects of our admiration."[6]

SCENES OF HORROR

As More's fate reminds us, the Church was not reformed without resistance, and many Protestants believed Catholicism showed its true colors only after its authority was challenged by Protestant reformers. Here Hume's critiques are at their most pointed: "England was soon filled with scenes of horror, which have ever since rendered the catholic religion the object of general detestation, and which prove, that no human depravity can equal revenge and cruelty, covered with the mantle of religion."[7]

Mary Tudor's "*calamitous* and *dishonourable* Reign" was, as one might expect, the favorite target of eighteenth-century anti-Catholic rhetoric. Although Oldmixon insists that "The Character of Queen *Mary* is far from being a Subject to be delighted in," most eighteenth-century historians did in fact take a perverse delight in heaping abuse upon her – not only in her official capacity, but even in her personal character. She was "naturally of a sour and obstinate temper," writes Hume, and "possessed all the qualities fitted to compose a bigot." Smollett concurs – "She was indeed a bigot to her religion in the most gloomy sense" – adding that "the characteristics of Mary were bigotry and revenge."[8]

The standard Protestant source of information on Mary and her persecution of Protestants was Foxe's *Book of Martyrs* (1554), which appeared eighteen times, in whole or in part, in the eighteenth century, often in lavishly illustrated editions.[9] Every literate Protestant could be expected to know it, at least by reputation. Burnet notes that since Foxe's accounts are so familiar, a modern historian need only list the names of martyrs, something he does for many pages. Mere names, though, are not enough for Hume, who describes the tortures in gruesome detail, often drawing from Foxe. Of Bishop Hooper's burning at the stake, he writes, "All his lower parts were consumed, before his vitals were attacked: One of his hands dropped off...He was heard to pray and exhort the people; till his tongue, swoln with the violence of agony, could no longer permit him utterance."[10] A similarly grotesque catalogue of burnings at the stake appears in Smollett's history, as Hooper, Taylor, Latimer, Ridley, and Cranmer meet their death, one after another: "Perhaps history cannot parallel a more infamous scene of unprovoked cruelty...Every person of humanity," he says, "whatever might be his persuasion in points of religion, was shocked at this barbarity."[11]

More important than simply enumerating cruelties, though, was placing them in a context. The consequences of the Marian Counter Reformation were not only doctrinal and liturgical, but cultural. The frequent use of the word "barbarity" to describe Mary's persecution suggests the historical and temperamental relationship between Catholicism and the barbarous Dark Ages. Mary caused a hiatus in the Protestant movement, interrupted the progress of the revival of learning, and returned England's culture to the Middle Ages. Thus Robert Anderson in 1792: "In the turbulent and sanguinary reign of Queen Mary, when the fires of persecution were kindled in Smithfield, and every part of England was polluted with murders, more atrocious than the slaughters of the most bloody civil war; the cultivation of polite literature was neglected amidst the calamities of the state."[12] Sixteenth-century Catholicism provided eighteenth-century Protestantism with a limitless supply of examples of what it most feared and abhorred.

THE RUFFIANS OF THE REFORMATION

Catholicism was the most obvious threat to the English Church both before and after the Reformation, and eighteenth-century Protestant commentators were nearly unanimous in attacking Mary for subjecting Britons to both her misguided faith and the rule of Rome. Most, however, agreed the other extreme was equally dangerous: the Protestant rebels (and their modern descendants) could be as perfidious as Mary herself. The writers of the eighteenth century, like those at the end of the sixteenth, therefore devoted the greater part of their energy to defending the Protestant Church from its Protestant enemies.

Johnson was deeply skeptical about "the rage of Reformation," and some of his most bitter comments were directed not at the Catholics but at their enemies. It is tempting to attribute such attitudes to imagined Catholic sympathies. Boswell, for instance, mentions that "he had a respect for *'the old religion'* as the mild Melancthon called that of the Roman Catholick Church." Johnson may have been more conservative in religious matters than many of his contemporaries, but his objection to radical Protestantism is owing not to any closet Catholicism, but to the destructiveness that so often accompanies radical movements of whatever sort. "No change in religion," he laments, "has been made with that calmness, caution, and moderation, which religion itself requires, and which common prudence shews to be necessary . . . Rage has been called in to the assistance of zeal, and destruction joined with reformation."[13] Others joined in this criticism of radical Protestantism. Swift's satirical account of the destructive violence of radical Protestantism is well known:

When He [Martin] had gone thus far, he demurred a while: He knew very well, there yet remained a great deal more to be done; however, the first Heat being over, his Violence began to cool, and he resolved to proceed more moderately in the rest of the Work . . . Brother *Jack* . . . stripping down a Parcel of *Gold Lace*, a little too hastily . . . rent the *main Body* of his *Coat* from Top to Bottom.[14]

The real reformers, of course, were more feared for tearing down churches than tearing coats, and the grim specter of Spenser's Kirkrapine lasted well into the eighteenth century. Things were worst in Presbyterian Scotland. On his trip there in 1773, Johnson looked at the "skeletons" of old churches, "which now stand faithful witnesses of the triumph of Reformation." "The change of religion in Scotland," he writes, "eager and vehement as it was, raised an epidemical enthusiasm, compounded of sullen scrupulousness and warlike ferocity." Boswell writes that his wistfulness became bitterness when "he beheld the ruins of religious magnificence," and he turned his invective toward the agent of the destruction: "I happened to ask where John Knox was buried. Dr. Johnson burst out, 'I hope in the high-way. I have been looking at his reformations.'" Johnson notes with mordant irony Knox's "merry narrative" of Cardinal Beaton's assassination by "the ruffians of the reformation."[15] He was unwilling to see an entire age relegated to the dustheap and churches reduced to bare ruined choirs.

Johnson's reputation as a High-Churchman is well known, but the chorus of condemnation was widespread among Anglicans across the religious spectrum. Hawkins, for instance, refers to "that furious bigot John Knox"; Smollett calls him "a violent asserter of purity in church-government"; and the *Biographia Britannica* praises John Aylmer for giving "a signal proof of his learning, moderation, and love to his native country, by penning a sober answer to an outrageous book, written by John Knox." John Lindsay's popular catechistical school history (1748) manages to attack him even in its index: "*Knox (J.)* a Schismatic and Incendiary." Gilbert Stuart, who rarely misses an opportunity to side with the Protestants, laments that Knox stirred the people "to madness by what was termed the abomination of idols and images," and complains of his "impatient and sanguine temper."[16]

The zealotry of the reformers is therefore often compared to the equally misguided zealotry of the Catholics. According to an eighteenth-century commonplace, extremes meet – never more wittily expressed than in Hogarth's "Credulity, Superstition and Fanaticism" (1762), in which a Dissenting preacher, St. Money-trap, loses his wig to reveal a Catholic tonsure. The solution lay neither in Catholicism nor in unbridled reform, but in a middle course – one devoted to the pursuit of spiritual truth, but still determined to preserve the fabric of the all-too-fragile state. England learned that hard lesson in the Civil Wars of the seventeenth century, and sought a solution in the age of Elizabeth.

REASON AND MODERATION

After Mary's disastrous reign, the English were understandably nervous about admitting to the throne another woman of uncertain right of succession and unknown religious and political sympathies. The ultimate measure of her success in managing the Reformation is evident in the statements of historians writing two centuries later. A school text is clear: when asked, "For what is she chiefly commended?" the student is taught to reply, "For having establish'd the protestant religion."[17]

Much of Elizabeth's fame is attributable to her apparent moderation in matters ecclesiastical. The Elizabethan Settlement came at the end of decades of disputes and wars begun in England under Henry VIII, and took England on a middle course between Mary's Catholicism and the radical Protestantism of Edward's reign – what Richard Hooker, Elizabeth's greatest apologist, calls "the middle point of evennesse and moderation."[18] This moderation consisted in careful navigation between the Scylla of Rome and the Charybdis of Geneva. Though Catholic power remained a threat, writes Strype in 1709, a new danger was emerging: "Another sort...were not satisfied with the Reformation of this Church, but would have it reformed again *by the Word of God*...These were men of more Zeal than Knowledge: Who afterwards throughout the Queen's Reign were the Causes of great Differences and Discords among the Queen's Protestant Subjects...These were those they called *Puritans*."[19] Swift explains that England has "been infested by two Enemies, the Papists and Fanaticks, who each, in their Turns, filled it with Blood and Slaughter." As Lindsay catechizes in his history: "*Q*. Did Queen *Elizabeth* meet with no other Opposition in the establishing of the Church of *England*? *A*. Yes; from Papists on the one Hand, and Puritans on the other."[20] The truth lay in between. This Anglican *via media* was for the eighteenth century the defining characteristic of Elizabeth's church governance. It was not easily reached or held, for extremists on either side attacked Anglicanism as a half-hearted compromise. Catholics lamented England's apostasy from orthodoxy; for Puritans, the Church of England represented a "leaden mean," mere lip-service to the doctrines of the Reformation. The tug-of-war between the two parties is evident throughout the early history of the Church of England, and both civil and ecclesiastical historians followed its progress with great interest in the eighteenth century.

Historians could discern anticipations of the Elizabethan *via media* even in the reign of Henry VIII, whom Rapin credited with "steer[ing] a kind of middle Course" in religious matters. Moderation, it seemed, came naturally to the English nation. The Elizabethan Settlement represents the codification of England's natural moderation into a reasoned middle course between what Strype calls "Papists and Gospellers."[21] Many of the early Articles of the faith, for instance, can be seen as negotiations of the middle ground between Catholicism and Calvinism – in doctrine, in liturgy, in discipline. Even the apparently single-mindedly Calvinist Articles are in fact compromises, as is often evident from the *yet* or *but* that balances the periods: in Article 11, "Of Good Works," for instance, the first clause pays homage to radical Protestantism, the second to traditional ethics:

Albeit that good works, which are the fruits of faith, and follow after justification, cannot put away our sins, and endure the severity of God's judgment: yet they are pleasing and acceptable to God in Christ, and do spring out necessarily of a true and lively faith, in so much that by them, a lively faith may be as evidently known, as a tree discerned by the fruit.

Hume noticed as much in his *History*, where he highlights the compromises in the convocation of 1536:

The two sects seem to have made a fair partition, by sharing alternately the several clauses. In framing the . . . articles, each of them seems to have thrown in its ingredient. The catholics prevailed in asserting, that the use of images was warranted by Scripture; the protestants, in warning people against idolatry, and the abuse of these sensible representations. The ancient faith was adopted in maintaining the expediency of praying to saints; the late innovations in rejecting the peculiar patronage of saints to any trade, profession, or course of action . . .[22]

And so on, through the various articles. The intellectual descendants of both the conservatives and reformers naturally tried to depict Elizabeth's "real" preferences, from which she was forced to sway by the demands of *Realpolitik*. But whatever her real sympathies and however discontented the extremists, she was able to keep her Church and state stable.

In a curious paradox, the favorite eighteenth-century avatar of Elizabethan moderation was Erasmus – for Pope, "good *Erasmus* in an honest Mean" – who, although a Dutchman who lived and died a Catholic and even attacked Luther, became a sort of honorary English Protestant, "the church father of Anglican moderation, the pioneer of reasonable religion."[23] Erasmus's anticipation of Protestant attacks on Church abuses was widely noted; Rolt, for instance, insists that "Erasmus, by shewing the absurdity and uselessness of school divinity, by recommending the study of the Bible and fathers, by discovering the errors and abuses which had crept into the church, and by ridiculing the barbarous ignorance of monks and priests, had a great hand in paving the way for the reformation."[24] Jortin makes him a proto-Protestant without the Puritan excesses: "Long before Luther made his appearance, Erasmus had censured the minute devotions, which the directors of consciences imposed upon the people."[25] This Erasmian moderation was a pose assumed by many eighteenth-century religious controvertists. A translator of the *Colloquies* (1725) writes of himself: "*Some* will have him to be a *Papist in Masquerade*, for going *so far*; *Others* again will have him to be too much a *Protestant*, because he will go *no farther*: So that he is crush'd betwixt the two Extremes, as they hung up *Erasmus himself*, betwixt Heaven and Hell."[26]

As this translator shows, the moderate sixteenth-century heritage allowed eighteenth-century Anglicans to view themselves as an eminently reasonable people in a world of irrational extremes. Louis Landa notes that "Many sermons were preached on the biblical text, 'Let your moderation be known unto all men,'" and both High- and Low-Church partisans tried to claim the reasonable middle. It reinforced their view of their own national character, between the mercurial Italians and the dour Germans; it allowed them to congratulate themselves on an enlightened political system that synthesized extremes, arising out of a constitution perfectly poised between republican anarchy and monarchical tyranny. Eighteenth-century moderation is both civil and ecclesiastical, for it is impossible to separate the political from the theological. As Edmund Burke argued in 1792, "The church and the state are one and the same thing, being different integral parts of the same whole." Eighteenth-century writers had before them many examples of the earthly consequences of divine disputes: the fires at Smithfield, the sixteenth-century French Wars of Religion, and most recently the English Civil Wars. Even later, the Glorious Revolution, the Hanoverian succession, and the 'Forty-five served as reminders that religious quarrels can have disturbing consequences. The connection between ecclesiastical and civil order was therefore plain for all to see: as Patrick Middleton put it in 1733, "The Peace and Safety of the State doth depend on the due Management of Religion and Ecclesiastical Affairs."[27]

Many eighteenth-century commentators remarked on this connection of church and state in the Reformation. Hume, for instance, points out that Elizabeth found the Puritans offensive not so much for their theology as for their "principles of civil liberty." More important, he saw the connection between Reformation theology and later politics. He is describing the lot of Mary, Queen of Scots, when he writes, "Nothing can be more unhappy for a people than to be governed by a sovereign, who is attached to a religion different from the established," calling it "scarce possible that a mutual confidence can ever, in such a situation, have place between the prince and his subjects." But the shift from the specific reference to Mary to the ostensibly generic "prince" and "his" suggest that his real attention is on the late seventeenth century, when James II nearly suffered a similar fate. Delarivier Manley draws her own connections between church and state, past and present, in 1714: "The Circumstances of Qu. *Elizabeth* much resemble those of Her present Majesty," Queen Anne; she adds that "there were many Factions at that time, both of *Papists* and *Puritans*, to neither of which she gave much Quarter ... yet She carried the Respect and Duty of her Subjects with her, even to the Grave."[28]

Moral lessons from the Reformation were drawn by those on both sides. The High-Church editor of an abridgment of Hooker's works, an anonymous "Divine of the Church of England," reminds all who will listen in 1705 that "the Crown and the Crosier" are linked. "*Forty One* is not yet out of the reach of our Remembrance," he writes, and reminds his readers that "We have seen the fatal Effects of [Puritanism] once, when without all manner of Right, they jostled out our Laws, and seized on the Government." Dissenters, he insists, are "a Herd of Men, whom nothing but Anarchy or a Common-wealth can please."[29] On the other side of the spectrum, a pseudonymous Nonconformist is determined to show the relevance of the sixteenth-century religious struggles in eighteenth-century politics. His hostile *Memoirs of Queen Anne* (1729) demonstrates an almost paranoid concern for "the ill Designs of the Popish Party in this Kingdom, who have been in continual Hopes ... to overturn the Reformation, and re-establish Popery." To impress his readers with the threat posed by the Catholics, he begins with an "Introduction: containing a short view of parties, from the Reformation to the Reign of Queene *Anne*," which likens the contemporary "Differences between the High Church and Low in *England*" to "Disputes between the *Lutherans* and *Calvinists* abroad."[30] The anonymous author of *A Protestant Memorial* (1713) likewise uses the example of Elizabeth's reign as a means of keeping the Papists down, and calls for the people

to exert their Zeal, now, and at all Times, (tho' always in a *fit* and *legal manner*) against the *evil Spirit of Popery*, which was cast out at the Reformation, but has ever since wander'd about, seeking for a Re-admittance... We have now a *new Motive* to this Zeal; the *Preservation of our most gracious Queen* ANN, being to be added to the *Vindication* of the most *gracious Queen* Elizabeth... There is a saying which is lately become familiar among us, *what has been, may be*. One *Pope Anathematiz'd* Queen *Elizabeth*, and another may Queen *Ann*.[31]

GLOOMY AND SCHOLASTIC DISQUISITIONS

The most significant lesson the eighteenth century learned from Elizabeth's reign was the value of a moderate religious course and the necessity of preserving civil peace. Against the background of the religious turmoil of Mary Tudor's reign and the Civil Wars of the seventeenth century, the age of Elizabeth seemed a model for all matters ecclesiastical. And the means to this end was the proper handling of adiaphorism, or "things indifferent," in church governance.[32]

The Church of England had never been especially doctrinal. Henry VIII's split with Rome was more political than theological; in 1534, England was a nominally Protestant nation without a Protestant theology. As later British commentators were pleased to point out, the English Church, like the English constitution, was derived not from a set of abstract *a priori* principles, but from the actual conditions of sixteenth-century life. The more recondite aspects of Reformation theology were held in low regard in the eighteenth century, perhaps as part of the legacy of Locke's empiricist rejection of the abstract Continental disputation. Pope's formulation is especially forceful: "For Modes of Faith, let graceless zealots fight." In that spirit Smollett blames Henry VIII for his excessive attention to "gloomy and scholastic disquisitions," and Hume grumbles at "the bigotry of theologians; a malady, which seems almost incurable," deriding such Continental theologians as Melanchthon, Bucer, Sturmius, and Draco as "wretched composers of metaphysical polemics."[33]

Rejection of Christian disputation, however, did not amount to a rejection of Christianity, for a non-doctrinal brand of Protestantism was favored throughout the eighteenth century. The rancorous polemicists' loss is Hugo Grotius's gain; like Erasmus, he wins praise for his ostensibly non-denominational Christianity. "Were all Christians to go upon this Principle," writes an anonymous editor of *The Truth of the Christian Religion* (1743), "we should soon see an End to all the fierce Controversies and unhappy Divisions, which now rend and confound the Church of Christ." His ingenious argument boils down to this: theological dispute is uncharitable, and controvertists "ought not to disturb that Peace and Unity which ought to be amongst all Christians, for the Sake of any Matters of Faith, any Differences of Opinion; because it is contrary to the known Law of Charity."[34] Grotius's moderation, even Latitudinarianism, was a kind of ideal for irenic eighteenth-century theologians.

It is unsurprising that England, having suffered so many disastrous consequences of religious disputations, should seek a sort of ecumenical Protestantism and avoid any doctrinal disagreements likely to upset the peace. Burnet backs up these concerns with a history lesson: too many divines were "diverted...by the *Disciplinarian Controversies*." The consequence was grave: "As Waters gush in, when the Banks are once broken, so the breach that these had made, proved fruitful. Parties were formed, Secular Interests were grafted upon them, and new Quarrels followed those that first begun the Dispute...Soon after that, we fell into the Confusions of *Civil War*."[35] Burnet's solution is to invoke the Elizabethan doctrine of things indifferent, and the most forceful sixteenth-century expression of adiaphorism and its role in civil government appears in the works of Richard Hooker. His *Laws of Ecclesiastical Polity* (1594–97), a systematic defense of moderation against its extremist rivals, remained the definitive statement of Elizabethan Anglicanism in the age of Johnson.

Its scope and authoritativeness made it a favorite text for later ages to invoke in similar disputes. The anonymous High-Church editor of the *Faithful Abridgment of the Works of...Richard Hooker* (1705), for example, uses the Preface as an opportunity for a scathing attack on modern Dissenters "in this hurry of Whigism," and hopes "to open the Eyes of some blind Zealots, who seek to ruin her Regimin contrary to Reason and Scripture." The Puritans have inflicted "extraordinary Gashes" on the Church, "and unless a speedy Assistance be brought in, I pray God she be not thrown down, and over-powered."[36]

Not all invocations of Hooker were so crudely partisan, and for most later readers the *Laws* offered a timeless and balanced statement of the principles of the Anglican faith. Hooker's Church depends on a distinction between essential and indifferent things; his concern was to remove matters inessential to salvation from the realm of dispute. It is important to distinguish this sort of Elizabethan adiaphorism from Lockean toleration. Locke addresses things indifferent, but insists that in such matters the choice should be left to the individual:

You will say: Will you then deny the magistrate what everyone allows him – power over indifferent things?... If anything is not useful to the commonwealth, however indifferent it may be, it cannot thereupon be established by law. Things however indifferent in their own nature are removed out of the reach of the magistrate's jurisdiction when they are brought into the church and the worship of God, because when used there they have no connexion with civil affairs.[37]

Hooker would have agreed with the principle that things with no relation to civil affairs should be out of the reach of the magistrate. He disagreed, however, on whether religious adiaphora posed such a threat. Rather than toleration, which grants the individual the choice in cases where there is no clear scriptural mandate, Hooker calls for the state to step in and rule on controversial matters: "Touching things which belong to discipline and outward politie, the Church hath authoritie to make canons, laws, and decrees." The effect is to admit that such questions are not essential to salvation, but to remove the threat of disorder by removing the questions from the realm of debate: "Nature, scripture, and experience it selfe, have all taught the world to seeke for the ending of contentions by submitting it selfe unto some judiciall and definitive sentence."[38]

The next age learned Hooker's lesson. The succession of bills on Dissent – the Toleration Act of 1689, the Occasional Conformity Act of 1711, the Schism Act of 1714, the annual Indemnity Acts beginning in 1727, each qualifying but not revoking its predecessors – represents a series of compromises between license and oppression, a careful navigation between toleration and despotism. The emphasis varies from bill to bill, but the larger picture remains constant: if you agree on such essentials as the Trinity and transubstantiation, you may believe what you will, provided you do not threaten the civil peace by clamoring in public about less central concerns. In these acts, we can discern the emergence of eighteenth-century England's distinctive blend of Latitudinarianism and Erastianism.

THE AUTHORITY OF THE CHURCH

This insistence on the state's right to legislate theology, especially matters indifferent, leads to one of the richest points of contact between the ecclesiastical world of the sixteenth century and the intellectual world of the eighteenth, the relationship between Hooker and Samuel Johnson.

Johnson's interest in religious matters is obvious to any observer, but his interest in church history may require some substantiation. Nicholas Hudson rightly points out that Johnson's "beliefs addressed modern issues and problems quite different from those which faced theologians of

the sixteenth and seventeenth centuries."[39] However much he responded
to contemporary events and crises, though, these responses were consistently informed by his extensive knowledge of the history of the Church
from Chrysostom to Wesley, and here the sixteenth-century was central.
In 1738, shortly after arriving in London, he began work on a translation
of Sarpi's *History of the Council of Trent*.[40] Two decades later, in his most
productive period, he wrote to Thomas Warton: "I have been thinking
about some literary business for an inhabitant of Oxford." He suggests
that his friend consider

1. An Ecclesiastical Hist. of England...
2. A Hist. of the Reformation (not of England only but) of Europe.

If Warton should decline the projects, Johnson conditions "that what you
do not make use of yourself shall revert to me, uncommunicated to any
other. The schemes of a writer are his property, and his revenue, and
therefore must not be made common" – evidence that, having finished
the *Dictionary*, Johnson was considering such projects for himself.[41]

Hooker would certainly have been a major figure in that ecclesiastical
history, for Johnson knew his works thoroughly. He is quoted by name
2,108 times in the first edition of the *Dictionary*, including under such
important words as *church*, *doctrine*, and *canon*. This makes him the tenth
most-quoted author in the entire work – in the company of Shakespeare,
Pope, and Dryden – and, to most modern readers, by far the least familiar
of the top ten. Johnson, moreover, apparently considered producing an
edition of Hooker's works.[42]

The influence of Hooker and his contemporaries on Johnson is now a
critical commonplace, but this importance has never been adequately as-
sessed.[43] The greatest of Johnson's concerns inherited from the Reformation is an established English Church with the power to legislate doctrine.
Such an official church was essential for Johnson, no believer in private
enthusiasm ("A vain belief of private revelation," says the *Dictionary*;
"a vain confidence of divine favour or communication"), which could
produce only chaos. As Johnson expresses it in one of his sermons, "The
prevailing spirit of the present age seems to be the spirit of scepticism
and captiousness, of suspicion and distrust, a contempt of all authority,
and a presumptuous confidence in private judgement; a dislike of established forms, merely because they are established, and of old paths,
because they are old."[44] One such hater of establishment was Milton,
of whom he writes, "To be of no church is dangerous." Although he
insists that "Tradition, sir, has no place, where the Scriptures are plain,"

he vigorously defends the binding power of tradition where it does not contradict Scripture. And his attitudes toward evangelical sects are the same as toward those who depart from the Church of England. He liked John Wesley, and even "owned that the Methodists had done good," but he believed that the "expulsion of six students from the University of Oxford, who were methodists" was "extremely just and proper. What have they to do at an University who are not willing to be taught, but will presume to teach?"[45]

Hooker's defense of a national church and its ability to make binding laws anticipates many of Johnson's opinions on church governance.[46] Indeed, Hooker influenced much of Johnson's thinking on the grounds of society. Maxwell provides Boswell with the following account:

Speaking of the *inward light*, to which some methodists pretended, he said, it was a principle utterly incompatible with social or civil security. "If a man (said he,) pretends to a principle of action of which I can know nothing, nay, not so much as that he has it, but only that he pretends to it; how can I tell what that person may be prompted to do? When a person professes to be governed by a written ascertained law, I can then know where to find him."[47]

Compare Hooker: "By following the law of private reason, where the law of publique should take place, they breede disturbance."[48] Johnson's invocation of "social or civil security" in a discussion of religious inner light shows how the secular and the ecclesiastical are bound together in his mind.

The clearest evidence of his debt to Hooker appears in a source unknown to early commentators, the Vinerian *Lectures on the English Law*, which Johnson helped his friend Robert Chambers to compose in 1768 and 1769. The extent of Johnson's contribution to the lectures has not been precisely determined, but it is safe to say he did not disagree with Chambers on fundamentals; moreover, the similarities between the *Lectures* and the *Laws* suggest the hand of someone deeply knowledgeable in Hooker's work. Hooker's influence is pervasive. One of Johnson's few direct quotations of Hooker outside the body of the *Dictionary* – "Change is not made without inconvenience, even from worse to better" – suggests the nature of this influence. Another close analogue, one suggestive of similar habits of mind if not of direct influence, comes in *The Life of Milton*: Milton "was much read; for paradox, recommended by spirit and elegance, easily gains attention: and he who told every man that he was equal to his King could hardly want an audience." Compare the opening of Hooker's *Laws*: "He that goeth about to perswade a multitude, that they are not so well governed as they ought to be, shall never want attentive and favourable hearers."[49]

Johnson and Hooker share more than a vague congenital conservatism: both feel threatened by unchecked disquisitions on fundamental questions. Though often depicted as a wrangler, Johnson often refused to quarrel at all on important questions, as Boswell notes:

> He was a sincere and zealous Christian, of high Church-of-England and monarchical principles, which he would not tamely suffer to be questioned ... His being impressed with the danger of extreme latitude in either [religion or politics], though he was of a very independent spirit, occasioned his appearing somewhat unfavourable to the prevalence of that noble freedom of sentiment which is the best possession of man.[50]

Hawkins finds Johnson "no friend to controversy," and mentions his "habitual reverence for the name of God," which led him to avoid "idle discussions of theological questions." It is more than close-minded prejudice. He writes approvingly that Thomas Browne "had read all the books against religion, [and] was, in the latter part of his life, averse from controversies. To play with important truths, to disturb the repose of established tenets, to subtilize objections, and elude proof, is too often the sport of youthful vanity, of which maturer experience commonly repents." Johnson dismisses such Scholasticism as "casuistical theology" in one of his sermons, and his evaluation of Joseph Priestley's works – "that they tended to unsettle every thing, and yet settled nothing" – recalls Hooker's argument that "They that seeke a reason of all things do utterly overthrow reason." Where Hooker writes, "Dangerous it were for the feeble braine of man to wade farre into the doings of the most High," Johnson and Chambers echo back, "This eternal and *archetypal* law is not however for the feeble spirit of mortals to pry into."[51]

We see the same sentiment elsewhere in Johnson's writings and conversation. Boswell records an example. When asked whether "it be wrong in the magistrate to tolerate those who preach against the doctrine of the TRINITY?" "Johnson was highly offended, and said, 'I wonder, Sir, how a gentleman of your piety can introduce this subject ... Permitting men to preach any opinion contrary to the doctrine of the established church, tends, in a certain degree, to lessen the authority of the church, and, consequently, to lessen the influence of religion.' "[52] This is evidence not of Trinitarian bigotry, but of a need to keep men's feeble brains from wading into the doings of the most High. Rather than seeking religious topics to dispute, Johnson actively seeks the common ground. Boswell, put off at their first acquaintance by "reports of his bigotry," was "agreeably surprized" at Johnson's declaration, "I think all Christians, whether Papists or Protestants, agree in the essential articles, and that their differences are trivial, and rather political than religious." It was not mere talk for victory: he writes in his "Life of Browne" that "Men may differ from each other in many religious opinions, and yet all may retain the essentials of christianity."[53] Although the rivals and allies had changed over the two and a half centuries since the *Laws* appeared, the spirit comes from Hooker. Both he and Johnson recognize the value of identifying and fortifying the common ground of Christian society, civil and ecclesiastical, and of discouraging reckless disputation about its underlying principles.

The problem with such a position is that it seems to leave no room for liberty of conscience. Hooker, as we have seen, was not calling for Lockean toleration; he and Johnson were acutely conscious of the difficulties that accompany religious toleration. In his discussion of *Areopagitica*, Johnson recognizes the dangers of both encouraging and restricting free speech:

If nothing may be published but what civil authority shall have previously approved, power must always be the standard of truth; if every dreamer of innovations may propagate his projects, there can be no settlement; if every murmurer at government may diffuse discontent, there can be no peace; and if every sceptick in theology may teach his follies, there can be no religion.[54]

Johnson tacitly approves of the role of a free press in the early history of English Protestantism: "In the Time of King *Edward the Sixth*, the Presses were employed in Favour of the *Reformed* Religion, and *small Tracts* were dispersed over the Nation," but "no sooner was Queen *Mary* resolved to reduce her Subjects to the *Romish* Superstition; but she... intirely prohibited *all* Presses... Under the Reign of Queen *Elizabeth*, when Liberty again began to flourish, the Practice of writing Pamphlets became more general." Boswell, however, records a contrary opinion:

Every society has a right to preserve publick peace and order, and therefore has a good right to prohibit the propagation of opinions which have a dangerous tendency. To say the *magistrate* has this right, is using an inadequate word: it is the *society* for which the magistrate is agent. He may be morally or theologically wrong in restraining the propagation of opinions which he thinks dangerous, but he is politically right.

Johnson believes in freedom of conscience, but is careful to distinguish this from freedom of expression. Swift likewise: "Liberty of Conscience is now-a-days not only understood to be the Liberty of believing what Men please, but also of endeavouring to propagate the Belief as much as they can, and to overthrow the Faith which the Laws have already established."[55]

Johnson's position amounts to a kind of moral Occasional Conformity: your conscience is your own, but you owe lip-service to the state. In this he follows Elizabeth: as Strype recounts, in 1570 she was called upon to seek out and persecute closet Catholics. She wrote: "'That the Queen would not have any of their Consciences unnecessarily sifted, to know what Affection they had to the old Religion': Which was in effect to allow them their Religion to themselves, if they would but be quiet, and make no Disturbances about it in the State."[56]

The Thirty-nine Articles provide a test case. A sentence from Bacon's *Letter of Advice... to the Duke of Buckingham* (pub. 1661) is important enough to be quoted three times in the *Dictionary*: "The doctrine in the thirty-nine articles is so orthodoxly settled, as cannot be questioned without danger to our religion, which hath been sealed with the blood of so many martyrs and confessors."[57] Boswell provides more evidence of Johnson's conviction that the state is competent to rule on things indifferent:

I mentioned the petition to Parliament for removing the subscription to the Thirty-nine Articles. JOHNSON. "It was soon thrown out. Sir, they talk of not making boys at the University subscribe to what they do not understand; but they ought to consider, that our Universities were founded to bring up members for the Church of England, and we must not supply our enemies with arms from our arsenal. No, Sir, the meaning of subscribing is, not that they fully understand all the articles, but that they will adhere to the Church of England."

To Boswell's objection that it would be "sufficient to subscribe the Bible," Johnson replies, "Why no, Sir; for all sects will subscribe the Bible; nay, the Mahometans will subscribe the Bible; for the Mahometans acknowledge JESUS CHRIST, as well as Moses, but maintain that GOD sent Mahomet as a still greater prophet than either."[58] He echoes Hooker's conviction that Scripture alone is not enough to establish doctrine; only an organized church can establish those principles.

These cases reveal Johnson's debt to the Elizabethan Anglicanism so forcefully described by Hooker. For both Hooker and Johnson, the state has a compelling interest in guiding the church on a middle course between potentially revolutionary extremes. It is therefore the state's responsibility to transfer the discussion of adiaphora from the realm of religious to that of secular policy – not because such matters are themselves necessary to salvation, but to protect both religious and civil society from the disputes that arise from unregulated debate. The individual conscience need not take its direction from Canterbury or Westminster; but civil peace, so ardently desired after so many decades of war, depends on learning the lessons taught in the age of Elizabeth.

CHAPTER 5

The ground-work of stile: language and national identity

"Every language," writes Johnson in the Preface to the *Dictionary*, "has a time of rudeness antecedent to perfection, as well as of false refinement and declension."[1] This pair – rise and fall, refinement and declension – suggests a linguistic peak, which occupied many eighteenth-century minds eager to find a rule by which to regulate their language. Johnson's century marks the first concerted and systematic effort to discover a "standard" English, a search in which the language of the age of Elizabeth looms large. History often works its way into discussions of linguistic propriety, and linguistic propriety often works its way into discussions of national identity. This chapter explores the linguistic trajectory of refinement and declension by placing Johnson's comments on the history of the language in the context of other such statements from the fifteenth through the eighteenth centuries.

Two further sentences from the Preface to the *Dictionary* provide a starting point for the investigation. The first: "I have studiously endeavoured to collect examples and authorities from the writers before the restoration, whose works I regard as *the wells of English undefiled*, as the pure sources of genuine diction." Johnson's concern is to justify his choice of illustrative quotations for his *Dictionary* – the first English dictionary to include them. The second sentence is perhaps equally familiar, its Johnsonian periods stretching to eighty-one words:

Our language, for almost a century, has, by the concurrence of many causes, been gradually departing from its original *Teutonick* character, and deviating towards a *Gallick* structure and phraseology, from which it ought to be our endeavour to recal it, by making our ancient volumes the ground-work of stile, admitting among the additions of later times, only such as may supply real deficiencies, such as are readily adopted by the genius of our tongue, and incorporate easily with our native idioms.[2]

Familiar as these passages are, their relation to one another has received little attention.[3] But their surprising proximity – one follows immediately on the other, without so much as a paragraph break – suggests a connection between these "undefiled" sixteenth-century writers and the source of subsequent pollution, "a Gallick structure and phraseology." Together, these comments on the history of English in the eighteenth century's most imposing work on the language provide an opportunity to discuss the relationship between the language of Johnson's day and that of the revival of learning.

THE PUREST AND MOST GENUINE LANGUAGE

Johnson calls the sixteenth- and early seventeenth-century writers "pure sources" and "undefiled," echoing Spenser's accolade for Chaucer. He thereby implies some sort of pollution, invoking the familiar Renaissance habit of castigating the undesirable as "impure." Purity of diction is by now a commonplace, a metaphor so thoroughly naturalized that it is nearly dead. But it was not always so, and Donald Davie's advice is salutary: "We have to be aware... of the force still latent in metaphors that sham dead."[4] Purity *versus* corruption, I have suggested, is a favorite theme of Renaissance humanists. Although they applied it to nearly every aspect of their culture, linguistic corruption was especially susceptible to the humanist critique, and evaluations of language as pure or corrupt were widespread in discussions of both Latin and the vernacular languages.

Treating a language as a substance capable of admitting adulteration was an idea first developed fully only in the fifteenth century. Antiquity indisputably had ideas of *good* and *bad* Greek and Latin: Aristotle, for instance, found the paramount stylistic virtues in writing that was σαφής (clear, perspicuous) and ἁρμόττων (fitting, appropriate), and Horace satirizes the then-current vogue for Greek coinages. Although Cicero mentions purity as one of the merits of style in *De Oratore*, he means by it something akin to Aristotle's criterion of appropriateness, and buries it in a long catalogue: "pure, Latine, plane, dilucide, ornate, apte, decore dicere." In any case, his praise of "copiose et ornate dicere" was far more important throughout antiquity. Quintilian criticizes writing sullied by "barbarismus" and "soloecismus," but in neither case is language praised for being pure – even barbarism is inappropriate rather than unclean.[5] Nor did medieval latinists think in terms of purity and corruption: such a dichotomy simply had not been made. Other divisions, of course, were common: language was pigeonholed as clear or muddled, decorous or inappropriate, belonging to the *genus grande* or *genus humile*. But Latin was not routinely conceived as a "true" medium in which "false" elements served as pollutants.

The first hints appear, fittingly enough, where some commentators see the first stirrings of the Renaissance spirit. Dante suggests this idea of purity when he says of the "illustris" vernacular: "It has indeed been elevated by the [*stilnovisti* poets], since it was chosen from so many rude words of the Latins, from so many perplexed constructions, from so many failed quotations, from so many country accents..."[6] But only with the humanist "recovery" of "real" Latin was the language of the intervening era widely regarded as corrupt, contaminated by medieval verbal pollutants. The enemy was the millennium and a half since the reign of Augustus: fifteen hundred years of linguistic development were turned into an aberration. Scholastic philosophers and medieval lawyers were rebuked as barbarians, and charged with infecting the learning and the Latin of the ancients with atrocious solecisms. Roger Ascham, for instance, objects that "For wordes, right choice is smallie regarded, true proprietie whollie neglected, confusion is brought in, barbariousnesse is bred vp so in yong wittes, as afterward they be, not onelie marde for speaking, but also corrupted in iudgement." Linguistic infections threaten to spread to morals. He therefore looks back to a healthy antiquity in admonishing English speakers: "Whan apte and good wordes began to be neglected, and properties of those two tonges [Latin and Greek] to be confounded, than also began, ill deedes to spring... newe and fond opinions to striue with olde and trewe doctrine." Thomas Campion in 1602 likewise blames "the illiterate Monks and Friers" in the "lack-learning times," when "Learning, after the declining of the *Romaine* Empire and the pollution of their language through the conquest of the *Barbarians*, lay most pitifully deformed till the time of *Erasmus, Rewcline*, Sir *Thomas More*, and other learned men of that age... [who] brought the Latine toong againe to light."[7]

When the old tongue was at last brought to light, many works of the Middle Ages were unceremoniously jettisoned. The result was an extensive effort to cure the Latin tongue by excising its tumors, to restore it to the full bloom of health it experienced in the first century B.C. Thus Vives, whose recurring question about each of the modern liberal arts in *De causis corruptarum artium* is "who first corrupted it with lies, and why?," longs for the purity of the first century, "when one could seek out a master of speech, most certain in his usage, from among the people (as in the time of Quintilian, and even of Cicero), and the usage of those who spoke poorly was generally refuted by analogy." J. C. Scaliger makes a similar point in a section "De imitatione et ivdicio": "Thus many things work their way into the poet's breast, but not all should be admitted."[8] Linacre's motto, *ad fontes*, suggests that the desire is to arrive at the pure source, to drink from waters yet unpolluted.

In the place of the barbarians were erected monuments to the Augustan prose writers, especially Cicero, whose style was the hottest commodity in the literary marketplace. Purity of style cannot be separated from nobility of thought. The classical authors whose styles were most highly regarded were almost always those whose ideas were most admired: as Edward Phillips put it in 1658, "All those ancient Authours that have written the best things, have left them to posterity in the purest and most genuine Language."[9] This assumption that the most interesting authors were necessarily the purest led to the practice of grounding a modern language in a body of old works, with one canon serving as the model for imitation both of style and of substance. The supposedly Ciceronian prose of the Renaissance, to be sure, often had little to do with Cicero's style. But it sounded authentic to fifteenth- and sixteenth-century ears, and that was enough.

In the most extreme, but in some ways the most representative, form of this project, radical Ciceronians such as Pietro Bembo would restrict the legitimate vocabulary to only those words that Cicero himself had used – Longolius in fact prided himself on using only the inflected forms found in Cicero's works. This extremism prompted reactions even from those friendly to humanism: Erasmus's *Dialogus ciceronianus* (1528) famously satirizes such absurd excesses.[10] But although slavishness was often disavowed, imitation of earlier styles was not, and Dolet's position was typical: "Cicero in his *de Oratore* says there could not be a standard of writing for all unless there were a model, therefore the chief thing in the art of speaking is that we try to imitate one person." We can hear the same thing in Camerarius ("I consider these ancient classics the best, and any departure from them I count disgraceful"), J. C. Scaliger's *Oratio pro M. T. Cicerone contra Disiderium Erasmum* (1537), and other works of the sixteenth century.[11]

The whole enterprise depends upon the belief in a period in which a language most nearly approaches its true genius, and the humanists thought they found it in the Late Republic and Early Empire, the years between Sulla's invasion of Rome and the death of Augustus. The sixteenth century therefore produced lexicons that drew illustrative quotations almost exclusively from this part of antiquity, not with the descriptive intentions that lie behind modern lexicographical corpora, but in the hope of regulating contemporary usage with that of the age of Cicero and Virgil. Terence's observation – "nullumst iam dictum quod non dictum sit prius" – became not a lament about the burden of the past, but a vow, a mustering of resolve, on the way to a proper style.[12]

Even those who followed Erasmus away from extreme Ciceronianism – Muret, Montaigne, Bacon – into what Morris Croll has denominated the "Attic" or "Baroque" style continued to respect the notion of linguistic purity. They plotted a palace coup to dethrone Cicero from his position as stylistic arbiter, only to replace him with a junta consisting of Seneca, Lucan, Persius, Juvenal, and other writers of the Silver Age.[13] So even as Cortesi rejects Poliziano's party-line Ciceronianism, he grants that "no one can at present speak with elegance and variety unless he place before him a model to imitate"; Erasmus, too, argues that "where correctness and precision of language are concerned, Varro is not inferior to Cicero, and Caesar ranks higher."[14] The principle of grounding modern style on that of a privileged earlier age remained intact. Whether they looked to the writers of the Augustan or the Silver Age, Renaissance thinkers based their conception of style on a privileged moment in the history of the language, and elevated the works of that age into classics.

The result, evident from our own historical vantage point, was the transformation of Latin from a living language to a dead one: the very fate Erasmus warned against. The Ciceronians demanded a linguistic self-consciousness which would have paralyzed any native speaker, and Latin's days as a spoken tongue were numbered: as C. S. Lewis puts it, "Before they had ceased talking of a rebirth it became evident that they had really built a tomb."[15] But this was far from the minds of most early humanists, for whom the regulation of modern speech by ancient rule promised to cure their language of its infirmities and to render it useful to their age.

FALSE REFINEMENT AND DECLENSION

The Ciceronian habit survived the radical stylistic and lexical experiments of the seventeenth century, and continued, albeit in altered form, into the eighteenth. Whether the particular passages cited above constitute sources for Johnson and his contemporaries is not the issue. The metaphors were so widespread that eighteenth-century readers would have had many opportunities of encountering them.[16] But whatever the channels through which these ideas flowed, subsequent eras inherited this Renaissance concern with linguistic purity; we can hear it clearly in Johnson's declaration that he has "laboured to refine our language to grammatical purity, and to clear it from colloquial barbarisms, licentious idioms, and irregular combinations."[17] As England began searching for its own canon of classics, it sought to ground its style on that of its best exemplars.

The quest for a vernacular English classic style was already underway in the Restoration. Thomas Sprat, a foe of the florid rhetorical habits of the Renaissance, asks, "Who can behold, without indignation, how many mists and uncertainties, these specious *Tropes* and *Figures* have brought on our Knowledg?" Yet he uses the same old metaphors in revealing his anxiety about the "infection" in the language: like the sixteenth-century anti-Ciceronians, Sprat resorts to the conceptual categories of his rivals. He hopes that "some sober and judicious Men, would take the whole Mass of our Language into their hands...and would set a mark on the ill Words." John Evelyn also hopes that the language might "be purg'd from things intollerable," and proposes "a Lexicon or collection of all the pure English words."[18] Sprat gives his thoughts on how this might be brought about, proposing a linguistic academy on the model of the scientific one whose history he is chronicling. His remedy is "a constant Resolution, to reject all the amplifications, digressions, and swellings of style: to return back to the primitive purity, and shortness, when men deliver'd so many *things*, almost in an equal number of *words*."[19] Note that the hated amplifications and swellings are the legacy of the sixteenth-century Ciceronians: but note, too, that the expurgatory metaphor is also theirs. His choice of models is different, but his insistence on "return[ing] back to the primitive purity" demonstrates exactly the same dynamic.

A similar call for an academy appears prominently in the most famous eighteenth-century jeremiad on linguistic impurity, Swift's *Proposal* of 1712. Swift finds "our Language...extremely imperfect...its daily Improvements are by no Means in Proportion to its daily Corruptions." The modern vitiated style was widespread: "These Corruptions very few of the best Authors in our Age have wholly escaped." He attributes this want of refinement partly to England's linguistic history: "The *Latin* Tongue in its Purity was never in this Island." The same concern with English as a linguistic mongrel – Muret's adjective "mixobarbarus" is fitting – can be heard in Defoe's invocation of "Your *Roman–Saxon Danish–Norman English*."[20]

George Campbell's *Philosophy of Rhetoric* (1776) makes much of an unadulterated English tongue. The third chapter of the second book, "Of Grammatical Purity," defines purity thus: "Pure English... implies three things: *first*, that the words be English; *secondly*, that their construction... be in the English idiom; *thirdly*, that the words and phrases be employed to express the precise meaning which custom hath affixed to them" – all of which is to say that pure English is English and only English. In further comments on the "different ways it may be injured," he castigates archaisms (*hight, cleped, uneath, erst, whilom*), neologisms (*volupty, opiniatre, sortie*), and "good words new-modelled" (*incumberment, portic, martyrised, eucharisty, analyse, connexity*). Too many such barbarisms lead to what Campbell attacks as "a sort of monkish gibberish."[21]

This anxiety that English was still threatened with monkish barbarism has important implications. Most eighteenth-century thinkers, it is true, regarded the English Renaissance as a progress away from the imperfections of the barbarous Middle Ages. But for many, the linguistic ascent from Chaucer and Lydgate to Shakespeare and Jonson had its mirror image in a subsequent decline. Henry Stern probably overstates the case in arguing that "the dominant theory of the eighteenth century was that a state of perfection had been reached in former times, that the English language was currently in a process of degeneration, and that measures were needed to restore its purity"[22] – no one "theory" seems quite so "dominant." But linguistic decline had been on English minds at least since Ascham:

The Latin tong, concerning any part of purenesse of it, from the spring, to the decay of the same, did not endure moch longer, than is the life of a well aged man, scarse one hundred yeares... And good cause why: for no perfection is durable. Encrease hath a time, & decay likewise, but all perfit ripenesse remaineth but a moment.

Compare Dryden's concern about his own native tongue:

That an Alteration is lately made in [English] or since the Writers of the last Age (in which I comprehend *Shakespear, Fletcher* and *Jonson*) is manifest... But, that this is an *Improvement* of the Language, or an alteration for the better, will not so easily be granted. For many are of a contrary opinion, that the *English* tongue was then in the height of its perfection; that, from *Jonsons* time to ours, it has been in a continual declination.

Swift fears the same thing: "From that great Rebellion to this present Time, I am apt to doubt whether the Corruptions in our Language have not, at least, equalled the Refinements of it."[23]

Eighteenth-century writers, that is to say, saw contrary movements since the age of Elizabeth: progressive refinement toward Waller and Dryden on the one hand, but a potentially unstoppable decline into babble on the other. Pope's formulation is only the most famous statement of a common anxiety: "And such as *Chaucer* is, shall *Dryden* be."[24] Swift's contribution to *Tatler* 230 is also well known: "I mean the continual Corruption of our *English* Tongue; which, without some timely Remedy, will suffer more by the false Refinements of Twenty Years past, than it hath been improved in the foregoing Hundred." Swift is more cautious than this suggests: "Whether our Language . . . will decline as fast as the *Roman* did, is a Question that would perhaps admit more Debate than it is worth"; and "the *English* Tongue is not arrived to such a Degree of Perfection, as, upon that Account, to make us apprehend any Thoughts of its Decay."[25] But whether or not the decline had begun or was inevitable, anxiety about the threat was real, and caused the eighteenth century to inherit the humanistic idea of subjecting their own language to the discipline of a privileged earlier form, from a time before the decay began.

Just as the humanists found their enemy in the barbarisms of the Middle Ages, many eighteenth-century purists resented the innovations of the seventeenth century, especially during the Civil Wars and Interregnum. The rhetoric of the eighteenth century is sometimes surprisingly similar to that of the fifteenth. Swift, for instance, complains that "During the Usurpation, such an Infusion of Enthusiastick Jargon prevailed in every Writing, as was not shaken off in many Years after." Chesterfield sees the newcomers as anarchists: "All words, good and bad, are jumbled indiscriminately together . . . The time for discrimination seems to be now come. Toleration, adoption and naturalization have run their lengths. Good order and authority are now necessary." Thus his advice to his son, in which he invokes the Terentian tag: "There is nothing truer than that old saying *Nihil dictum quod non prius dictum.*"[26]

Johnson's differences from Chesterfield are well known, but to judge by the front matter of the *Dictionary*, Johnson was attuned to the same discourse of linguistic and cultural corruption. "Every language," as we have seen, "has a time of rudeness antecedent to perfection, as well as of false refinement and declension." Languages participate in the general cultural progress, as Johnson says in an echo of the metaphor of cultural maturity: "Language proceeds, like every thing else, thro' improvement to degeneracy." Like Swift, he withholds comment on whether the

English language had already in fact begun its decline, hoping to avoid "any credulous confidence in the superior wisdom of past ages, or gloomy persuasion of the degeneracy of mankind."[27] But the metaphors of the humanist tradition fill both the Preface and the History, where Johnson imagines his obligation "to guard the avenues of [his] languag[e], to retain fugitives, and repulse intruders," however futile it may be to fortify English against linguistic vandals.[28] The intruders are those without a pedigree: only those words grounded in good, old usage are considered legitimate. Thus one critic remarks of Johnson's attitude toward unauthorized diction: "Johnson sees words without a past as a mob of rebellious bastards."[29] Bastardy is the right word: illegitimate words are degraded. Johnson labels *cuddy* "a low bad word," and notes that it is "without etymology," while *crambo* is "a cant word, probably without etymology." A language is authorized by its past.

The question, then, for Johnson and his contemporaries was *which* past to choose. Rome's golden age was easy to identify: the Italian humanists had made the choice, and later ages ratified it. The project to subject contemporary vernacular usage to that of privileged old authors was already in full swing on the Continent. As early as the sixteenth century, Bembo found modern models for Italian style in Petrarch and Boccaccio.[30] Both of these figure prominently, along with all the major names in Italian literature, in the "Tavola de nomi degli autori o de' libri citati in quest' opera" of the Accademia della Crusca's *Vocabolario* (1612).[31] Richelet likewise supports his *Dictionnaire françois* (1680) with "l'usage... des bons auteurs de la langue françoise," most from the reign of Louis XIV, and states his intention to regulate modern language by the best usage: "J'ai fait un Dictionnaire François afin de rendre quelque service aux honnêtes gens qui aiment notre Langue. Pour cela j'ai lu nos plus excellens Auteurs."[32]

English writers, though, were more troublesome, for no domestic age of Augustus, Boccaccio, or Louis XIV had yet been identified. Even those who agreed that language had begun its fall differed on the time of the language's golden age. Searches had been going on for some time. While the proponents of the Ciceronian and Baroque styles were debating classical models, the vernacular was receiving a similar scrutiny: in the sixteenth century, "Many Elizabethan writers judged the language of Chaucer, Lydgate, and Gower to be such a peak."[33] The eighteenth-century search for a model on which to base a modern style recalls and amplifies these sixteenth-century debates. In this age of profound linguistic self-consciousness, the search for a standard by which to regulate the language produced competing claims for various periods from the earliest times through the age of Anne.

ORIGINAL TEUTONICK CHARACTER

Johnson leaves no doubt as to the identity of some of the modern-day barbarians in his *Dictionary*, and hints at one common choice for a model of properly pure English. "The whole fabrick and scheme of the *English* language," he writes, "is *Gothick* or *Teutonick*"; but "Our language... has ... been gradually departing from its original *Teutonick* character, and deviating towards a *Gallick* structure and phraseology."[34] The French, then, are the invaders, the poisoners of the pure Saxon streams. English is in a unique position among the European languages in having two parents, one Germanic, one Romance. By comparison with such relatively homogeneous languages as French and German, English has an obvious standard of what constitutes purity. The fit was indisputably imperfect, but for some the need for an authorizing corpus of pure diction was enough to put Old English, at least tentatively, in the position of Augustan Latin.

Interest in Saxon antiquities was never really popular: only a small cadre of dedicated antiquarians could read Old English, and few translations were available to make such works accessible to a wider public. But scholarly interest in the roots of the English language was considerable, and from at least the late sixteenth century this study was associated with British national identity. Camden, for instance, writes that "The English tongue is extracted, as the nation, from the Germans the most glorious of all now extant in Europe for their morall, and martiall vertues, and preserving the libertie entire." Phillips points out that the "*Teutones* or *Germans*, being the very first people that ever inhabited *Germany*, have continued in the possession of it to this very day uncorrupted, unsubdued and (as their language, so themselves) unmixed with any forraigne Nation."[35]

Against such a background, later additions to the language – particularly those from French sources – could be seen as impurities. An anonymous sixteenth-century reader inscribed the plan of a history of the language on the flyleaf of an Old English vocabulary by Laurence Nowell, "by the w^ch, and suche like it may appeare, how, and by what steps, our language is fallen *from* the old Inglishe, and drawn nearer to the frenche."[36] Not long after, write two modern critics, Sir John Cheke and

Thomas Wilson believed "The English language should be kept pure. More of the native words – the simple Anglo-Saxon words – should be employed; and words of foreign origin should be rejected."[37] Camden distinguishes two varieties of English, "the *Antient English-Saxon*, and the *Mixt*," and remarks, "Great verily was the glory of our tongue before the Norman Conquest." Even when the number of valuable Latin and French imports was acknowledged, as in Phillips's work, the Saxon words had the advantage of being "the more essential," and while the "German tongue is the ground-work upon which our language is founded," the Romance words are "rather the superstructure then the foundation."[38] Framing the debate in these terms subsumes both anti-French attitudes and attacks on latinate inkhorn terms: in both cases, the Saxon purity is being corrupted by intruders. This praise of Gothic vigor continued into the eighteenth century.[39]

We should be precise about the crime of which the French are accused. Though no great etymologist, Johnson of course knew that countless English words are of French origin. When he writes, therefore, of "a *Gallick* structure and phraseology," he means something more than "French words": "Single words may enter by thousands, and the fabrick of the tongue continue the same, but new phraseology changes much at once; it alters not the single stones of the building, but the order of the columns." Nor is barbarity inherited from a word's roots, for a legitimate English word can come from illegitimate parents: "I have not been very careful to observe," Johnson writes, "whether the *Latin* word be pure or barbarous, or the *French* elegant or obsolete." The danger Johnson sees is that, in the century or so before the *Dictionary*'s publication in 1755, English was being shaken at its very foundations. The offenders are modern authors, providing quarter for the unwanted foreign words "by their knowledge of foreign languages, or ignorance of their own, by vanity or wantonness, by compliance with fashion, or lust of innovation."[40] So Johnson calls *souvenance* "A French word which with many more is now happily disused." *Gout* ("taste") is "An affected cant word"; *frisky* and *gob* are "low"; *to transpire* 2 is "a sense lately innovated from *France*, without necessity"; *to give* ("to rush, to fall on") is "A phrase merely French, and not worthy of adoption"; *ruse* is "A French word neither eloquent nor necessary."

This resentment of French intrusions cannot, however, be attributed to simple anti-Gallic prejudice. Johnson's respect for French writers, beginning with Scaliger and Thuanus and running through his own age, is sincere. The problem lies not with the French language itself, but with its intrusion into English, where it does not belong. Languages, it seems, are mutually corrupting, a point Johnson makes about Italian when he writes to Baretti: "Your English stile still continues in its purity and vigour... Its purity must be continued by close attention. To use two languages familiarly, and without contaminating one by the other, is very difficult."[41] As he explains in the *Dictionary*, "A mixture of two languages will produce a third distinct from both; and they will always be mixed... He that has long cultivated another language, will find its words and combinations croud upon his memory; and haste or negligence, refinement or affectation, will obtrude borrowed terms and exotick expressions."[42]

TEMPLE, OR LOCKE, OR TILLOTSON

Whatever the attraction of old Gothic vigor, however, it was a troublesome standard. We have noted already the way one set of works tends to be used as both literary and linguistic classics at the same time. But *Beowulf*, though known to Laurence Nowell in the sixteenth century and Robert Cotton in the seventeenth, remained unpublished until 1815, and no other work was available to play the role of popular Saxon classic. Perhaps partly for want of a great body of literature, Teutonic words were routinely taken to task for their barbarism: Swift, for instance, refers to "a Tendency to lapse into the Barbarity of those *Northern* Nations from whom we are descended, and whose Languages labour all under the same Defect."[43]

Many in the early eighteenth century therefore sought the language's acme in the decades immediately before them. The evidence is lexicographical. Although Johnson was the first actually to produce an English dictionary with illustrative quotations, he was not the first to consider it, and his selection of quotations from the sixteenth and early seventeenth centuries would not have been everyone's choice. Addison, for instance, planned a dictionary in which Tillotson, "the chief standard of our language," was to have provided the illustrative quotations. Pope, after asking "whether a word is English or not" and resolving to rely on "nothing but authority," looked to the late seventeenth century for his models: "Is [the word] in Sir William Temple, or Locke, or Tillotson? If it be, you may conclude that it is right." The list of authorities for his planned dictionary includes more names from after the Restoration than before it: "Lord Bacon, Hooker, Hobbes, Ben Jonson, Lord Clarendon, Barrow, Tillotson, Dryden, Sir William Temple, L'Estrange, Locke, Sprat, Atterbury, Congreve, Addison, Vanbrugh, Swift, Lord Bolingbroke..."

Hooke and Middleton ... Spenser, Shakespeare, Fletcher, Waller, Butler, Milton ... Prior."[44]

But the qualities that made Old English a good choice made the late seventeenth century a bad one. Johnson's reference to "false refinement" echoes the castigation of foppish and epicene French beaux popular since the Restoration, and catches the tone of many accusations against the late seventeenth century. The affected language of a frenchified culture would simply not satisfy the need for an English golden age. Swift, as we have seen, traces the beginning of the problem to "the great Rebellion," and lays out the charges against Restoration English: "To this succeeded that Licentiousness which entered with the *Restoration*; and from infecting our Religion and Morals, fell to corrupt our Language ... The *Court*, which used to be the Standard of Propriety, and Correctness in Speech, was then, and I think hath ever since continued the worst School in *England*."[45]

WELLS OF ENGLISH UNDEFILED

Anglo-Saxon and Restoration English could, if necessary, be conscripted to serve as pure sources of literary English diction, but neither was an adequate surrogate for Augustan Latin. Another option, though, proved more suitable: the undefiled wells of "the writers before the restoration." The age of Elizabeth, it turns out, provides not only the source of the metaphor, but also the best model of linguistic purity.

We have seen earlier commentators and would-be lexicographers looking for models of a pure style in the Gothic ages and the late seventeenth century. But in collecting his own quotations, Johnson resolved to turn to the Renaissance, when the language reached its zenith: specifically, the 1580s through the 1650s, from Sidney to the Restoration. He was well prepared to do so. The *Dictionary* shows, perhaps better than any of his other works, both the depth and the breadth of Johnson's reading in these authors. Later writers like Dryden and Pope are quoted often, of course, but among the fifteen most-quoted authors in the *Dictionary* are seven canonical authors of the English Renaissance: in order of frequency, Shakespeare (first), Milton (third), Bacon (fourth), Spenser (ninth), Hooker (tenth), Browne (twelfth), and Sidney (fourteenth). The thousands of quotations from the Bible come from the 1611 Authorized Version.

This, the "long" age of Elizabeth, is for Johnson England's linguistic golden age. Its authors provided the model for his own writing: Hawkins traces Johnson's style to "our old English writers, such as Sir Thomas More, Ascham, Hooker, Spenser, archbishop Sandys, Jewel, Chillingworth, Hales, of Eton, and others," and Boswell notes that "The style of Johnson was, undoubtedly, much formed upon that of the great writers in the last century, Hooker, Bacon, Sanderson, Hakewell, and others; those 'GIANTS.' "[46] Some of the *Dictionary*'s most characteristically "Johnsonian" words – *adscititious, dignotion, vermiculation* – are supported by quotations from authors such as Burton and Browne, and are owing to Johnson's professed aim in *The Rambler*: "I have familiarized the terms of philosophy by applying them to popular ideas, but have rarely admitted any word not authorized by former writers."[47] These "former writers" occupy the same place in the *Dictionary* that Cicero's contemporaries held in Renaissance lexicons. Johnson's "studious" search for "examples and authorities from the writers before the restoration" is an expression of the eighteenth-century desire to authorize the language by reference to a corpus of canonical British texts.

He was not alone. As early as 1658, Edward Phillips recommended "for the avoiding of... gross words... onely this in general, To be ever conversant in the best Authours, as Sir *Philip Sidney*, Sir *Thomas More*, Sir *Walter Rawleigh*, my Lord *Verulam, Ben Johnson*." Dryden praises "divine *Shakespeare*" for arriving at such a pure language: "Words and Phrases must of necessity receive a change in succeeding Ages: but 'tis almost a Miracle that much of his Language remains so pure." Edward Howard praises Ben Jonson in similar terms: "He gave our *English* Tongue firmness, greatness, enlarged and improved it, without patching of *French* words to our speech, according to some of our modern Pens." For Swift, "the Period wherein the *English* Tongue received most Improvement" could be said "to commence with the Beginning of Queen *Elizabeth*'s Reign, and to conclude with the great Rebellion in Forty-two": after the Restoration, though, "Licentiousness... from infecting our Religion and Morals, fell to corrupt our Language." Hurd, whose temperament is often far from Johnson's, agrees with him at least on this point: he finds Elizabethan English "pure, strong, and perspicuous, without affectation."[48]

USE AND ELEGANCE

Tracing the ascent of this standard and justifying its primacy is the business of Johnson's Preface and History. The "time of rudeness antecedent to perfection" took more than a millennium, from the fifth century to the end of the sixteenth. Indeed, in its earliest days, English had little to recommend it. "We know nothing of the scanty jargon of our barbarous ancestors," writes Johnson, but "The Christian religion always implies or produces a certain degree of civility and learning; [early English speakers] then became by degrees acquainted with the *Roman* language, and so gained, from time to time, some knowledge and elegance, till in three centuries [after 450] they had formed a language capable of expressing all the sentiments of a civilised people." Thus after the language "began to be adapted to civil and religious purposes," it became "artless and simple, unconnected and concise."[49] The Angles, Saxons, and Jutes benefited from their exposure to Latin, rising from their "rudeness" some time in the eighth century.

The Norman Invasion brought about the next phase: the terms of philosophy and science entered the language along with an infusion of Norman French. Few in the eighteenth century apart from Thomas Warton had anything to say about the poetry of the eleventh through fourteenth centuries. There was, however, far more interest in the final stage of refinement, which began in the late fourteenth century: "From the time of Gower and Chaucer, the English writers have studied elegance, and advanced their language, by successive improvements."[50]

By the end of the sixteenth century, the process had reached its peak, and from the writers of that time a pure and copious language may be collected:

From the authours which rose in the time of *Elizabeth*, a speech might be formed adequate to all the purposes of use and elegance. If the language of theology were extracted from *Hooker* and the translation of the Bible; the terms of natural knowledge from *Bacon*; the phrases of policy, war, and navigation from *Raleigh*; the dialect of poetry and fiction from *Spenser* and *Sidney*; and the diction of common life from *Shakespeare*, few ideas would be lost to mankind, for want of *English* words, in which they might be expressed.[51]

Here are the same assertions for Elizabethan English that were made for Augustan Latin, and also, less successfully, for Saxon and Restoration English: its purity provides a model for contemporary usage. It retains the vigor of the Gothic ages but anticipates the refinement of Temple, and offers just the kind of classical purity the eighteenth century sought.

A small but representative sample of the words in the *Dictionary* gives a rough sense of Johnson's practical approach to the words of the English Renaissance. Of the 103 words in the first edition beginning with *na-*, all but five – over ninety-five percent – are attested in the *OED* for the period from Sidney to the Restoration.[52] Johnson adduces quotations for eighty-three of these words, and of those, forty-two are supported with quotations from that period (and several others with quotations from Milton).

Elizabethan English, we should note, was hardly free from Gallic impurities. The late sixteenth century probably saw a greater influx of Romance words than the middle eighth or the middle eighteenth, for that matter: that much was evident to Camden, who writes that "wee within these 60 yeares, have incorporated so many Latine and French [words], as the third part of our tongue consisteth now in them."[53] But we can set aside the question of whether Johnson's historical sense was accurate when he wrote that in Shakespeare's day "the Saxon was still visibly mingled in our diction."[54] (We must also set aside the irony of the sesquipedalian Lexiphanes – accused in his own day of writing Latin words with English terminations – calling for a Germanic English.) Johnson's extolling the Saxon roots of English over the French intrusions inverts the traditional hierarchy which placed Romance over Germanic languages, a hierarchy already in place in antiquity (as when Tacitus calls the savage Britons "those who used to reject the Latin language"[55]) and reinforced by the sack of cultured Rome by the Teutons. Just as he inverts the centuries-old hierarchy of Romance over Germanic languages, he associates not only "use" with the basic Saxon vocabulary, but appropriates even traditionally latinate "elegance" for the English authors, leaving little to be desired from outsiders. Elizabeth's age was the new standard. As Robert DeMaria notes, "In the social order of the *Dictionary* poetry and learning are the true measures of nobility...The giants before the flood in this lineal descent are the Elizabethans, and their progeny pay them proper homage throughout the *Dictionary*."[56]

The implications for the eighteenth-century study of language are worth noting. The language of the age of Elizabeth for the first time was considered to have a character of its own, to be more than a step on the way to something else. For the first time the language achieved "a stile which never becomes obsolete, a certain mode of phraseology so consonant and congenial to the analogy and principles of its respective language as to remain settled and unaltered." It was therefore for the first time worthy of an attention not merely antiquarian. This is one of the seeming paradoxes in Johnson's attitude toward antiquated language. On the one hand he justifies the exclusion of obsolete words from his *Dictionary*: "Nor are all words which are not found in the vocabulary, to be lamented as omissions"; "What makes a word obsolete, more than a general agreement to forbear it?" On the other hand, according to Boswell, he complained about modern editions: "An authour's language... is a characteristical part of his composition, and is also characteristical of the age in which he writes. Besides, Sir, when the language is changed we are not sure that the sense is the same." This is how Johnson justifies the preservation of forms like "hugger-mugger":

That the words now replaced are better, I do not undertake to prove; it is sufficient that they are Shakespeare's: if phraseology is to be changed as words grow uncouth by disuse, or gross by vulgarity, the history of every language will be lost; we shall no longer have the words of any authour; and... we shall in time have very little of his meaning.

"The history of our language, and the true force of our words," he writes elsewhere, "can only be preserved, by keeping the text of authours free from adulteration."[57]

This concern with a historically specific state of the English language was new to the eighteenth century, but not confined to Johnson. Although even early seventeenth-century antiquarians preserved older orthography in transcriptions of medieval manuscripts and inscriptions, as in Weever's *Ancient Funerall Monuments* (1631), English works published after roughly 1500 had never received similar treatment. By the end of the eighteenth century, by contrast, the need for old-spelling editions was widely acknowledged, and original spelling was used even in some popular editions. Hughes recognizes that the language of the English Renaissance had a distinct character, one that was worth preserving, in producing the first old-spelling edition of a modern English text, that of Spenser (1715). He resolves not only "to preserve the Text entire, but to follow likewise, for the most part, the old Spelling. This may be thought by some too strict and precise; yet there was a Necessity for it, not only to shew the true State of our Language, as *Spenser* wrote it, but to keep the exact Sense."[58] George Sewell followed Hughes's practice in an old-spelling edition of Surrey and Wyatt (1717). Soon such editions of modern English works were widespread, and by century's end they were almost the scholarly norm. The *Six Old Plays* (1779), for instance, are in old spelling, and Joseph Ritson's policy is to introduce "no alteration... either in the language or the orthography" of the works in *The English Anthology* (1793–94). Jonathan Richardson goes further still, arguing that the 1674 edition of *Paradise Lost* "ought to be the Model of Some Future Edition, and follow'd Letter for Letter and Point for Point." Edward Capell would extend the policy to minor sixteenth-century works like Overbury's *Wife* and even to popular ballads like "The Nut-Brown Maid": "Every departure from [the first edition], how minute soever, is at once offer'd to the eye" in a footnote.[59]

This concern for the language of the last age is also expressed in other ways. The effort which evidently went into Hughes's glossary of 777 Spenserian words, for instance, reveals the same desire to historicize the language. Starnes and Noyes call the 1730s "a dictionary-conscious age," in which editors "even went to the length of affixing a glossary to any work whose language was at all unusual," many of them period- or author-specific. So Anderson includes a thirteen-page appendix of Spenserian English to his edition of Spenser's works, and Sewell likewise appends a glossary of 174 "Old Words" to Pope's edition of Shakespeare, ranging from the familiar (*to carol*, a horse's *withers*, *dank*) through the perverse (*quern*, *oursbutt*). When Fairfax's translation of Tasso's *Jerusalem Delivered* was reprinted in 1749, it came with a six-page glossary of words such as *brast*, *kest*, and *nathless*; Ritson's *English Anthology* of 1793–94 is accompanied by a twenty-page "Glossary of Obsolete or Difficult Words." The most impressive such lexicon appears in the first volume of Edward Capell's *Notes and Various Readings to Shakespeare* (1779–83) – part index, part concordance, part glossary to the works of Shakespeare and his contemporaries, cataloguing over three thousand obsolete words, senses, and constructions and noting where they occur in Shakespeare's works. Marcus Walsh half-facetiously refers to Johnson's *Dictionary* as "the most important glossary to any edition of Shakespeare."[60]

RECOURSE TO FOREIGN WRITERS

In the impressive claims Johnson makes for the language of this age, we can discern his striving for a minimally adequate vocabulary – "admitting... only such as may supply real deficiencies" – such as we see in the last *Rambler*: "I believe that whoever knows the English tongue in its present extent, will be able to express his thoughts without further help from other nations." He returns to the same theme in *Idler* 91, attacking "the prejudice which seems to prevail among us in favour of foreign authors," and asserting, "There is, I think, not one of the liberal arts which may not be competently learned in the English language... The more airy and elegant studies of philology and criticism have little need of any foreign help."[61]

This self-sufficiency recalls Sprat's dream "to return back to the primitive purity" in which "men deliver'd so many *things*, almost in an equal number of *words*," and has a long history before Johnson. Camden, for instance, praises pure Anglo-Saxon for its sufficiency: "Great verily was the glory of our tongue before the Norman Conquest in this, that the olde English could expresse most aptly, all the conceiptes of the minde in their owne tongue without borrowing from any." The same tone runs through his declaration of linguistic self-sufficiency:

Pardon me and thinke me not overballanced with affection, if I thinke that our English tongue is (I will not say as sacred as the Hebrew, or as learned as the Greeke,) but as fluent as the Latine, as courteous as the Spanish, as courtlike as the French, and as amorous as the Italian ... Neither hath any thing detracted more from the dignitie of our tongue, than our own affectation of forraine tongues.[62]

Sir John Cheke's letter prefixed to Sir Thomas Hoby's *Courtier* reads, "I am of this opinion, that our own tung shold be written cleane and pure, unmixed and unmangeled with borrowings of other tunges."[63] Samuel Daniel "cannot but wonder at the strange presumption of some men, that dare so audaciously aduenture to introduce any whatsoeuer forraine wordes, be they neuer so strange."[64] And in the eighteenth century, Sewell, addressing the diction of the preeminently British poet, takes aim at those who would anglicize Greek compound epithets (such as "far-shooting") when there is perfectly good English that will do just as well: "I wish the Patrons of this Practice would give us any Reason for flinging in this unnatural foreign Mixture into our Language, when we have Words of Signification, and Sound sufficient to answer our Ideas. What occasion is there for Adulteration, when we have current Coin enough of our own?"[65] Ephraim Chambers makes a similar plea in his *Cyclopædia* (1728), suggesting a hierarchy of the languages that might influence English: "Nothing could be more desirable than an *index expurgatorius*, to clear the language of superfluous words and synonyms; to expunge the modern French and Italian terms in the several arts, where we have Latin and Greek ones; and even the Latin and Greek ones, where we have English or Saxon ones, equal in sound and significancy."[66] Hugh Blair admits that "Barren languages may need such assistance, but ours is not one of these."[67] George Campbell argues that "A liquor produced by the mixture of two liquors of different qualities will often prove worse than either." Latin lacked the beauty of Greek, but was "vitiated" rather than improved by the intrusion of Hellenisms, and for that reason eventually "lost almost entirely ... that beauty and majesty which we discover in the writings of the Augustan age." Greek resistance to foreign admixtures, on the other hand, preserved "the Greek tongue in its native purity for such an amazing number of centuries."[68] Campbell clearly links English vogues for fashionable French words to the collapse of Augustan Latin into barbarism.

The opinion was not quite universal. Thomas Blount's *Glossographia* (1656) considers "our best modern Authors" those "who have both infinitely enriched and enobled our Language, by admitting and naturalizing thousands of foreign Words."[69] Two years later, Edward Phillips looked forward to at least some foreign imports: "The interspersion of forraign words, especially coming from the more southerly and civil Climates, [will] conduce to the sweetning and smoothing of those harsh and rough accents which are peculiar to the most northerly Countries." But even he wonders whether this influx is entirely for the better – "Whether this innovation of words deprave, or inrich our English tongue is a consideration that admits of various censures" – and admits that "the Saxon, or German tongue is the ground-work upon which our language is founded." He goes on: "The mighty stream of forraigne words that hath since *Chaucers* time broke in upon it" has "not yet wash't away the root"; "it is our happinesse that being a terror to other nations, we are now free from invaders that formerly altred our Language."[70]

With this notion of minimal sufficiency – "Thus needless is all recourse to foreign writers" – we move beyond the history of the language and into the history of the nation. The following passage from 1684 is nothing like a source for the Preface to the *Dictionary*, but Johnson's writings share at least some superficial characteristics with the Marquess of Halifax's third-person self-portrait: "But for the earth of *England*, though perhaps inferiour to that of many places abroad, to him there is divinitie in it, and he would rather dye than see a spire of English grasse trampled down by a foreign Trespasser."[71]

His nationalism has lexicographical cousins. John Cannon, one of the more cautious commentators on Johnson's politics, is unequivocal: "In the *Dictionary*...a national purpose was clear from the outset." Sledd and Kolb too discover "patriotic purposes" in Johnson and the other two great early modern lexicographical projects, the Italian *Vocabolario* and the French *Dictionnaire*: "Each has discovered a golden age for the native language: the fourteenth century for Italian, the seventeenth century for French, from the time of Sidney to the Restoration for English."[72] The *Grand dictionnaire*'s dedication to the king, an obvious place to celebrate the nation, delivers fulsome praise to the monarch by associating France's political preeminence with its linguistic superiority: "Que l'on remonte de siecle en siecle, on ne trouver a rien de comparable au spectacle qui fait aujourd'huy l'attention de l'Univers: Toute l'Europe armée contre vous, & toute l'Europe trop foible... La superiorité de vostre Puissance l'a desja renduë la Langue dominante de la plus belle partie du monde."[73] The same national pride shows up in England. Camden ties language to national identity, praising "our Ancestors stedfastnes" for "retaining their own tongue. For as before the Conquest they misliked nothing more in King *Edward* the Confessor, than that he was Frenchified, & accounted the desire of forraine language, then to be a foretoken of the bringing in of forraine powers." This reveals the connection between an uncorrupted language and a sense of nationhood, and hints at the role of a dictionary in the creation of a national idenitity: Edward Phillips in fact refers to "the renown and glory of the Nation, which cannot but be much advanced by such like [lexicographical] indeavours." Chesterfield, in puffing Johnson's soon-to-be-published *Dictionary*, therefore believed the French and Italian dictionaries "now do so much honour to the two nations," and hoped Johnson's lexicographical canonization of the authors of England's golden age would have the same effect: "I confess that I have so much honest English pride, or perhaps prejudice about me, as to think myself more considerable for whatever contributes to the honour, the advantage, or the ornament of my native country." Johnson has similar thoughts of British renown in mind when he discusses the sixteenth century: "Our own language has from the Reformation to the present time, been chiefly dignified and adorned by the works of our divines, who... have undoubtedly left all other nations far behind them." His goals are clear: "I have devoted this book... to the honour of my country, that we may no longer yield the palm of philology without a contest to the nations of the continent." He makes a similar claim for English pride in praising Warton "for the advancement of the literature of our native Country" in clarifying "the authours which are yet read of the sixteenth Century."[74]

Not everyone agrees that this is what Johnson was doing in the *Dictionary*. Daisuke Nagashima finds the History of the English Language less nationalistic than many similar writings: "Johnson clearly distinguishes 'the Saxon (Old English)' from 'the present *English*'...Johnson's basic purpose in the history... lies in displaying the historical changes, rather than the continuous identity, of his mother tongue." The point is well taken. DeMaria, however, correctly notes that "Johnson tried harder than earlier general lexicographers to pay attention to the Germanic roots of English... [and] elevate[d] the importance of the Teutonic element in English." The recurring emphasis on Teutonic roots does little to bear out Nagashima's claim, and even if Johnson does not consistently trace English back to the age of the Egg Kings, Elizabeth's England provides both a linguistic and a political normative standard. As is evident in chapter 3, the victory over the Spanish Armada was still a defining moment in the English national story nearly two centuries later: "Call Britannia's glories back to view; / Behold her cross triumphant on the main, / The guard of commerce, and the dread of Spain."[75] The language of the period has obvious nationalistic associations.

Cannon pithily sums up some of the traps into which we might fall when we drag nationalism into the eighteenth century: "The concept of nationalism has been almost as troublesome to historians as the practice of it has been to rulers." The conventional view was clearly formulated half a century ago: "Nationalism, as we understand it, is not older than the second half of the eighteenth century. Its first great manifestation was the French Revolution."[76] Others, though, are not so sure. Linda Colley's influential work on eighteenth-century British national identity suggests that nationalism is (like periodization) a structuralist enterprise: Britain, she writes, "was an invention forged above all by war." The French were "an obviously hostile Other and encouraged them to define themselves collectively against it...Men and women decide who they are by reference to who and what they are not."[77]

If national identity, then, proceeds through the exclusion of the foreign and the insistence on the adequacy of the national culture, it has unmistakable similarities to the discourse of purity and contamination. The early humanists, it is true, formulated a trans-European rather than a national identity, no doubt because the fragmentation of the Italian principalities (and later the thriving tramontane humanism) made identification with a single nation-state difficult, and a shared language made internationalism easy. But even by the late sixteenth century, the same celebration of purity and castigation of barbarism found a place in nationalistic discourse: one need look no further than John of Gaunt's "fortress built by nature for herself, against infection." Camden early likened linguistic miscegenation to religious subjection to Catholicism: "Hence it is that so many Latine words remain in the French, Spanish, and other tongues, as also from the Popes practise, who imposed the Latine tongue in the divine Service, as a token of subjection to the Romane Sea."[78] Some of the enemies changed in the next few centuries, but the idea remained the same. Colley therefore makes the point: "French contamination had been an evil since the Norman Conquest and could be thrown

off now only by Britons becoming more moral and more united...
Allowing Frenchisms to infiltrate the English language" was "nothing
less than cultural treason, a vicious squandering of true identity."[79]

John Barrell may overstate the case when he argues "Johnson's appeal
to the 'orthography of our fathers' is closely related to that deference to
the wisdom of our political forefathers," but he is on the mark when he
says "good usage is to be defined nationalistically"[80] – or at least that
good usage and nationalism proceed by similar means in the eighteenth
century, and that both look backwards. In both explicitly political nationalism and the celebration of "our ancient volumes," the same habit
of mind is at work: both seek a foundation on which English linguistic or
political authority can rest, and they work by characterizing the foreign as
impure. The only difference lies in the synchronic versus the diachronic
application of this paradigm: nationalism applies the metaphors of purity and corruption spatially; the extolling of Renaissance authors applies
them chronologically. Both seek to justify and to constitute a privileged
point, temporal or geographical, as normative by treating any deviation
from it as barbaric corruption.

Johnson's age, that is to say, used the previous age to understand,
authorize, and regulate itself, just as the humanists situated themselves in
history by referring to their beloved antiquity and despised Middle Ages.
As Elizabeth's age began to assume a coherent identity, writers looked
backwards to understand and regulate their language. The sixteenth
century's insecurity about its latinity and cultural identity was eased only
by appeals to Cicero and his contemporaries; the eighteenth century's
insecurities about its language and national identity were likewise eased
by Shakespeare and his. Eighteenth-century linguistic histories entangle
these historical judgments with logical and aesthetic judgments so tightly,
in fact, that it is difficult to separate them. Languages, it seems, *need* such
privileged moments, for golden ages can cut many of the Gordian knots
that appeals to logic or beauty cannot untie. Eighteenth-century writers
used a fifteenth-century metaphor to celebrate sixteenth-century authors
in order to borrow some of their political glory. The linguistic, national,
and historical identity of an era can be constituted through the sort of
cultural historiography Johnson employs in his *Dictionary*, and this is one
of the ways in which the age of Johnson worked to define itself through
the age of Elizabeth.

CHAPTER 6

Studied barbarity: Jonson, Spenser, and the idea of progress

The early eighteenth century was proud of its poetry, and convinced of its superiority to what came before it. In place of rude stories in faltering meter, Pope's readers had available to them a body of elegant, refined, and eminently proper poetry. Even the enemies of Dryden and Pope – and there were many – could not deny the excellence of their versification. Nearly everyone agreed the verse of the later seventeenth century showed tremendous advances in both technique and decorum over that of the sixteenth, to say nothing of the thirteenth or fourteenth, and that Denham, Waller, and Dryden had achieved mastery where their predecessors had failed.

Things had been worst, of course, in the Gothic ages. Impressing readers with the darkness of the Dark Ages was therefore *de rigueur* for early eighteenth-century writers such as Addison, for whom the Middle Ages were a time of "Darkness and Superstition... when pious Frauds were made use of to amuse Mankind, and frighten them into a Sense of their Duty. Our Forefathers... loved to astonish themselves with the Apprehensions of Witchcraft, Prodigies, Charms and Enchantments."[1] Although "Prodigies, Charms and Enchantments" would be worthy of praise a century later for, say, Coleridge and Keats, for Addison they deserved only vilification. Most early eighteenth-century critics saw little else in the Middle Ages, and those few whose interest in medieval authors extended beyond mere antiquarianism valued primarily their anticipation of what was to come. The poetic tradition they admired was a teleological progression from medieval rudeness to modern politeness, and the cultivated verse of Denham, Dryden, and Pope was the standard by which earlier poets were measured. Even Thomas Warton, the most devoted and sympathetic eighteenth-century reader of medieval English literature, writes that his *History of English Poetry* "exhibits without transposition the gradual improvements of our poetry."[2]

To chart this course from medieval barbarity to modern enlightenment is to tell a story of progress. But in England, at least, it was not a story of progress toward an ideal republic, nor a heavenly city of eighteenth-century philosophers. Most discussions of eighteenth-century progress focus on the French rationalist tradition, and are therefore only minimally applicable to English literary history. Where "progress" appears in an English context, it is usually associated with Whiggish versions of history. What, exactly, "progress" means in this poetic context is worth settling with some precision.

THIS PROGRESS OF ENGLISH POETRY

The revival of learning was long in coming: it "did not immediately arrive at its meridian," writes Johnson, "and tho' day was gradually increasing upon us, the goblins of witchcraft still continued to hover in the twilight."[3] It did not arrive in full force even in the age of Elizabeth, for (as we have seen) even Shakespeare's contemporaries were sometimes staggeringly unenlightened. Such a conception of poetic excellence depends on a characterization of the literature and culture of the Middle Ages as rough, crude, barbarous. When they were not childishly enraptured by the supernatural, medieval authors were concerned with the local and temporary trivia of life rather than enduring truths. They were not yet masters of their own language.

Things had changed by the early eighteenth century. Readers at that time were pleased to trace the progress of their national poetry from its rude beginnings in Chaucer and Langland to its modern refinement. Elizabeth Cooper thus opens her *Muses Library* (1738) with a clear statement of progress: "Philosophers in a Series of Fossils, begin with Nature in her crudest State, and trace her, Step by Step, to the most refin'd. – In this Progress of *English* Poetry we must do the same." A work of the same year, Thomas Hayward's *British Muse*, arranges its extracts chronologically under each topical heading, "to shew the graduate IMPROVEMENTS of our *Poetry* and *Language*." These "improvements" include propriety of diction, smoothness of versification, and suitability of matter. The most important of them, however, is captured in that favorite term of late seventeenth- and early eighteenth-century criticism, *decorum*. This sort of decorum is evident in the mastery of the qualities found first in Wyatt and Surrey, later in Ben Jonson, Denham, Waller, and preeminently Dryden and Pope. Nearly all moderns have a leg up on the Renaissance: Dryden writes of the authors of the last age, "Our Ladies and our men now speak more wit / In conversation than those Poets writ." He writes elsewhere that Elizabethan authors, "had they liv'd now, had doubtless written more correctly... The... errors which I tax'd in the most correct of the last Age, are such, into which we doe not ordinarily fall." Charles Gildon insists in 1710 that "our very Farce Writers deserve more Esteem, than the... Plays of an hundred Years ago, as having as much Nature, more Design and Conduct, and much more Wit."[4]

Dating the beginning of this progress toward decorum precisely is difficult. The sixteenth was the pet century of most Englishmen, but some suggest poetic progress began much earlier. Warton extends his interest back to the classically learned ecclesiastics of the twelfth century, and Johnson calls Chaucer "the first of our versifyers who wrote poetically." Not long after their deaths, Wyatt and Surrey were treated as harbingers of the new poetics, and retained the titles throughout the seventeenth century. By the eighteenth, it was conventional to salute them as major figures in England's poetic progress – thus Pope's praise of "noble *Surrey*," "one of the first Refiners of the *English* Poetry" with a "Matchless... Pen" – though, to be sure, they were actually little read.[5]

THE MOST LEARNED AND JUDICIOUS POET

Ben Jonson is among the most important chapters in progressive English literary history. In him, eighteenth-century readers could discern a turning point, an advance toward Waller, Dryden, and Pope. In spite of Pope's reported conversational remark on Jonson – "What trash are his works, taken all together!" – for most, he was a shining example of the clear advancement since the Dark Ages. Dryden, for example, considered him "the greatest man of the last age." For Thomas Shadwell, even that title was inadequate, and he attacks Dryden for tempering his praise of "The Mighty Prince of Poets, learned BEN, / Who alone div'd into the Minds of Men."[6]

When in 1675 Edward Phillips called Jonson "the most learned, judicious and correct, generally so accounted, of our *English* Comedians," he set the terms for subsequent discussions of the dramatist, which show remarkable uniformity. Peter Whalley, for instance, notes in 1756 that "he is universally allowed to have been the most learned and judicious poet of his age." For Robert Anderson (who had few scruples concerning unattributed quotation), he is "universally allowed to have been the most learned and judicious poet of his age," "one of the greatest dramatic poets of the last age," and "the first that brought critical learning into vogue."[7] Samuel Johnson in 1747 discusses his near-namesake in similar terms: "Then JOHNSON came, instructed from the school, / To please in method, and invent by rule."

> His studious patience, and laborious art,
> By regular approach essay'd the heart;
> Cold approbation gave the ling'ring bays,
> For those who durst not censure, scarce cou'd praise.
> A mortal born he met the general doom,
> But left, like Egypt's kings, a lasting tomb.[8]

But if these are compliments, they are perhaps back-handed, and they exemplify an early stage in a significant trend: beginning late in the seventeenth century and accelerating in the 1730s and 1740s, Jonson's fame went into decline.[9] Whalley asks, "Is not this agreeable Display of [Shakespeare's] Genius . . . infinitely preferable to that studied Regularity and lifeless Drawing practised by our latter Poets?" Collins gives this answer in 1743: "Too nicely *Johnson* knew the Critic's Part; / Nature in him was almost lost in Art."[10]

To trace Jonson's reputation from Dryden through the Romantics is to trace the history of late eighteenth-century aesthetics. This is not just another case of a poet's reputation rising or falling: such turns of fortune's wheel happen all the time. To challenge Jonson's excellence had larger consequences. He had been admired precisely because he anticipated the eighteenth century's conception of poetic excellence, and demonstrated that the advancements in refinement and decorum begun in Chaucer's day were continuing to the present. If, however, it turned out that Jonson made no strides forward – if his road was a dead end – could literature be said to have advanced at all since Chaucer? Or was there some other poet who embodied an alternative narrative? Shakespeare is the obvious foil to Jonson's "studious patience, and laborious art," but his story is much bigger than Jonson's and has been often recounted. We can sharpen this progressive aspect of Jonson's reception by looking at a less likely poet, and no poet introduced more complications into this neat teleology than Edmund Spenser.

THE MYSTICK TALE, THAT PLEAS'D OF YORE

Where did Spenser fit into this progressive paradigm? He was certainly far more important for the eighteenth century than such primitives as John Skelton, dismissed by Pope as "low and bad" and by Winstanley as "only a rhymer."[11] The influence of *The Faerie Queene* on eighteenth-century poets was considerable; Earl Wasserman finds *The Faerie Queene* "the most prolific source of poetic Elizabethanism in the eighteenth century," and Eithne Henson considers its author "probably the most important influence on the English conception of romantic landscape."[12] But this importance did not translate into widespread popularity, at least early in the century. Although Spenser could be said to have pleased long, his ability to please many was less certain. Johnson notes that Hughes's edition of 1715, influential as it was, "did not much revive the curiosity of the publick; for near thirty years elapsed before his edition was reprinted."[13] In spite of Spenser's importance for poets like Pope and Cowper, *The Faerie Queene* appeared in print only nine times in the eighteenth century: compare this to fifty printings of Shakespeare's complete plays and over a hundred of *Paradise Lost*.

This relative unpopularity can be explained by his position in the age's nascent conception of the revival of learning. Like Skelton, Spenser sat uncomfortably in a tradition that valued authors who looked forward to Dryden, and he was therefore a problem for the eighteenth century. Somewhere between medieval rudeness and modern civilization, Spenser perversely refused to let go of what appeared to be vulgar errors, and could not be reconciled with progressive critical bromides. Even Richard Hurd, one of Spenser's most zealous eighteenth-century apologists, admits Spenser and Ariosto "were seduced by these barbarities of their forefathers; were even charmed by the *Gothic* Romances."[14] This peculiar failure of Spenser's judgment led to surprisingly scathing attacks, of which Addison's dismissal is typical: "But now the mystick tale, that pleas'd of yore, / Can charm an understanding age no more."[15]

The apparent lapses in Spenser's taste can be arranged under three heads: design, allegory, and language. Most upsetting for early eighteenth-century readers was his disregard for the Aristotelian unity of action.[16] The romance design, with its Ariostan *entrelacement* and multiple heroes, was disdained by most early eighteenth-century critics. The issue is not new with the eighteenth century; it has a long history in the Renaissance itself, especially in the debates between the followers of the supposedly medieval and barbarous Ariosto and those of the classical and decorous Tasso.[17] Spenser's debt to these poets and to others across the epic–romantic spectrum was immense, but many readers, both upon the *Faerie Queene*'s original publication and long after, saw in it only the apparently unstructured romantic design of Ariosto: Thomas Warton notes in his influential *Observations on the Fairy Queen of Spenser* (1762) that "Spenser made an unfortunate choice, and discovered but little judgment, in adopting Ariosto for his example, rather than Tasso, who had so evidently exceeded his rival."[18] Even Warton is more sympathetic than most of his predecessors, for the romantic model was little regarded before the middle of the eighteenth century. Rymer, for instance, tempers his praise of Spenser with criticism for following the "unfaithful guide" of Ariosto, and suggests that while "they who can love *Ariosto* will be ravish'd with *Spencer*," "men of juster thoughts lament that such great Wits have miscarried in their Travels for want of direction to set them in the right way." Dryden, too, admits "*Spencer* has a better plea for his *Fairy-Queen*, had his action been finish'd, or had been one," while Hughes writes that "That which seems the most liable to Exception... is the Model." (Other romances fared little better; the editor of the 1787 edition of Sidney's *Defence of Poetry* notes that it was first published "at the end of so tedious and unnatural a Romance as the *Arcadia*."[19])

Allegory, another holdover from the Dark Ages, has a complicated eighteenth-century history, and Spenser was at the center of many of the debates. Many scorned it outright as a technique fit only for children or a childish age. Rymer, for example, continues his criticism of Spenser by disparaging his allegory: "It was the vice of those Times to affect superstitiously the *Allegory*; and nothing would then be currant without a mystical meaning."[20] Others, more generous to allegory itself, found little to praise in Spenser's handling of it. Sir William Temple complained in 1690 that "his Design was Poor, and his Moral lay so bare, that it lost the effect; 'tis true, the Pill was Gilded, but so thin, that the Colour and Taste were too easily discovered." Addison's complaint that "The long-spun allegories fulsom grow, / While the dull moral lyes too plain below" is a variation on the same theme. As with the early eighteenth-century disdain for the Ariostan model, the distinction here is between a privileged classical taste and a debased modern one. Allegory on classical models – whether Plato, Prodicus, Cebes, or others – was widely admired, even by Addison himself. As a genre, however, it was decidedly inferior to and incompatible with epic: "Beautiful extended Allegories are certainly some of the finest Compositions of Genius," writes Addison, but they "are not agreeable to the Nature of an Heroic Poem."[21]

Language rounds off the list of objections, for Spenser's metrical "imperfections" and his archaic diction were his most obvious failings. When Rymer said "We must blame the *Italians* for debauching great *Spencer's* judgment; and they cast him on the unlucky choice of the *stanza*, which in no wise is proper for our Language," he initiated what became an eighteenth-century critical commonplace. Warton repeats the objection: "Spenser, in chusing this stanza, did not sufficiently consider the genius of the english language."[22] Samuel Wesley admits Spenser has progressed beyond Chaucer's linguistic barbarity, but makes clear the long way Spenser's numbers had to go before reaching the refinement of those of 1700:

> SPENCER more *smooth* and *neat* than Chaucer, and none than He
> Could better skill of *English Quantity*;
> Tho by his *Stanza* cramp'd, his *Rhimes* less chast,
> And *antique Words* affected all disgrac'd.[23]

Pope, in addition to finding the *Shepheardes Calender* "sometimes too allegorical," blames Spenser for a stanza "not always well chosen" and "contrary to the practice of the old Poets."[24] Hughes lists some of the reasons for the stanza's failure: "The same Measure, closed always by a full Stop, in the same Place, by which every Stanza is made as it were a distinct Paragraph, grows tiresom by continual Repetition, and frequently breaks the Sense, when it ought to be carry'd on without Interruption."[25] Spenser's language before mid-century, in short, was considered more perverse than charming.

GREAT MIXTURES OF BEAUTY AND BARBARISM

For all his problems, though, Spenser had his partisans and defenders. Apologists valued his luxuriantly fertile imagination, a quality much in demand in what Wasserman calls "an age...often acutely aware of the deficiency of its own inventive powers." Hughes writes that the *Faerie Queene*'s "chief Merit...consists in that surprizing Vein of fabulous Invention...The Author seems to be posses'd of a kind of Poetical Magick." Shiels concurs: in "fertility of imagination, few of our English authors have approached him."[26]

Imagination, it was nearly universally admitted, was Spenser's claim on our attention, but for many this was an inadequate answer to the larger failings mentioned above. Some of his defenders, in searching for an apology for his peculiarities, may have done his case more harm than good. Hughes, invoking the historicist defenses of Shakespeare we saw earlier, justifies Spenser's perverse choice of a model by grounding it in a debased popular taste: "At the time when he wrote, the *Italian* Poets, whom he has chiefly imitated...were in the highest vogue, and were universally read and admir'd." This admiration, many critics were pleased to think, was indeed only a "vogue," a temporary aberration in the progression toward modern polite literature. Addison reminds us of Spenser's "barb'rous age; / An age . . . yet uncultivate and rude," and Hughes agrees when he observes that even the best wits of the age of Elizabeth were not far removed from medieval barbarism: "At the time when our Author wrote, the Remains of the old *Gothick* Chivalry were not quite abolish'd" – a "*Gothick* Chivalry" responsible for quaint jousts and tournaments, but which now, like so many works of Gothic architecture, lay in ruins.[27]

The best case that could be made for Spenser – at least by those who adopted the traditional canons of taste – was that he was not so bad as he might have been, given the handicaps he took upon himself. Warton grants Spenser the faint praise that "the FAIRY QUEEN is not so confused and irregular as the Orlando Furioso." Likewise Spenser's allegory. However barbarous itself, as Hughes suggests, it at least makes the absurd palatable: "The perpetual Stories of Knights, Giants, Castles, and Enchantments," Hughes writes, "wou'd indeed appear very trifling, if *Spenser* had not found a way to turn them all into Allegory." Spenser's debased age explains his language as well. Hughes considers Spenser metrically proficient only by comparison with others of his day. In versification, "tho he is not always equal to himself, it may be affirm'd, that he is superior to all his Cotemporaries."[28] This paradox – "not always equal to himself," but "superior to all his Cotemporaries" – frustrated eighteenth-century critics, who found that Spenser's poetical power, for all its faults, could be neither denied nor resisted.

The best English critics were never so rule-bound as their French or Italian counterparts, and insisted their critical principles were generalizations about the great works of the past, not narrow-minded *a priori* prescriptions. Many, however, saw their work as the codification of poetic excellence into rules and principles – in Pope's formulation, "Nature methodiz'd." Progress for them is defined, therefore, as movement toward the ideal established in the rules. But Spenser, educated in the classics in an increasingly enlightened age, rejected many of the principles the eighteenth century held not only dear but self-evident, and thereby threw the entire critical project into doubt. Dryden offers an early expression of this frustration:

The *English* have only to boast of *Spencer* and *Milton*, who neither of them wanted either Genius or Learning, to have been perfect Poets; and yet both of them are liable to many Censures. For there is no Uniformity in the Design of *Spencer* . . . Had he liv'd to finish his Poem . . . it had certainly been more of a piece; but cou'd not have been perfect, because the Model was not true.[29]

He decides finally in the Dedication to the *Aeneis* that a little more education in the modern canons of taste would have tipped the balance: "*Spencer* wanted only to have read the Rules of *Bossu*." Hughes, rejecting the appeal to more education, spells out his puzzlement: "It may seem strange indeed, since *Spenser* appears to have been well acquainted with the best Writers of Antiquity, that he has not imitated them."[30] For many, these best models are self-evident, and no transitory vogue of taste should be enough to lead a poet of Spenser's parts down the wrong path. Warton opens his *Observations* with an expansion of this paradox:

When the works of Homer and of Aristotle began to be restored and studied in Italy, when the genuine and uncorrupted source of antient poetry and antient criticism were opened, and every species of literature at last emerged from the depths of Gothic ignorance and barbarity; it might have been expected, that, instead of the romantic manner of poetical composition introduced and established by the Provencial bards, a new and more legitimate taste of writing would have succeeded. With these advantages it was reasonable to conclude, that unnatural events, the machinations of imaginary beings, and adventures entertaining only as they were improbable, would have given place to justness of thought and design, and to that decorum which nature dictated, and which the example and the precept of antiquity had authorised. But it was a long time before such a change was effected.[31]

This is an exceptionally clear account of Spenser's resistance against the "more legitimate taste," a taste which appeared, from the point of view of the middle eighteenth century, to be progressive.

Faced with this resistance, even Spenser's defenders had to admit he was incompatible with the paradigm of literary history as progress from barbarism to modernity. This recognition, when it was not repressed, contributed to the changes in critical sensibility over the course of the century: as David Hall Radcliffe notes, "Spenser's authority became a standing challenge to the 'rules' adopted by Davenant, Rymer, and their followers."[32] Hughes was among the first to formulate a coherent aesthetics different from the classical inheritance, an early stage in the development of a new Romantic sensibility. He suggests, unusually for his age, that classical standards (or what passed for classical standards early in the century) may be inadequate for measuring Spenser:

Men of Critical Learning, if they had thought fit, might have given us Rules about Allegorical Writing, as they have done about Epick, and other kinds of Poetry; but they have rather chosen to let this Forest remain wild, as if they thought there was something in the Nature of the Soil, which cou'd not so well be restrain'd and cultivated in Inclosures.[33]

The agricultural metaphors, familiar from so many discussions of the joys of "cultivation," are here used in a radically new way. Cultivation in fact may not be the unquestioned good it had been thought to be. The rules are likened to "Inclosures," and bring with them all the political baggage of actual enclosures – rules that serve only to consolidate the power of the already powerful at the expense of those whose voices are not heard. Hughes's fondness for the wild forest anticipates developments in taste nearly three-quarters of a century away.

Another of Hughes's metaphors is architectural. What was censure in Rymer – "I have thought our Poetry of the last Age was as rude as our Architecture"[34] – is praise in Hughes: "The whole Frame of it wou'd appear monstrous, if it were to be examin'd by the Rules of Epick Poetry, as they have been drawn from the Practice of *Homer* and *Virgil*." Poetry predates the rules, which have no value independent of the works from which they are drawn. Hughes insists that the choice of models determines the result: if Spenser were to be examined by Virgil's rules, he would necessarily appear retrograde. But the subjunctive "were" sets us up for another possibility, as Hughes continues:

But as it is plain the Author never design'd it by these Rules, I think it ought rather to be consider'd as a Poem of a particular kind, describing in a Series of Allegorical Adventures or Episodes the most noted Virtues and Vices: to compare it therefore with the Models of Antiquity, wou'd be like drawing a Parallel between the *Roman* and the *Gothick* Architecture. In the first there is doubtless a more natural Grandeur and Simplicity: in the latter, we find great Mixtures of Beauty and Barbarism, yet assisted by the Invention of a Variety of inferior Ornaments; and tho the former is more majestick in the whole, the latter may be very surprizing and agreeable in its Parts.[35]

In other words, if one gets to choose the models from which the rules are drawn, the results "may be very surprizing." He turns from the classical models beloved by the French to a home-grown tradition, to native woodnotes wild, and thereby places Spenser into the long-running dialogue on the merits of an irregular native British literature.[36]

Pope picked up both the argument and the metaphor in his defense of the pre-eminently British poet, Shakespeare: "To judge . . . of *Shakespear* by *Aristotle*'s rules," he writes in 1725, "is like trying a man by the Laws of one Country, who had acted under those of another." He concludes his Preface by saying,

One may look upon his works, in comparison with those that are more finish'd and regular, as upon an ancient majestick piece of *Gothick* Architecture, compar'd with a neat Modern building: The latter is more elegant and glaring, but the former is more strong and more solemn. It must be allow'd, that in one of these there are materials enough to make many of the other. It has much the greater variety, and much the nobler apartments, tho' we are often conducted to them by dark, odd, and uncouth passages. Nor does the Whole fail to strike us with greater reverence, tho' many of the Parts are childish, ill-plac'd, and unequal to its grandeur.[37]

This "strong" and "solemn" aesthetic of Gothic and British literature grew, with the help of others like Upton, Warton, and Hurd, over the course of the century. Spenser's poems provided, like Shakespeare's resolutely unclassical plays and Percy's ballads, a rallying cry for a generation of Romantic critics engaged in rewriting the early eighteenth century's progressive version of literary history.

ENCHANTRESSES OF THE SOUL

Samuel Johnson witnessed this change in critical sensibility, but more important, he was a major participant in it. Neither a caricature Neo-classicist nor a simple Hurdian enthusiast for the Gothic, he thought carefully about the competing claims of the progressivist version of literary history and the more resolutely primitive Gothic taste.

Johnson's interest, even fascination, with Spenser was lifelong. One of his passions was for the genre of Spenser's greatest work: romance of every sort was a favorite subject, and Percy tells Boswell that "when a boy he was immoderately fond of reading romances of chivalry, and he retained his fondness for them through his life." Eithne Henson, surveying Johnson's reading in the genre, finds him "addicted to chivalric romance," including Spenser's. Spenser was for him, though, more than a spinner of romantic tales. In 1787, Hawkins listed Spenser along with More, Ascham, Hooker, Sandys, and others as seminal influences on Johnson's style. Watkins asserts "few men have known Spenser more thoroughly than Johnson," and argues that "He certainly looked upon Spenser as having succeeded in giving England a great poetry comparable, if not superior, to that of the Italian and French Renaissance."[38]

Johnson produced no edition or biography of Spenser, nor did he provide any extended close readings. But comments scattered throughout his works and letters give ample support to Watkins's contention that he valued Spenser's works highly, from the beginning of his career to the very end. One of Johnson's earliest surviving letters requests that the copy of Spenser he left at Oxford be sent to him; on his death,

Spenser's works were found in his library.[39] Spenser provides thousands of quotations in the *Dictionary*, and Johnson expressed interest in writing a *Life of Spenser*, abandoning the project only for want of new material.[40] Another projected but never attempted work is listed by Boswell as "The Palace of Sloth, – A Vision,"[41] a title that suggests Spenser's characteristic blend of romance and allegory. Spenser's position in eighteenth-century criticism generally and Johnson's thought specifically has received little attention,[42] but tugging on these Spenserian loose ends reveals a thread woven across the entire fabric of Johnson's criticism.

The notion of progression is important for Johnson, who often contrasts the naïveté of earlier ages with Elizabethan enlightenment: we have seen in the Preface to the *Dictionary*, for instance, "Every language has a time of rudeness antecedent to perfection," and therefore "I have been cautious lest my zeal for antiquity might drive me into times too remote, and croud my book with words now no longer understood." Versification, too, is a progressive science, as Johnson notes of poetry after Dryden and Pope: "New sentiments and new images others may produce, but to attempt any further improvement of versification will be dangerous. Art and diligence have now done their best, and what shall be added will be the effort of tedious toil and needless curiosity."[43] Prosody had achieved perfection, and earlier attempts at versification were necessarily inferior by comparison. For Johnson, language is to be measured by eighteenth-century standards.

The "rudeness" is not only linguistic, for taste follows a course parallel to language. Elizabethan taste, as Hughes suggested, had not entirely abandoned its medieval trappings. Johnson makes the case for literary development in a passage from the Preface to Shakespeare we have already seen: "Nations, like individuals, have their infancy. A people newly awakened to literary curiosity, being yet unacquainted with the true state of things, knows not how to judge of that which is proposed as its resemblance ... The study of those who then aspired to plebeian learning was laid out upon adventures, giants, dragons, and enchantments."[44] This movement toward "the true state of things" was still in its early stages when Shakespeare and Spenser wrote. These "adventures" make another appearance in a description of the eighteenth century's advances over the fiction of the previous centuries. Scaliger found Pontanno's works "filled with the same images," entirely dependent on "his lillies and his roses, his satyrs and his dryads ... In like manner, almost all the fictions of the last age will vanish, if you deprive them of a hermit and a wood, a battle and a shipwreck." He continues by expressing the same bewilderment at the Elizabethans' fascination for "giants, dragons, and enchantments" that baffled Hughes and Warton: "Why this wild strain of imagination found reception so long, in polite and learned ages, it is not easy to conceive." The best Renaissance writers slew these dragons by departing from the merely fanciful medieval romances – Shakespeare especially trades "the pleasures of sudden wonder" for "the stability of truth" – and moved closer to "the true state of things," that is, to modern taste.[45]

The turning point comes in the last few decades of the sixteenth century, and "*Sidney*'s work" is therefore the *Dictionary*'s "boundary, beyond which I make few excursions. From the authors which rose in the time of *Elizabeth*, a speech might be formed adequate to all the purposes of use and elegance." And Spenser, one of the most important of "the authors which rose in the time of *Elizabeth*," is for all his problems an important figure in the Renaissance progression toward the modern taste. In *Idler* 91, for instance, Johnson "consider[s] the whole succession [of poets] from Spenser to Pope, as superiour to any names which the continent can boast." The Preface to the *Dictionary* puts Spenser in similarly distinguished company: "the dialect of poetry and fiction" from Spenser and Sidney, combined with the terms of Hooker, Bacon, Raleigh, and Shakespeare, is nearly all the English language needs. Johnson reveals Spenser's importance in his chronicle of the language, for he appears nearly three thousand times in the *Dictionary*, to which are admitted only "writers of the first reputation." Spenser moreover gives Johnson his designation for "the writers before the restoration, whose works I regard as *the wells of English undefiled*."[46]

But for all his fondness for Spenser, Johnson saw the same problems as his contemporaries, and they produced in him the same tensions and frustrations. His often lavish praise for Spenser's merit must be weighed against his censure of the "studied barbarity"[47] of *The Shepheardes Calender* – "barbarity," defined in the *Dictionary* as the nominal form of both *barbarous* and *barbaric*, means both "A form of speech contrary to the purity and exactness of any language" and "Brutality; savageness of manners; incivility," exceptionally harsh criticism of an admired poet.

His final estimation, insofar as it can be reconstructed from his works, is more tempered than those of most of his contemporaries, for he refused to let *a priori* notions of progress and periodization direct his reading. Rule-based criticism was important for him, as shown in his comment on the object of critical inquiry: "It is . . . the task of criticism to establish principles; to improve opinion into knowledge." This includes rendering the past intelligible by building historical narratives and constructing inevitably teleological accounts. But though the rules and schemata have their place, the empiricist critic must also

distinguish those means of pleasing which depend upon known causes and rational deduction, from the nameless and inexplicable elegancies . . . which may well be termed the enchantresses of the soul. Criticism reduces those regions of literature under the dominion of science, which have hitherto known only the anarchy of ignorance, the caprices of fancy, and the tyranny of prescription.[48]

"Enchantresses," "anarchy," "caprices," "tyranny" – the richly metaphorical language begins to suggest the world of the romances themselves. These "enchantresses" are especially intriguing; they recall Hughes's "Poetical Magick," and the second of two definitions in the *Dictionary* – "A woman whose beauty or excellencies give irresistible influence" – suggests that their power borders on the erotic. Indeed, the enchantress may recall the sole occurrence of the word in Spenser, where men's souls have been similarly seduced:

> These seeming beasts are men indeed,
> Whom this Enchauntress hath transformed thus,
> Whylome her louers, which her lusts did feed,
> Now turned into figures hideous,
> According to their mindes like monstruous.[49]

Johnson wants, where possible, to explain away these "enchantresses of the soul" by annexing their territory into the realm of literary history, to subject them to reason as Guyon does the Bower of Bliss. But he recognizes – perhaps uncomfortably – that some authors cannot, and should not, be thus subdued. Guarding against "the tyranny of prescription," therefore, is as important as reducing literature to rules.

PLEASING VEHICLES OF INSTRUCTION

Of the three categories considered above – design, allegory, and language – Johnson says nothing about Spenser's design, but we can speculate on his opinions. Although he was instrumental in removing the unities of time and place from English criticism, he preserved one Neoclassical unity – "nothing is essential to the fable, but unity of action"[50] – and here even Spenser's apologists admit he is manifestly deficient. But up rises Johnson's critical empiricism: "Since the end of poetry is pleasure, that cannot be unpoetical with which all are pleased." Although unity of action is often more effective than seeming chaos, design need not follow *a priori* rules to be pleasing, and even if Spenser's own popularity was small, romances with no regard for Aristotelian unity had retained countless readers for centuries. This critical honesty accounts for his fondness for the medieval romances widely scorned by the educated; Reynolds recalls with some surprise that "he chose for his regular reading the old Spanish romance of *Felixmarte of Hircania*, in folio, which he read quite through" during a visit in 1764. Of Spenser's design he likely would have said something similar to his comment on Milton's blank verse: "I cannot wish his work to be other than it is; yet like other heroes he is to be admired rather than imitated."[51]

This critical candor accounts for many of Johnson's departures from the taste of his age. Though Spenserian allegory was widely condemned, Spenser the allegorist was dear to him. Johnson, it is true, follows Addison's *Spectator* 273 in condemning the "unskilful" allegorical episode in book two of *Paradise Lost* as "undoubtedly faulty" and "one of the greatest faults of the poem." He censures both Cowley and Dryden for being inept allegorists: of the *Davideis* he says "Every reader feels himself weary with this useless talk of an allegorical Being," while *Absalom and Achitophel* is "defective" because "allegories drawn to great length will always break." Carey McIntosh, for these and other reasons, finds that "Johnson sticks pretty much to the party line" in questions of allegory.[52]

But Johnson is surprisingly tolerant of the intrusion of allegorical writing even into heroic poetry. In this respect Spenserian imitation may be admissible. He says nothing about the allegory of the two most prominent Spenserian imitators in the *Lives*, Thomson and Shenstone; but although the mode could be abused, Johnson held that "To imitate the fictions and sentiments of Spenser can incur no reproach, for allegory is perhaps one of the most pleasing vehicles of instruction."[53] Any reader of Horace would know that a "pleasing vehicle of instruction" is too valuable to be rejected on any but the firmest grounds, and a prejudice toward Prodicus is not enough. Johnson was himself an allegorist: McIntosh counts nine developed allegories in his works, and if some of his uses of personification can be counted, this total goes much higher.[54] These allegorical writings owe much to Spenser – which is not, of course, to discount the influence of other allegorists: Johnson borrows his model for *The Vision of Theodore* not only from Addison but from Prodicus and Cebes as well.[55] Among British authors, Bunyan was another obvious source, but even he is a conduit for Spenserianism: Johnson "praised John Bunyan highly," says Boswell, and found it "remarkable, that [*Pilgrim's Progress*] begins very much like the poem of Dante; yet there was no translation of Dante when Bunyan wrote. There is reason to think that he had read Spenser."[56]

Specific textual parallels in Johnson's allegories make his debt to Spenser clear. The allegory of *Rambler* 96, for instance, is more elaborate than anything in Bunyan: "Truth was the daughter of Jupiter and Wisdom; Falsehood was the progeny of Folly impregnated by the wind. They advanced with equal confidence to seize the dominion of the new creation, and as their enmity and their force were well known to the celestials, all the eyes of heaven were turned upon the contest."[57] Compare it, moreover, to the genealogy of Orgoglio in *The Faerie Queene*:

> The greatest Earth his vncouth mother was,
> And blustring *Æolus* his boasted sire,
> Who with his breath, which through the world doth pas,
> Her hollow womb did secretly inspire,
> And fild her hidden caues with stormie yre,
> That she conceiu'd . . .   (i.vii.9)

Rambler 102 takes Addison rather than Spenser as its immediate model – the "Vision of Mirzah" from *Spectator* 159 is the most significant source – but note Johnson's invocation of "the 'Gulph of Intemperance,' a dreadful whirlpool, interspersed with rocks, of which the pointed crags were concealed under water, and the tops covered with herbage, on which Ease spread couches of repose, and with shades, where Pleasure warbled the song of invitation."[58] The passage has enough echoes of Guyon's approach to the Bower of Bliss in *Faerie Queene* ii.xii – where we find gulfs (stanzas 3 – 5), rock-filled whirlpools (stanzas 2–4, 7–8), crags (stanza 4), and luxuriant Sirens (stanzas 14–17) – to suggest the correspondence of images is more than coincidental.

His *Vision of Theodore* is especially reminiscent of Spenser's allegory. The "regions of Desire," "caverns of Despair," and "bowers of Content" combine allegory with romantic trappings in a mode most readily associated with Spenser. Spenser has no special claim on allegorical combat, but the "attacks of the Appetites [and] the Passions" on Reason sometimes echo the assault on the House of Alma in *Faerie Queene* ii.x–xi. And the "bowers of Intemperance" recall once again the Bower of Bliss in book two, of which the guiding virtue is Temperance.[59]

OBSOLETE TERMS AND RUSTICK WORDS

Propriety of language is for Johnson a more vexed problem than design or allegory. Eighteenth-century discussions of Spenser's archaic diction are part of a much larger discourse on the anxiety over linguistic instability and mutability. We have already considered Pope's memorable formulation: "And such as *Chaucer* is, shall *Dryden* be." Robert Shiels, ghostwriter of most of the *Lives of the Poets* attributed to Theophilus Cibber, develops the theme when he writes that readers of Langland and Chaucer must "lamen[t] the unhappiness of a fluctuating language, that buries in its ruins even genius itself; for like edifices of sand, every breath of time defaces it, and if the form remain, the beauty is lost." Hughes's exposition is more systematic: "It is a Misfortune... which attends the Writers of *English* Poetry, that they could hardly expect their Works shou'd last long in a Tongue which is daily changing... Our Poets... shou'd imitate judicious Statuaries, that chuse the most durable Materials, and shou'd carve in *Latin* or *Greek*, if they wou'd have their Labours preserv'd for ever." He admits only "two Antient *English* Poets, *Chaucer* and *Spenser*, who may perhaps be reckon'd as Exceptions to this Remark."[60] Addison will not admit even Chaucer:

> *Chaucer* first, a merry Bard, arose,
> And many a story told in rhime, and prose.
> But age has rusted what the Poet writ,
> Worn out his language, and obscur'd his wit:
> In vain he jests in his unpolish'd strain,
> And tries to make his readers laugh in vain.[61]

Johnson's relation to this model of linguistic progress is complicated. Linguistic mutation has obvious disadvantages, not least that it renders the older poets unreadable. This is part of what he means in this letter to Warton on his *Observations on the Fairy Queen*: "The Reason why the authours which are yet read of the sixteenth Century are so little understood is that they are read alone, and no help is borrowed from those who lived with them or before them. Some part of this ignorance I hope to remove by my book [the *Dictionary*] which now draws towards its end."[62] He notes that Hughes, in spite of being "well qualified as a judge of the beauties of writing," was not entirely equal to the task he set himself in his edition of Spenser and "Discourse on Allegorical Poetry" because he "perhaps wanted an antiquary's knowledge of the obsolete words."[63]

But Pope's angst has an obverse: that language does not mutate randomly, but partakes in a constant evolution toward perfection, a progress that mirrors the progressive version of literary history espoused by so many. Chaucer's language in this model is incomprehensible only insofar as it is defective. Change, far from being a cause for lamentation over a fleeting past, can be a mark of civilized progress: "The language most likely to continue long without alteration, would be that of a nation raised a little, and but a little, above barbarity." Some words can therefore be relegated to the dustheap with impunity: "Nor are all words which are not found in the vocabulary, to be lamented as omissions." Some writers have resisted such change, it is true, but Johnson sees such efforts as fundamentally misguided and unreasonably prescriptive. Swift, for instance, "allows that new words must sometimes be introduced, but proposes that none should be suffered to become obsolete. But what makes a word obsolete, more than a general agreement to forbear it?"[64] The studied preservation of archaic language is not mere naïveté, but an effort to keep the "nation raised a little, and but a little, above barbarity."

I argued in the previous chapter that the English language, partly through its abandonment by degrees of its archaic words, achieved a kind of perfection in the sixteenth century, by which time the process of refinement had burnt out most of the medieval barbarisms. We have already seen that "From the authors which rose in the time of *Elizabeth*, a speech might be formed adequate to all the purposes of use and elegance." No party-line ancient or modern, Johnson considers language neither fundamentally degenerative nor progressive, but he does see in it a kind of development or trajectory: "Every language has a time of rudeness antecedent to perfection, as well as of false refinement and declension." This is not historical relativism but its opposite; it suggests an ahistorical linguistic ideal, an ideal to which ages succeed or fail in attaining. The sixteenth century marks the beginning of this linguistic perfection, for by this time enough barbarisms had been shed that the language achieved a degree of fixity: "Of the works of Sir *Thomas More* it was necessary to give a larger specimen, both because our language was then in a great degree formed and settled, and because . . . his works were considered as models of pure and elegant style."[65] From Chaucer, through More, and into the sixteenth century, poetic language in particular continued its ascent. In Shakespeare's day it was still riddled with solecisms. In the *Dictionary*, Johnson labels at least twenty-three words "low" or "bad," and yet adduces quotations from Shakespeare: examples include *to budge* ("a low word," illustrated with quotations from *The Tempest* and *Coriolanus*), *fraughtage* ("a bad word," in *The Comedy of Errors*), *pat* (as an adjective, "This is a low word, and should not be used but in burlesque writings," in *Midsummer Night's Dream* and *Hamlet*), and *to unpay* ("a low ludicrous word," in *2 Henry IV*). Things were, however, getting better in the seventeenth century. Johnson approvingly quotes Prior's account of poetic development: "Denham and Waller...improved our versification, and Dryden perfected it," and he finds Prior himself "one of the first that resolutely endeavoured at correctness." He elaborates on the culmination of the process in Dryden:

There was...before the time of Dryden no poetical diction: no system of words at once refined from the grossness of domestick use and free from the harshness of terms appropriated to particular arts...Those happy combinations of words which distinguish poetry from prose had been rarely attempted; we had few elegances or flowers of speech: the roses had not yet been plucked from the bramble.

The traditional botanical metaphor has been refined further, from agriculture to gardening. "The new versification, as it was called, may be considered as owing its establishment to Dryden; from whose time it is apparent that English poetry has had no tendency to relapse to its former savageness." Still, that "former savageness" cannot be ignored by the lexicographer, who necessarily serves the reading public, and who must therefore reconcile competing theoretical and practical demands. Johnson is obliged to record archaisms in the *Dictionary*, but only those that remain useful for authors still read: "Of antiquated or obsolete words, none will be inserted, but such as are found in authors, who wrote since the accession of Elizabeth."[66]

Some figures from the *Dictionary* demonstrate how he translated this theory into practice. Of the 777 words (or senses of words) Hughes includes in his "Glossary Explaining the Old and Obscure Words in *Spenser*'s Works,"[67] Johnson defines 534 in the first edition of the *Dictionary*. He mentions Spenser in 424 of them (nearly 80 percent), adducing a total of 407 quotations from Spenser for 354 words and mentioning Spenser without a quotation for another 70.[68] This body of quotation provides a convenient sample of Johnson's Spenserian quotations, and provides an insight not only into his use of Spenser for the *Dictionary* but also into his thoughts on Spenser and linguistic archaism generally.

A starting point is the source of the quotations within Spenser's works. Of the 407 illustrative quotations from Spenser in this sample, 257 (63 percent) are from *The Faerie Queene*, 71 (18 percent) from the *Shepheardes Calender* (usually identified in the *Dictionary* as "*Pastorals*"), 26 (6 percent) from *Mother Hubberds Tale*, 7 (2 percent) from the prose *A View of the Present State of Ireland*, and 45 (11 percent) from the other works, including "Epithalamion," "Amoretti," and "Muiopotmos."[69]

Since Hughes's catalogue lists only words obsolete in the eighteenth century, we should expect Johnson to label most of them archaic, but he identifies only 108 of the 534 words he defines as "obsolete," "out of use," "used by old authors," and the like. The identification of obsolete words is inconsistent; perhaps in some cases a lone quotation from Spenser is enough to identify a word as not in current use. The words identified as obsolete provide 37 percent of the *Shepheardes Calender* quotations, compared to 25 percent of those from *The Faerie Queene* (and much smaller numbers from the other works), suggesting Johnson naturally found the pastorals the richest source of old usages.

The quotations from *The Faerie Queene* reveal something of the way Johnson worked. Of the 257 illustrative quotations from that poem, 138 come from book one, 116 from book two, only one each from books three, four, and six, and none at all from book five or the *Mutability Cantos*.[70] The cantos Johnson mined most thoroughly may suggest the episodes he found particularly interesting. The 257 *Faerie Queene* quotations are drawn from all twenty-four cantos of the first two books, of which eight cantos are quoted thirteen or more times: I.i (Redcrosse, Una, and Error), I.ii (Archimago), I.iv (the House of Pride), I.v (Sansfoy), II.i (Mordant and Amavia), II.iii (Braggadocchio), II.ix (the House of Temperance), and II.x (the chronicles of Fairyland). At the bottom of the list are I.iii (Una, Abessa, and Kirkrapine) with five quotations, II.iv (Furor) with four, and II.xi (the assault on Temperance) with only one.

Although Johnson doubtless had Hughes's glossary on hand when he compiled the *Dictionary* – he cites it in his definition of *hilding* – there is little evidence that he relied on it heavily when he began his work, as few definitions in the early part of the *Dictionary* show direct influence. As he proceeded through the alphabet, however, he came increasingly to depend on him. He sometimes simply defines a word that appears in the later books of *The Faerie Queene* and mentions only "Spenser" without a quotation or specific citation, information he could have gathered simply by browsing the glossary without consulting Spenser's works, and in the later part of the alphabet he increasingly provides unattributed but nearly verbatim quotations from Hughes.[71]

These figures from the *Dictionary* provide useful raw material, but to tell what to make of these obsolete words, we must turn to more obviously evaluative criticism. There we see that Johnson finds Spenserian archaizing perversely retrograde, especially in the fashionable Spenserian imitations of the eighteenth century, which he saw as the successor to the earlier vogue for Pindaric odes. "It would indeed be difficult," he says, "to exclude from a long poem all modern phrases, though it is easy to sprinkle it with gleanings of antiquity." Johnson uncomfortably watches faddish archaism gaining popularity, as his light-hearted but pointed attack on Thomas Warton's "Uncouth words in disarray" makes clear. Even Prior, whose greatest praise is "correctness," falls prey to this easy archaizing: "His imitation of Spenser, which consists principally in *I ween* and *I weet*, without exclusion of later modes of speech, makes his poem neither ancient nor modern."[72]

Johnson faults not only Spenser's epigones ("O imitatores, servum pecus!"), who "are indeed not very rigid censors of themselves," but Spenser himself, whose diction he, like Ben Jonson, found to be "no language": "His stile was in his own time allowed to be vicious...darkened with old words and peculiarities of phrase, and...remote from common use." "Diction," he warns, "being the first vehicle of the thoughts, first presents itself to the intellectual eye; and if the first appearance offends, a further knowledge is not often sought." *The Shepheardes Calender* therefore especially draws Johnson's scorn for its "obsolete terms and rustick words, which they very learnedly call Dorick"; this "studied barbarity" calls forth a bitterly ironic jab: "Surely at the same time that a shepherd learns theology," he writes acidly, "he may gain some acquaintance with his native language."[73] Johnson's dismissal of Spenser's archaizing in such harsh terms shows his concern at discovering major failings in a major poet, a poet who could not be rescued from "the nameless and inexplicable elegancies which appeal wholly to the fancy."

Poetic language is more than diction, and Johnson is able to "conside[r] the metrical art simply as a science,"[74] a positivist science in which the clear failures of the past should be abandoned, and in which modern poets can advance by degrees beyond their precursors. Spenser's unmusical stanza and versification were therefore especially loathsome, particularly among the imitators, who "seem to conclude, that when they have disfigured their lines with a few obsolete syllables, they have accomplished their design...Perhaps...the stile of Spenser might by long labour be justly copied; but life is surely given us for higher purposes than to gather what our ancestors have wisely thrown away."[75] In spite of his general praise of Spenser, therefore, he is "very far from extending the same respect to his diction or his stanza," which he said (in terms recalling Rymer's complaint decades earlier) was "formed in imitation of the Italian poets, without due regard to the genius of our language." It is "at once difficult and unpleasing; tiresome to the ear by its uniformity, and to the attention by its length."[76]

JUST REPRESENTATIONS OF GENERAL NATURE

That Spenser could draw both the highest approbation and the most stinging irony leads us to seek Johnson's larger notions of cultural progress since the revival of learning, one that admits Spenserian allegory but not Spenserian diction, one that shares some of the qualities of the progressivist model but remains always wary of reducing all literary history to naïve teleology. A candidate for the kind of progress he saw since the last age appears throughout his works; one clear statement comes in his praise of Homer: "His positions are general, and his representations natural, with very little dependence on local or temporary customs, on those changeable scenes of artificial life, which, by mingling original with accidental notions, and crowding the mind with images which time effaces, produce ambiguity in diction, and obscurity in books."[77] Here is one of Johnson's favorite pairs of polar opposites, generality *versus* "accident." Johnson saw the revival of learning as Europe's passage from one pole to the other. The opposition of particularity and generality is mapped onto literary history, with the late sixteenth century at the center. Shakespeare is of course the best example from the age of Elizabeth: he pleases many and pleases long because of his "just representations of general nature," which are contrasted with "particular manners." Faux medieval diction is a recollection of the "remote allusions and obscure opinions" of a justly forgotten age. Thus Hume: "Homer copied true natural manners ... But the pencil of the English poet [Spenser] was employed in drawing the affectations, and conceits, and fopperies of chivalry, which appear ridiculous as soon as they lose the recommendation of the mode."[78] These are Johnson's targets in his attacks on Spenser's obfuscatory archaism, which leads only to "obscurity in books," and which time justly "effaces" – the same process Johnson uses to discard the useless archaisms from the *Dictionary*.

Generality and "unadulterated nature," on the other hand, are dissociated from "changeable scenes of artificial life" with their "accidental notions" – the very business of allegory, which works by moving from the specific to the general. Allegory educates us in generality, teaching us to rest not on the "local and temporary customs" of the Middle Ages but on the "stability of truth,"[79] the timeless truth of generality. Insofar as Spenser resorts to *glaive* for sword and *haqueton* for armor, he is toying with the minutiae of the past; but when he pits the swords and armor against one another in a representation of moral conflict, he approaches the truth to which all great poetry aspires.[80] The revival of learning amounts to the abandonment of "the accidents of transient fashions or temporary opinions" and the revival of general nature, the nature that appears in Shakespeare at his most "universal."[81]

The revival of learning therefore marks a kind of progress: it is Europe's accession to general nature, its abandonment of the peculiarities of archaism. But even the most mature literature has room for the generality of allegory, the bridge between the details consigned to antiquarians and the universal nature valuable to every reader. Spenser more than any other poet is the wedge that splits allegory from archaism, and reveals with special clarity the way in which Johnson's empirical criticism comes to terms with Renaissance poetic progress.

CHAPTER 7

The last age: Renaissance lost

With Milton, the age of Elizabeth reaches its apogee and its end. In the decades after Milton's death, as *Paradise Lost* became part of the national canon, British readers first perceived a difference between their age and the last. Milton's epic stood at the center of the many discourses – political, theological, poetic – that contributed to this epochal division. Recognizing the historicity of the past was essential to eighteenth-century political and poetic self-conceptions, for by the middle of the eighteenth century, the distant Milton was the most painful reminder of everything the age of Johnson was not.

A NEW SCENE

This awareness of distance from the sixteenth and seventeenth centuries marks one of the largest shifts in literary and intellectual historiography since the Quattrocento humanists rethought the patristic scheme of periodization in secular terms. We saw earlier how the eighteenth century adopted the Renaissance's sense of modernity; it is time now to see how they revised it.

Petrarch and Ficino saw in their own works the beginning of a new age; Johnson and his contemporaries likewise saw in the middle seventeenth century the closing of that age and the opening of another – their own. Indistinct at first, it became a commonplace beginning in the 1730s, and by the end of the eighteenth century the line was firmly in place. The era of Spenser, Shakespeare, and Milton was "the last age."

There are many references, even contemporary with Dryden, to the "last age," but because "age" has all the ambiguity of Latin *saeculum*, such evidence requires caution. Sometimes "the last age" is charged with millenarian meanings – the final age – as when Sanderson speaks of "Decads, Centuries, Chiliads of novel Tenents, brought in in this last Age."[1] It is sometimes simply a synonym for "century": Johnson's fourth

143

sense of *age* in the *Dictionary* is "The space of a hundred years; a secular period; a century." An eighteenth-century reference to "the last age," then, can refer simply to the seventeenth century, comprising Jonson and Donne along with Dryden and Newton under a single rubric. Another sense of "age," however, is less strictly confined to arbitrary century boundaries, for Johnson's first definition is "Any period of time attributed to something as the whole, or part, of its duration: in this sense, we say, the age of man, the several ages of the world, the golden or iron age." This is Dryden's sense when he refers, in 1672, to "the Dramatique Poetry of the last Age," and Etherege's when four years later he invokes "the Forms and Civilities of the last Age": the past was being divided into periods to render it more comprehensible.[2] And in this sense, eighteenth-century writers no longer felt themselves part of the modernity first described by the early humanists. The age of Elizabeth had passed.

If it is true that Johnson's contemporaries considered themselves part of an age distinct from what we call the Renaissance, there must be some moment or event in the seventeenth century to mark the division between the two ages. Before searching for *the* dividing line, however, we should note that periodization can vary from nation to nation and genre to genre. The English drama, for instance, had a convenient and unmistakable line of division in which the extrinsic factors of political history and the factors intrinsic to the works themselves corresponded neatly: the closing of the theatres in 1642 marked the end of one age, and their opening in 1660 marked the beginning of another. Thus Dryden invokes "the last Age" in the Epilogue to *All for Love* (1678), Rymer in the same year refers to "the tragedies of the last age," and Buckingham's *General Key to the Writings of the British Poets of the Last Age* (1723) lumps together "*Johnson, Shakespear*, and *Beaumont*," referring to all Elizabethan, Jacobean, and early Caroline drama as if it were coeval.[3]

In nondramatic poetry, however, no such moment presented itself, and the problem was more vexed. Many eighteenth-century readers therefore looked to the most obvious epochal watershed, not in literature but in politics. The Civil Wars have long marked one *terminus ad quem* of the Renaissance: as Jonathan Richardson put it in 1734, "The Year 1660, as all the World knows, Open'd a New Scene in *England*."[4]

BETWIXT TWO AGES CAST

Epochal ruptures of this sort are often the source of great cultural anxiety. Dryden, however, saw not a threat but an opportunity: "'Tis well an Old

Age is out, / And time to begin a New." Like the early humanists, he hoped to claim the liminal position between ages for his own: "Let him retire, betwixt two Ages cast, / The first of this, and hindmost of the last." But while his claim to be "The first of this" age is as good as any of his contemporaries' (even today he is typically the first major figure in anthologies and survey courses on the long eighteenth century), subsequent histories usually give not Dryden but Milton the position of "hindmost of the last." Milton, wrote Thomas Love Peacock in 1821, "may be said to stand alone between the ages of gold and silver."[5] The preeminent poet of the middle seventeenth century stood on the fault line between the two ages.

Perhaps the best way to place Milton in literary history is to begin by asking where he places himself – a difficult matter, because periodization is often visible only in retrospect. What evidence there is suggests Milton accepted without significant qualification the humanist tripartite history, with ancient, medieval, and modern ages, and considered himself part of the same modernity as Erasmus and Shakespeare. As the tripartite model of history gave way to a new four-term model, Milton's successors more often than not put him on the earlier side of the divide, even though his most important work appeared after the Restoration. William Lauder's catalogue of "Dates of the Authors Quoted in the Essay, in Comparison with the Date of Paradise Lost" is revealing: it contextualizes *Paradise Lost* among works from Johannes Quintianus (1514) through Milton's immediate predecessors, placing him at the end of a pageant of Renaissance poets. Elizabeth Cooper puts Milton at the end of her own (very different) list of poets beginning with Surrey, Buckhurst, and Spenser – a list which stops shy of Dryden, and therefore makes Milton the apex and terminus of the tradition. Thomas Gray's abandoned plan for his history of English poetry, as noted above, places Spenser in the "Second Italian School (of Ariosto, Tasso, &c:)," and lists its other English practitioners: "Drayton, Fairfax, Phin: Fletcher, Golding, Phaer, &c.: this school ends in Milton." A "*third Italian* School" is roughly contemporary but runs a parallel course, comprising "*Donne*, Crashaw, Cleveland; carried to its height by Cowley, & ending perhaps in *Sprat*." A sharper epochal line is drawn between these Italian schools and the "*School of France*, introduced after the Restoration"; Gray's fourth (and final) part therefore contains "Waller, Dryden, Addison, Prior, & Pope," who represent modernity.[6]

Further evidence for Milton's placement in the last age is his rapid transformation into a vernacular classic, a national monument second only to Shakespeare. Milton's classicization in fact preceded

Shakespeare's: the transformation began only a few years after *Paradise Lost* appeared. The relationship of textual criticism to historiography was taken up in some detail in chapter 1, but the point is considerably simpler here: the classical editorial treatment given to *Paradise Lost* early in its history bespeaks a status analogous to the works of antiquity. Patrick Hume's annotations on *Paradise Lost* (1695), as we have seen, were the first such treatment of a text published after 1500, and make it clear that Milton's epic can be properly appreciated only when placed in an academic context and read historically, even though three decades had not yet passed since its first publication. (The classical treatment of a modern text is more evident still in Bentley's notoriously eccentric *Paradise Lost*, which shows that some eighteenth-century readers went too far in their association of English and Roman classics.[7]) Other scholarly tools make the same point: in 1741, Alexander Cruden published *A Verbal Index to Milton's Paradise Lost*, something never before accorded to a modern English author, followed in 1749 by Newton's "Verbal Index" in his *Paradise Lost*. Milton's near-contemporaries – Dryden, Waller, Pope – although of comparable importance did not receive similar treatment until much later: they were great poets, to be sure, but great *modern* poets, not yet classics.[8]

Another sign of Milton's classic status (and Shakespeare's) is the number of adaptations of his works to a later idiom. Dryden's *State of Innocence* most clearly indicates how far apart their two worlds were in spirit, if not in time. The play was written in 1674 (though unpublished until 1677), the same year as the twelve-book *Paradise Lost*. But the thoroughly un-Miltonic tone of lines like Dryden's "What ho, Asmoday!" speaks volumes about the difference in the tenor of the two ages. "It is not hard to imagine," quips Joseph Levine, "what Milton would have thought of the enterprise had he lived to see it accomplished." Anne Ferry, not content with leaving it to the imagination, calls *The State of Innocence* "an offensive vulgarization."[9]

Other adaptations of Milton's works, more or less radical, followed. John Dalton's *Comus* was published in 1735, "Altered from Milton's mask and now adapted to the stage"; a fourth edition was called for within three years, and no fewer than thirty-three editions were published by the century's end. W. Howard produced a verse paraphrase of the first book of *Paradise Lost* in 1738, and Andrew Jackson rewrote the same book a year later in rhyming couplets. A prose paraphrase of the entire epic by George Green Smith, also bearing the title *The State of Innocence* – in fact Dupré de Saint-Maur's translation of *Paradise Lost* from Milton's English into

French, turned back into English – appeared in 1745.[10] Smith followed this with *A New Version of the Paradise Lost; or, Milton Paraphrased* in 1756. Some adaptations were musical: Benjamin Stillingfleet turned *Paradise Lost* into an oratorio in 1760, and William Jackson produced *Lycidas, A Musical Entertainment* in 1767. In 1773, an Edinburgh publisher released James Buchanan's *First Six Books of Paradise Lost, Rendered into Grammatical Construction.*

It is helpful in these cases to distinguish adaptation from imitation – terms which do not reflect eighteenth-century usage, but which add some useful precision. Contemporary works can be *imitated* as easily as classics, as evidenced by the vogue for ballad opera after Gay, or the more significant popularity of sentimental domestic fiction after Richardson. An *adaptation*, on the other hand, implies translation from the idiom of one age to another, and its defining characteristic is the negotiation of the distance between the two. We see this sort of translation when Pope follows Horace or Donne, when Johnson reworks Juvenal, or when Cibber and Tate adapt Shakespeare. It is to ages what translation is to language. Such rewritings seem contrary to the spirit of careful textual scholarship, in which the goal is to preserve an author's words, yet the two phenomena spring from a single source: the sense that the works belong to a distant age, and cannot be approached as if they were contemporary. Two contrary solutions offer themselves: antiquarian and scholarly attention to the exact words of the original to bring the audience to the text, or adaptation to bring the text to the audience, both already familiar means of dealing with the texts of the ancient world.[11] Adaptation, therefore, as much as scholarly care, places Milton in the company of the classics.

It is not only the editing or adapting of Milton's text, however, that shows Milton's relegation to the last age: eighteenth-century writers often tell us as much. Joseph Warton, for instance, "consider[s] the high rank which Milton has deservedly obtained among our few English classics," and his brother argues that Milton "may be reckoned an old English poet, and therefore requires that illustration, without which no old English poet can be well illustrated." Garrick associates the two most important English classics in his celebration of Johnson's achievement in the *Dictionary*: "First Shakspeare and Milton, like gods in the fight, / Have put their whole drama and epick to flight." Like Garrick, Johnson places Milton in a tradition begun in Elizabeth's time: "Milton was the first Englishman," he writes, "who, after the revival of letters, wrote Latin verses with classick elegance," not granting exceptions even for "Haddon and Ascham, the pride of Elizabeth's reign." Likewise his notes to Shakespeare: in following his professed hope of "comparing the works of Shakespeare with those of the writers who lived at the same time, immediately preceded, or immediately followed him," Johnson includes Milton (and Erasmus) among Shakespeare's contemporaries, as when he observes, "The old *English* writers often confound the active and passive adjectives. So *Shakespear*, and *Milton* after him, use *inexpressive* from *inexpressible*."[12] Milton "immediately followed" Shakespeare, and both were "old *English* writers."

This teaming-up of Shakespeare and Milton is telling, for it reveals the way many Britons thought about England's two greatest poets. Milton's works are routinely treated as if they were contemporary with the works of the great Elizabethans. We still sometimes have to remind ourselves that Milton's epics are in fact far from Elizabethan. *Paradise Lost* is contemporary with Dryden's *Annus Mirabilis*, chronologically closer to Pope than to Shakespeare.[13] Other seventeenth-century poets undergo the same split, the effects of which are still with us: Marvell, Cowley, Crashaw, Traherne, and Vaughan are consigned to the last age, while their contemporaries, Denham, Waller, and Pomfret, belong to the next. Mere chronology, then, is clearly not at issue for these eighteenth-century readers. For them, Shakespeare and Milton, however distant in time, belong to the same age in spirit.

BLAME THE REBEL

Spirit, however, raises countless problems, for placing Milton in the company of Shakespeare and Spenser demands a wide rift between political and aesthetic history. This is a curious fate for such a political poet. Few poets, even those with revolutionary sympathies, figure so prominently in actual revolutions: Milton served the Commonwealth with his scholarship and lamented its passing in his verse. Yet the strange disjunction between the two halves of his character in eighteenth-century writings is unmistakable.

Eighteenth-century critics had no widely accepted model of the relationship between political and cultural history – which is not to suggest that later ages, our own included, have had better luck. This relationship has long posed difficulties to literary historians, unsure of how to associate politics and aesthetics without drifting into the Scylla of naïve ahistoricism or the Charybdis of historicist reductionism, and Milton was the most difficult case-study. And at the very time readers were first insisting on historicizing their understanding of English authors, Milton was being removed from his actual historical moment and transplanted into the late sixteenth century. This is partly owing to the widespread distaste for his role in the Civil Wars. A small group of committed readers from Toland to Shelley, and an increasing number after mid-century, never allowed the radical Milton to disappear entirely; they lauded Milton's political commitment, turning him into the poet of Liberty. Such were pleased to dwell on his republican sympathies, and made much of the connection between his politics and his poetics.[14] For them, Milton's political involvement was of a piece with his poetic grandeur, and his less savory involvement in politics and controversy could be brushed under the carpet.

For less radical readers, however, those less savory aspects remained. Milton, after all, was an apologist for regicide. Antipathy on political grounds was therefore common in the decades after his death. William Winstanley denigrates Milton in 1687: "His fame is gone out like a Candle in a Snuff, and his Memory will always stink, which might have ever lived in honourable Repute, had not he been a notorious Traytor, and most impiously and villainously bely'd that blessed King *Charles* the first." Yalden, writing in 1698, agrees: "These sacred lines with wonder we peruse, / And praise the flights of a seraphic muse, / Till thy seditious prose provokes our rage, / And soils the beauties of thy brightest page." The result was a desire to keep the two sides of the man separate: as Thomas Warton puts it, "The poet should be distinguished from the enthusiast." An anonymous contributor to a university magazine sums it up pithily: "I blame the rebel, but the bard admire."[15]

In the eighteenth-century reception of Milton, the prose works, which best reveal his involvement in the politics of the middle seventeenth century, are conspicuous by their absence: the bard completely edged out the rebel. Milton's poetry, *Paradise Lost* above all, was read far more often than what Yalden called his "seditious prose." Only one of the prose works achieved anything like popularity in the eighteenth century, and that a surprising one: *Considerations touching the Likeliest Means of Removing Hirelings out of the Church* appeared on its own eight times between 1717 and 1797. The other publications of Milton's prose between Toland's 1698 *Works* and 1800 can be enumerated easily: *The Doctrine and Discipline of Divorce* appeared in 1715;[16] *Areopagitica* appeared in 1738, as did the *Declaration against Spain* (perhaps owing to the anti-Spanish sympathies of the 1730s) and an edition of the prose *Works*.[17] *Of Education* was published in Glasgow in 1746, in London in 1751, and in Berwick-upon-Tweed in 1753. Another prose *Works* appeared in 1753,[18] which seems to have satisfied all late-century curiosity about the prose; thereafter, the only works to appear were *Eikonoklastes* in 1756 and 1770, an abridged *Tenure of Kings and Magistrates* in 1784, *A Treatise of Civil Power* in 1790, and *A Ready and Easy Way* in 1791. In the same period, *Paradise Lost* appeared in roughly a hundred editions. The eighteenth-century trend, in sum, is the separation of Milton the celebrated poet from Milton the denigrated prose writer.

Some tried to rationalize this partition. Many critics believed mundane matters of statecraft were incompatible with the poetic spirit: it was distasteful to imagine England's grandest poet stooping to serve as Cromwell's Latin secretary. Thus Jonathan Richardson complains that Milton's "Poetry was Long Suspended whilst he was, as He thought, Combating in the Cause of God, and his Country's Liberty." Thomas Warton laments that "the vigorous portion of his life... those years in which imagination is on the wing, were unworthily and unprofitably wasted on temporary topics, on elaborate but perishable dissertations in defence of innovation and anarchy." This concern only intensified over the course of the eighteenth century, as the Renaissance ideal of the courtier poet, effortlessly synthesizing literature with statecraft (think of Sidney's invocation of "Sweet poesy, that hath anciently had kings, emperors, senators, great captains... not only to favour poets, but to be poets"), gave way to the Romantic conception of the solitary, even feckless, genius. Poets could be legislators only if they remained unacknowledged. At century's end, therefore, Anderson echoes the popular complaint that worldly matters distracted Milton from his poetical work: "From this period [around 1644] to the restoration, our Author was so deeply engaged in the controversies of the times, that he found no leisure for polite learning."[19]

Even Johnson – who, though no courtier, was much more involved in public life than many writers – gives several extended developments of this incompatibility of high culture and practical affairs. The *Life of Milton* holds that "While he was obliged to divide his time between his private studies and affairs of state, his poetical labour must have been often interrupted." He notes more generally that "faction seldom leaves a man honest, however it might find him," and that "An Age of War is not often an Age of Learning; the Tumult and Anxiety of Military Preparations seldom leave Attention vacant to the silent Progress of Study, and the placid Conquests of Investigation."[20]

The effect of such discussions is evident: they wrench Milton especially, and to a lesser degree the other great writers of the Renaissance, out of their age, and turn them into transcendent figures divorced from the political conditions under which they lived. While Johnson, Warton, and (later) Malone were developing a historicist sense of their literary past, others were working more successfully to universalize the great writers of the last age. The apotheosis of Shakespeare, most visible in the Shakespeare Jubilee of 1769, is the best example of a favorite poet wrested from his historical situation. Dobson traces the rise of "the timeless and transcendent Bard" in Garrick's Jubilee: Shakespeare is "for the first time... praised as the 'man of all men,' directly inspired by nature to voice the universal truths of humanity."[21] Milton was likewise torn from the seventeenth century in a process that split the man of letters from the man of the world.

BLASTS OF MALIGNITY

Not everyone was comfortable with this attempt to remove Milton from his age, and a few critics struggled to keep the two Miltons together. No one in the middle eighteenth century paid more attention to his republicanism and his role in the Civil Wars than Samuel Johnson, who put the political Milton at the center of his life of the poet.

For this he received little praise. Johnson has become unfairly famous for his hostility to Milton; one modern defender of Milton actually confesses to a facetious but "strong urge to punch... Dr. Johnson" for his criticism.[22] The attacks were at their most virulent in the decades after the publication of the *Life of Milton*. William Cowper, for instance, asserts that "Johnson's treatment of Milton is unmerciful to the last degree," adding that "A pensioner is not likely to spare a republican." Pattison, too, labels Johnson "a literary bandit... who conspired with one Lauder to stamp out Milton's credit."[23] Francis Blackburne's *Remarks on Johnson's Life of Milton* (1780) typifies the vehemence some critics directed at him: "Dr. Johnson's see-saw meditations, the shifty wiles of a man between two fires, who neither dares fight nor run away... His strictures on Milton's poetry... are tainted throughout with the effects of an inveterate hatred to Milton's politics." He sums up with a suggested epitaph for Johnson: "HERE LYES THE GRAND EXEMPLAR OF LITERARY PROSTITVTION."[24]

There is, however, no evidence of "inveterate hatred" to Milton's poetry, whatever Johnson thought of his politics. Scholars have catalogued echoes of Milton in Johnson's own works,[25] and his esteem is evident in his insistence that Milton should have priority over Pope in having a monument in St. Paul's: "Why, Sir, as Pope was a Roman Catholick, I would not have his to be first. I think Milton's rather should have the precedence. I think more highly of him now than I did at twenty. There is more thinking in him and in Butler, than in any of our poets." Milton's scholarship "places him in the first rank of writers and criticks." Most tellingly, Johnson calls *Paradise Lost* "a poem which, considered with respect to design, may claim the first place, and with respect to performance the second, among the productions of the human mind."[26] As Paul Fussell observes, "This is a remarkable flux of enthusiasm from Johnson, a man who was constantly reminding his friends that nothing damaged an object or person so severely as excessive praise. We should be mindful of this warm conclusion of the *Life of Milton* when we encounter his earlier scorn for Milton's republicanism."[27] Johnson did indeed disdain Milton's politics, and worried that "they who contemplated in Milton the scholar and the wit were contented to forget the reviler of his King." He accuses Milton of "adopt[ing] the puritanical savageness of manners," and writes that "Nothing can be more just than that rebellion should end in slavery: that he, who had justified the murder of his king, for some acts which to him seemed unlawful, should now sell his services and his flatteries to a tyrant, of whom it was evident that he could do nothing lawful."[28] The politics are inseparable from the man: "His political notions were those of an acrimonious and surly republican . . . Milton's republicanism was, I am afraid, founded in an envious hatred of greatness, and a sullen desire of independence; in petulance impatient of controul, and pride disdainful of superiority . . . His predominant desire was to destroy rather than establish."[29] The sentiments he describes hardly make the political Milton a suitable candidate for inclusion in the *Dictionary*, where Johnson "was desirous that every quotation should be useful," and so he often simply ignores him.[30] In a different forum, however, Johnson did not shrink from confronting the Puritan. He approaches the controvertist without flinching: Milton "began to engage in the controversies of the times, and lent his breath to blow the flames of contention." Whereas others shrank from this political Milton, Johnson was unusually engaged with him. Boswell writes that "His just abhorrence of Milton's political notions was ever strong. But this did not prevent his warm admiration of Milton's great poetical merit, to which he has done illustrious justice, beyond all who have written upon the subject."[31] He did not dismiss the poet out of an antagonism for the republican.

In short, Johnson approaches Milton's politics as a moralist and a historian, and his poetry as a moralist and a critic. He recognizes, however, as few of his age did, that the two are different categories, and that while both should be present to the reader, neither should dominate or substitute for the other. Jean Hagstrum puts it best: Johnson is not often "found to express – perhaps because he did not always find it to be actually true, however much he may have wanted it to be – that favorite idea of Renaissance criticism, the 'impossibility,' in Ben Jonson's language, 'of any mans being the good *Poët*, without first being a good *Man*.'"[32] In the end, he was able to take Milton on precisely because Milton was in the process of achieving classic status, and was passing beyond criticism: the merely contemporary can be allowed to pass without criticism because it is likely to fade, but the reputation of a classic, particularly at the time it is being canonized, requires great care. It was because Milton was of the last age that Johnson was able to criticize him: *nil nisi bonum* may be a valid principle for the recently dead, but it was neither necessary nor desirable among our modern classics. "The everlasting verdure of Milton's laurels," he writes, "has nothing to fear from the blasts of malignity."[33] Thus Piozzi's defense of her friend's judgment: "After this it is to be hoped, that a certain class of men will talk no more of Johnson's malignity."[34]

THE SUBLIMITY OF HIS THOUGHTS

Johnson, though, was the exception, not the rule. In most eighteenth-century discussions, Milton was not a political poet but a poet of the sublime. Addison's formulation from 1712 is well known: "*Milton*'s chief Talent, and indeed his distinguishing Excellence, lies in the Sublimity of his Thoughts." John Dennis, writing in 1721, likewise argues that "*Milton*...carried away the Prize of Sublimity from both Ancients and Moderns," and calls sublimity "his distinguishing and Characteristick Quality...which sets him above Mankind." Several decades later, Collins resorts to the Miltonic sublime to describe Milton: "High on some Cliff, to Heav'n up-pil'd, / Of rude Access, of Prospect wild, / Where, tangled round the jealous Steep, / Strange Shades o'erbrow the Valleys deep..."[35] Even Johnson describes Milton's power as the product of "an imagination in the highest degree fervid and active, to which materials were supplied by incessant study and unlimited curiosity. The heat of Milton's mind might be said to sublimate his learning, to throw off

into his work the spirit of science, unmingled with its grosser parts...
The characteristick quality of his poem is sublimity."[36] It may seem that
readings of Milton that emphasize supposedly timeless sublimity over
historicity are themselves thoroughly ahistorical, as when Gray writes
"He pass'd the flaming bounds of Place and Time."[37] But the sublime is
in fact deeply implicated in history. Sublimity serves as its own epochal
marker, and is more bound up in history than it seems at first glance. The
syllogism was simple, if not entirely valid: Milton was sublime; Milton
was of his age; ergo, the age was sublime.

Readers found the Miltonic sublime in many authors of the last age,
most notably in Shakespeare.[38] We have seen that the two were treated as
contemporaries; the eighteenth century went further, and treated them
as two similar expressions of the character of the age. The styles of the
two were often conflated into one generic antique high style. Rowe's
declaration, for example, that *Jane Shore* (1714) was "Written in Imitation
of Shakespear's Style" has confused many. A few near-quotations aside –
"the long Train of Frailties Flesh is Heir to" – there is little that can be
called Shakespearean in lines like these:

> The drowzy Night grows on the World, and now
> The busie Craftsman and o'er-labour'd Hind
> Forget the Travail of the Day in Sleep:
> Care only wakes, and moping Pensiveness,
> With meagre discontented Looks they sit,
> And watch the wasting of the Midnight Taper.
>
> (II.i)

We can distinguish echoes of Milton (especially "Il Penseroso"), perhaps
anticipations of Young and Gray, but little of Shakespeare. There is even
more of Milton in these lines:

> I can place thee in such abject State,
> As Help shall never find thee; where repining,
> Thou shalt sit down, and gnaw the Earth for Anguish,
> Groan to the pitiless Winds without Return,
> Howl like the Midnight Wolf amidst the Desart,
> And curse thy Life in Bitterness of Misery.   (IV.i)

Compare Milton: "Into the womb / That bred them they return, and
howl and gnaw / My Bowels, thir repast"; "There they him laid /
Gnashing for anguish and despite and shame."[39] That Rowe could call
this Shakespearean cannot be attributed simply to his ignorance: having
edited Shakespeare's plays, he knew them better than nearly any of

his contemporaries. His imitation suggests that he heard in his original something lost to us.

The sublime side of Shakespeare interests Collins, too: he invokes Fear as "Thou whose Spirit most possest / The sacred Seat of *Shakespear*'s Breast," and notes that "In musing hour his Wayward Sisters found / And with their terrors drest the magic Scene!" In his professed Shakespearean imitations, he gives us verses such as "No wailing Ghost shall dare appear / To vex with Shrieks this quiet Grove," "His shroud, which death's cold damps destroy," and "Pale pansies o'er his corpse were plac'd." He echoes Milton's "one greater Man" to give Shakespeare's arrival a millennial ring: "The beauteous Union must appear at length, / Of *Tuscan* Fancy, and *Athenian* Strength: / One greater Muse *Eliza*'s Reign adorn, / And ev'n a *Shakespear* to her Fame be born!" Shakespeare is repeatedly subsumed under the rubric of the Miltonic sublime. Johnson's knowledge of the two authors was more extensive than Rowe's or Collins's, yet even he associates Shakespeare with Milton's essential attribute when he calls Shakespeare "the first considerable authour of sublime or familiar dialogue in our language."[40]

The sublime is not confined to Shakespeare and Milton, but is an almost universal characteristic of the best poetry of the age. Joseph Warton divides English poets into four classes, the first containing only the Renaissance triumvirate: "In the first class, I would place our only sublime and pathetic poets, Spenser, Shakespeare, and Milton." He thereby groups the three most imposing canonical poets of the last age under the rubric of sublimity. Anderson grants even the decorous Ben Jonson "a strong, and sometimes sublime vein of poetry" in addition to his "sterling wit, moral satire, and unrivalled erudition," although a less "sublime" poet than Jonson is hard for modern readers to imagine.[41]

These descriptions of a sublime age can be best understood against the background of another epochal divide, one often discussed in the eighteenth century: that between Homer's Greece and Virgil's Rome. When Milton is placed in a poetic tradition, it is usually that of the ancient epic poets, as Dryden's epigram of 1688 makes clear:

> Three *Poets*, in three distant *Ages* born,
> *Greece, Italy,* and *England* did adorn.
> The *First* in loftiness of thought Surpass'd;
> The *Next* in Majesty; in both the *Last*.
> The force of *Nature* cou'd no farther goe;
> To make a *Third* she join'd the former two.[42]

Milton is here associated with the ancient classics, yes; but Homer and Virgil have additional meanings to which most eighteenth-century readers were attuned. Johnson's verdict typifies most commentary on the two greatest poets of the ancient world: "The discriminative excellence of Homer is elevation and comprehension of thought, and that of Virgil is grace and splendor of diction." The opposition is widespread, appearing, for example, in Sir William Temple's *Of Poetry* and *Spectator* 160. Homer and Virgil are famously compared in *Spectator* 417: Homer "strikes the Imagination wonderfully with what is Great, [Virgil] with what is Beautiful... *Homer*'s Epithets generally mark out what is Great, *Virgil*'s what is Agreeable." Pope's comparison is similar: "*Homer* was the greater Genius, *Virgil* the better Artist... *Homer* hurries and transports us with a commanding Impetuosity, *Virgil* leads us with an attractive Majesty: *Homer* scatters with a generous Profusion, *Virgil* bestows with a careful Magnificence." It therefore comes as no surprise to see Milton associated more often with the fiery and inventive Homer than with the decorous Virgil. Addison, remember, declares that "*Milton*'s chief Talent, and indeed his distinguishing Excellence, lies in the Sublimity of his Thoughts," but he significantly goes on to award Milton only the silver medal: "In the Greatness of his Sentiments he triumphs over all the Poets both Modern and Ancient, *Homer* only excepted."[43]

If Milton's age is Homeric, where is the Virgilian contrast to be found? For many readers, the decades after Milton's death, in which propriety became a central poetic concern, played Rome to Milton's Greece. Milton's Homeric sublimity, then, serves an important function in literary periodization, for he can be contrasted with modern Virgilian decorum. When Gray describes his four schools of English poetry, he provides the neatest summary by associating Milton and his sublime age with early modern Italy, and Pope and his "correct" age with seventeenth-century France. This distinction suggests the analogy that seems to underlie many comments on Milton and his near-contemporaries who lie on the other side of the epochal boundary: Homer is to Virgil as Milton is to Waller; the sublime Greek is to the decorous Roman as the old school of Italy is to the new school of France. Milton's timelessness was characteristic of his time.

UNDER THE SHADE OF EXALTED MERIT

Characterizing the last age means characterizing the present, for to define the last age by its sublimity is to define the present by its lack.

This lack is most evident when Milton is compared not with the classics, but with his contemporaries. An anonymous contribution to the *Athenian Mercury* is typical: "*Milton* was the *fullest* and *loftiest, Waller* the *neatest* and most *correct* Poet we ever had."[44] When this appeared in 1692, "neatest and most correct" was no small praise. But as we have seen in tracing the trajectory of Jonson's reputation over the course of the eighteenth century, the increasingly faint praise began to turn into damnation. Milton's sublimity is all the more striking when set beside the works of his Restoration contemporaries: there is little Miltonic grandeur in Butler, Denham, or Waller, whose strengths lie elsewhere. It was just at this time – and, I believe, partly for this reason – that the poets of the middle seventeenth century were consigned to their respective periods, where they remain today, enshrined in anthologies and survey courses.

By the middle of the eighteenth century, poets and critics were pointedly aware of the distance between Milton's age and their own. Gray writes of the influence of Italy on the epic poets Spenser and Milton, but notes that "this School expired soon after the Restoration, and a new one arose on the French model, which has subsisted ever since." The result? "But ah! 'tis heard no more— / Oh! Lyre divine, what daring Spirit / Wakes thee now?" Collins too notes that after Shakespeare's masculine age, "With gradual Steps, and slow, exacter *France* / Saw Art's fair Empire o'er her Shores advance." Even William Lauder, attempting to deflate Milton's reputation, echoes the popular take on the passing of Milton's age: "*Cowley, Waller, Denham, Dryden, Prior, Pope*, in comparison with *Milton*, have bore no greater proportion than that of dwarfs to a giant." The most famous attack on the dwarfs, Joseph Warton's *Essay on Pope* (1756), defines poetry itself as the sublime poetry of the last age: "The sublime and the Pathetic are the two chief nerves of all genuine poesy." This has the effect of answering his own question, "What is there sublime or very Pathetic in POPE?" Only one answer is possible: "In that species of poetry wherein POPE excelled, he is superior to all mankind: and I only say, that this species of poetry is not the most excellent one of the art."[45]

Warton's evaluation of Pope is often treated as a sort of harbinger of Romantic criticism, but it is not out of place in the critical climate of the middle eighteenth century.[46] Even Johnson, whose *Life of Pope* rushes to Pope's defense, seems to agree (albeit reluctantly) with Warton's fundamental assumptions. His response to Warton's challenge – "If Pope be not a poet, where is poetry to be found?" – seems to place Pope outside any narrative of post-Miltonic poetic decay: "Let us look round upon the present time, and back upon the past...the pretensions of Pope will be no more disputed." And yet his look back upon the past does not reach very far, for a few pages earlier in the *Life* Johnson makes a telling exclusion: "It is not to be inferred that of this poetical vigour Pope had only a little, because Dryden had more, for every other writer since Milton must give place to Pope."[47] Pope and Dryden rule their respective domains, but the words "since Milton" imply that both must give place not only to Milton, but also to many of his predecessors – otherwise Johnson would have written not "since" but "except Milton." Here the two figures pressed into service as avatars respectively of "Augustan" and "Romantic" criticism agree: Johnson simply leaves implicit what Warton says outright, placing Pope below "*Spenser, Shakespeare*, and *Milton*," but "above other modern English poets."[48] Modern poets, even the best, cannot stand comparison with the "poetical vigour" of the last age.

In short, the age of sublimity had passed. The awareness of its passing increased in intensity over the course of the century, coming to a head in the often-described Romantic rejection of Pope's decorous poetry in favor of the unbridled energy of Milton and other sublime figures of the past, whether real (Homer) or imagined (Ossian).[49] Such feelings did not have their origin in Wordsworth's "Preface," nor even in the works of such Pre-Romantics (so-called) as the Wartons, Gray, and Collins. As early as the beginning of the eighteenth century, there was a sense that a sublime age had closed. Nicholas Rowe makes a fairly conventional lament for lost sublimity in the Prologue to *Jane Shore*:

> Those venerable ancient Song-Enditers
> Soar'd many a Pitch above our modern Writers...
> Our Numbers may be more refind than those,
> But what we've gain'd in Verse, we've lost in Prose.

He continues with a familiar praise of "Immortal Shakespear": "With rough, majestick Force he mov'd the Heart, / And Strength, and Nature made amends for Art." Collins's verse too is filled with expressions of desire to recapture the sublimity of the previous age in his poetry: "Hither again thy Fury deal," he apostrophizes to Fear; "Teach me but once like Him to feel." But he laments that poetry after Waller can only look back wistfully at the sublime age of Milton and Spenser:

> My trembling Feet his guiding Steps pursue;
> In vain – Such Bliss to One alone,
> Of all the Sons of Soul was known,

And Heav'n, and *Fancy*, kindred Pow'rs,
Have now o'erturn'd th' inspiring Bow'rs,
Or curtain'd close such Scene from ev'ry future View.

Shakespeare's "beauteous Union...of *Tuscan* Fancy, and *Athenian*
Strength" is gone: "In vain our *Britain* hop'd an equal Day! / No second
Growth the Western Isle could bear, / At once exhausted with too rich a
Year."[50] Other poets felt its absence. Joseph Warton writes that Addison
was "inexpressibly chagrined... because he was deeply conscious that
his own CAMPAIGN...contained no strokes of...genuine and sublime
poetry."[51]

Epic in particular served as a generic reminder of the passing of sublimity. Critics and poets after Milton continued to praise and encourage
the epic: Dryden, for instance, writes that in a heroic poem, "all things
must be Grave, Majestical and Sublime." A century later, Johnson agrees
that "the first praise of genius is due to the writer of an epick poem, as
it requires an assemblage of all the powers which are singly sufficient
for other compositions." He believed his century might produce more
epic poetry: "I am persuaded that, had Sir Isaac Newton applied to
poetry, he would have made a very fine epick poem."[52] Still, it was an
inescapable fact that no one *had* made a very fine epic poem in some
time. Dryden and Pope could write translations of epics and mock-epics,
but not one original heroic poem – such is now the conventional critical
wisdom.[53] Pope planned to write his epic *Brutus* in Milton's blank verse,
but as Johnson notes, "He laid aside his Epick Poem, perhaps without
much loss to mankind."[54] The disappearance of natural sublimity leaves
the modern age ill prepared to write an epic.

This is not to say no epics were written. Johnson liked Blackmore, who
actually did write epic poems – six of them, if we include *The Creation* –
well into the eighteenth century. But Johnson's remarks on his success in
Milton's mode are revealingly ambivalent:

His head still teemed with heroick poetry, and (1705) he published *Eliza* in ten
books. I am afraid that the world was now weary of contending about Blackmore's heroes, for I do not remember that by any author, serious or comical, I
have found *Eliza* either praised or blamed. She "dropped," as it seems, "dead-
born from the press." It is never mentioned, and was never seen by me till I
borrowed it for the present occasion.[55]

How to account for this? One of the most convincing explanations of the
inability to produce a successful epic appears in *Rambler* 86: "It is, indeed,

always dangerous to be placed in a state of unavoidable comparison with excellence... He that succeeds a celebrated writer, has the same difficulties to encounter; he stands under the shade of exalted merit, and is hindered from rising to his natural height, by the interception of those beams which should invigorate and quicken him."[56] Walter Jackson Bate quotes this passage in *The Burden of the Past and the English Poet*. Consider, too, Young's assertion of 1759: "Why are *Originals* so few? not because the Writer's harvest is over, the great Reapers of Antiquity having left nothing to be gleaned after them; nor because the human mind's teeming time is past, or because it is incapable of putting forth unprecedented births; but because illustrious Examples *engross, prejudice*, and *intimidate*."[57] One need not resort to a Freudian model of an anxiety of influence to appreciate Milton's position in eighteenth-century poetic consciousness. *Pace* Bloom, Milton does not cripple eighteenth-century poets so much as remind them that their age is not his. Few poets were paralyzed by Milton; Dustin Griffin rightly reminds us that "Milton's influence on the major English writers from Dryden to Johnson and Cowper was a creative one." But more than any other figure, Milton reminded eighteenth-century poets of their belatedness. "Modernity," says Griffin, "was a condition which one simply had to acknowledge... Certain kinds of poetry were no longer possible."[58] The last age set the standard that modernity had to live up to.

The first hint of the burden Milton was to exert on his successors appears in Marvell's "On Paradise Lost" (1674):

> None will dare
> Within thy Labours to pretend a share.
> Thou hast not miss'd one thought that could be fit,
> And all that was improper dost omit:
> So that no room is here for Writers left,
> But to detect their Ignorance or theft.[59]

Praise of this sort is not to be taken literally, for in dedications a man is not upon oath. The terms in which it is expressed, however, are significant: the only "room... left" is to make inferior copies. Sneyd Davies says as much in his "Rhapsody to Milton":

> Thy Hell,
> Copied by other Hand whate'er, will lose
> It's Terrors; and thy Paradise it's Sweets,
> Soil'd by rude Touch. – Enough then to admire,
> Silent admire: and be content to feel:

> Or, if we follow thy bright Track, advance
> With Reverence, and shew that not Desire
> To Rival, but Resemble, is our Aim:
> Resemble thee, tho' in inferior Strain.[60]

He goes on: "For O! great Pattern to succeeding Times!"

But following a pattern, even a great one, was passing out of fashion. It is no coincidence that, just at the time that poets and critics were struggling with their inescapable debt to Milton, a new aesthetics was being formed, one that placed a premium on originality. Young is direct: "*Originals* are the fairest Flowers: *Imitations* are of quicker growth, but fainter bloom."[61] Johnson praises Milton for this very quality:

The highest praise of genius is original invention. Milton cannot be said to have contrived the structure of an epick poem ... But of all the borrowers from Homer Milton is perhaps the least indebted. He was naturally a thinker for himself, confident of his own abilities and disdainful of help or hindrance; he did not refuse admission to the thoughts or images of his predecessors, but he did not seek them. From his contemporaries he neither courted nor received support.[62]

Milton paradoxically becomes more Homeric through his distance from Homer.

The eighteenth-century would-be epic poet, it seemed, was left with only imitation, but imitating Milton seemed both impossible and undesirable. So Dryden says of imitation of his predecessors in general: "There is scarce an Humour, a Character, or any kind of Plot, which they have not us'd. All comes sullied or wasted to us... This therefore will be a good Argument to us either not to write at all, or to attempt some other way. There is no bayes to be expected in their Walks."[63] This warning that Milton exceeds the grasp of imitators, and that we are left only with imitating his faults, recalls Erasmus's warning in the *Ciceronian*: Cicero's "virtues, because they are great, approximate to faults. It is inevitable that imitation falls short when it tries only to follow a model, not surpass it. Consequently, the more determinedly you aim to copy Cicero, the nearer you come to a fault."[64] In both cases, the concern is to avoid slavish imitation of the past – the great works of the past deserve our admiration, but in our debased age, we are unable to compete with them on their own terms.

Eighteenth-century writers did excel in at least two forms, satire and the novel. Neither, however, was held to be an Elizabethan genre, and therefore contemporaries were ambivalent about both. "No Satires, properly so called," notes Thomas Warton, "were written till towards the latter end of the queen's reign, and then but a few... Satire is the poetry of a nation highly polished." Elsewhere he refers to "Satire, that bane of the sublime." His brother argues that "WIT and SATIRE are transitory and perishable," contrasting them with Milton's "NATURE and PASSION."[65] The new prose narratives were impure mixtures of the genres of the past, and these bastard forms received little respect.

HEADS UPON CHERRY-STONES

We have seen that the rise of decorum from the Middle Ages through the Renaissance and into modernity was a source of pride: a progression of correctness toward "elegance." Most poets of the eighteenth century dated the rise of elegance to the middle seventeenth century: "Late, very late, correctness grew our care," writes Pope, "When the tir'd nation breath'd from civil war."[66] In elegance, the best poets of the eighteenth century could compete with the best poets in history, excepting only Virgil.

Elegance was the one area in which the eighteenth century felt itself to excel, and yet, as the decades passed, poets and critics increasingly began to suspect that the greatest poetry had little use for it. Johnson's definition of *elegance* is revealingly ambivalent, and anticipates the great sea-change in eighteenth-century aesthetics: elegance is "Beauty of art; rather soothing than striking; beauty without grandeur." It was a poor substitute for what had been lost since the last age: as Hurd laments, "What we have gotten by this revolution... is a great deal of good sense. What we have lost is a world of fine fabling." In 1724, Allan Ramsay notes that "*Readers* of the best and most exquisite Discernment frequently complain of our *modern Writings*, as filled with affected Delicacies and studied Refinements, which they would gladly exchange for that natural Strength of Thought and Simplicity of Stile our Forefathers practised," and turns to the Scottish writers from the sixteenth century – "Times that are past, and that exist no more" – for a corrective.[67]

Their forefathers had little time for elegance. "Milton," Johnson explains, "was a genius that could cut a Colossus from a rock; but could not carve heads upon cherry-stones." He "sometimes descends to the elegant, but his element is the great. He can occasionally invest himself with grace; but his natural port is gigantick loftiness." Johnson's own age, by contrast, was not one of lofty epic poems, but of smaller efforts. "The natural progress of the works of men," writes Johnson in *Idler* 63, "is from rudeness to convenience, from convenience to elegance, and from elegance to nicety." The age feared that its elegance was dwindling into mere nicety. So Johnson complains of the late Metaphysical poets, "Nor was the sublime more within their reach than the pathetick… What they wanted however of the sublime they endeavoured to supply by hyperbole."[68] Prior "had apparently such rectitude of judgment as secured him from every thing that approached to the ridiculous or absurd; but… judgment in the operations of intellect can hinder faults, but not produce excellence. Prior is never low, nor very often sublime." Ditto Waller: "The general character of his poetry is elegance and gaiety. He is never pathetick, and very rarely sublime."[69]

Few moderns aspired higher than elegance and gaiety. Goldsmith's Lien Chi Altangi, the Citizen of the World, finds "the practice of the last age" superior to that of his day, and faults the moderns because they "are more employed in describing to the imagination than striking at the heart."[70] A similar lament about modern poetry appears in Headley's *Select Beauties* (1787), a book Stuart Curran calls "the key instrument in the [Romantic] Renaissance revival":

If we seriously and impartially examine the cluster of poetical names that shone, and were concentered in the space of ninety-one years from the accession of Elizabeth inclusively, to the restoration of Charles the second, and compare them with those who have respectively flourished from that time to this, a period of an hundred and thirty-eight years, we shall find the phalanx of older classics but little affected by a comparison with the more modern muster-roll.[71]

So this is where the eighteenth-century investigation into the revival of learning ended up: in the recognition that the grandeur of the past left the moderns in the shadows. What began as an attempt to characterize the age of Shakespeare and Elizabeth became a way of characterizing the present, sometimes as an advance over what came before it, but increasingly as a bronze successor to a golden age. Perhaps modernity was no better than the Middle Ages over which learning had triumphed some three centuries earlier. Yes, the modern age was more refined and more elegant – but was it really any better than the barbarous ages the humanists had taught the eighteenth century to despise? In politics, in religion, and above all in poetry, the age of Johnson chastised itself for failing to live up to the standard set by the age of Elizabeth. Those who came after Johnson used this standard to attack the eighteenth century, when Johnson's intellectual stock plummeted and the Elizabethans received a kind of sublime apotheosis. Keats's complaint of 1818 is typical:

"Modern poets differ from the Elizabethans in this. Each of the moderns like an Elector of Hanover governs his petty state, and knows how many straws are swept daily from the Causeways in all his dominions and has a continual itching that all the Housewives should have their coppers well scoured: the ancients were Emperors of vast Provinces."[72] The moderns are petty, domestic, feminized; the Elizabethans – now unselfconsciously given the honorific "ancients" – are grand, sublime, and preeminently masculine.

It is wrong, however, to associate this sense of modernity's inadequacy exclusively with Romanticism, for hints of it appeared much earlier. The deficiency of post-Miltonic poetry was a concern even in the late seventeenth century, when people first began to treat the Renaissance as the last age. More than a century before Keats, for instance, Dryden complained:

> Strong were our Syres; and as they Fought they Writ,
> Conqu'ring with force of Arms, and dint of Wit;
> Theirs was the Gyant Race, before the Flood;
> And thus, when *Charles* Return'd, our Empire stood.
> . . .
> Our Age was cultivated thus at length;
> But what we gain'd in skill we lost in strength.
> Our Builders were, with want of Genius, curst;
> The second Temple was not like the first.[73]

Evident here is the central artistic anxiety of the eighteenth century: that in describing the passing of the last age, they described the passing of the golden age. Modernity was initiated by a "Flood" at the Restoration, and things have not been the same since. Declarations of modernity, as noted at the beginning of this study, are most often used defiantly to proclaim the superiority of the present to the past. Over the course of the century, though, as the sixteenth century came to seem increasingly distant from the modern world, the age of Johnson became ever more wistful in its longing for the age of Shakespeare and Milton, and it became time for a new modernity to declare itself.

Joseph Warton puts it most directly, in "The Enthusiast": "What are the lays of artful Addison, / Coldly correct, to Shakespear's warblings wild?"[74] The answer is obvious, and perhaps even Johnson would have agreed. The strides in elegance that had produced a Pope and an Addison were a cause for celebration, to be sure. But the age feared it was left only to cut heads upon cherry-stones.

Notes

1. O'Brien, *Narratives of Enlightenment*, p. 142.
2. Croce, *Theory and History of Historiography*, p. 112; Brown, "Periods and Resistances," p. 309. Brown's essay is the introduction to a special issue of *Modern Language Quarterly* 62, no. 4 (Dec. 2001), *Periodization: Cutting Up the Past*, which appeared just as this book was going to press.
3. As Wellek explains, "'Period' is a term which cannot be discussed in isolation: a single period, though we may elect to study it to the exclusion of others, is a period only within a series of periods" ("Periods and Movements," p. 74). It is thus no surprise that one of the most influential modern voices on periodization is Claude Lévi-Strauss, who writes, "Insofar as history aspires to meaning, it is doomed to select regions, periods, groups of men and individuals in these groups and to make them stand out, as discontinuous figures, against a continuity barely good enough to be used as a backdrop" (*Savage Mind*, p. 257). See also Chandler, *England in 1819*, pp. 3–93; Japp, *Beziehungssinn*, p. 13; Schmidt, "On Writing Histories of Literature," p. 282; Bürger, "On Literary History," p. 202; and Blumenberg, *Legitimacy of the Modern Age*, pp. 457–81.
4. Benjamin's term "Jetztzeit" – "now time" – hints at the importance of the *now* in periodization (see *Illuminationen*, p. 276). As Vogler observes, "The perennial goal of historical thought can be seen to be a mode of self-definition in the form of a narrative in which a 'modernity' defines itself over against a past perceived as essentially *different*" ("Romanticism and Literary Periods," p. 135).
5. The scheme of six ages corresponding to the six days of creation is described most influentially by Augustine: see *Confessions* 1.3.13 (1:7–8), with O'Donnell's commentary (11:52–56), and William M. Green, "Augustine on the Teaching of History," pp. 322–24. Jean Bodin famously rejected Daniel's four monarchies in the seventh chapter of his *Methodus* (pp. 291–302). One of the more extensive accounts of this shift in historical paradigms is Falco, *La Polemica sul medio evo*, pp. 29–41. See also Croce, *Theory and History of Historiography*, pp. 112–13 and 213–14; Collingwood, *Idea of History*, pp. 49–58; and Kemp, *Estrangement of the Past*, pp. xi and 104.

6. The best twentieth-century assessment of his importance is Theodor Mommsen, "Petrarch's Conception of the 'Dark Ages.' "
7. Kerrigan and Braden, *Idea of the Renaissance*, p. 3.
8. Michelet, *Renaissance, Réforme*, in *Œuvres complètes*, vII:51. Burckhardt and Pater are similarly direct: see, for instance, *Civilization of the Renaissance in Italy*, p. 81, and *Renaissance*, pp. 1–2.
9. Hazlitt, *Collected Works*, v:173. Eighteenth-century periodization is the subject of de Grazia's *Shakespeare Verbatim*, especially pp. 94–131, and Lipking's *Ordering of the Arts in Eighteenth-Century England*.
10. See, for instance, *Rambler*, v:75–76 (no. 158).
11. Thomas Warton, *History of English Poetry*, IV:414, 420, 418.
12. Cited in Sir John Davies, *Poetical Works* (1773), p. iii.
13. Bell, *Poets of Great Britain*, xv:vi. The claim that Elizabeth's age is "the most shining part of the English history" is thoroughly conventional; see, for instance, Rolt, *Lives of the Principal Reformers*, p. 196.
14. Johnson, *Shakespeare*, vII:87.
15. Thomas Warton, *History of English Poetry*, III:490–91, 408, 490.
16. Anderson, *Works of the British Poets*, 1:4.
17. Evelyn, *Diary*, III:304 (26 November 1661); Rymer, *Tragedies of the Last Age Consider'd*, title page, p. 142, etc.
18. Frye, *Anatomy of Criticism*, p. 62. Kerrigan and Braden make a similar point: "This nascent self-periodization is generally reproachful" (*Idea of the Renaissance*, p. 78).
19. The scheme appears in Ruffhead's *Life of Pope*, p. 425, and is discussed in Lipking, *Ordering of the Arts*, pp. 334–38.
20. Gray, *Correspondence*, III:1122–24 (to Thomas Warton, 15 April 1770). For the relation of Gray's sketch to Warton's *History*, see Fairer, "Origins of Warton's *History of English Poetry*," esp. pp. 45–49.
21. Headley, *Select Beauties*, p. xiv.
22. Robert Griffin, "The Age of 'The Age of' Is Over," perceptively notes some of the problems with "the age of Johnson."
23. "While he knew his Shakespeare and Ben Jonson, he was but imperfectly acquainted with the rest of Elizabethan literature" (Hollis, *Dr. Johnson*, p. 78). See also Watkins, *Johnson and English Poetry before 1660*, p. 5, n. 4.
24. Bate, *Samuel Johnson*, p. 540; "Prologue Spoken at the Opening of the Theatre in Drury-Lane, 1747," in Johnson, *Poems*, p. 87. The three most extensive surveys of Johnson's interest in the Renaissance, two old, one recent, are Watkins, *Johnson and English Poetry before 1660*, esp. pp. 1–15, 58; Houston, *Dr. Johnson*; and DeMaria, *Life of Samuel Johnson*. Throughout this study I have depended on all of them, especially DeMaria.
25. The editors of the Yale *Rambler* note of the quotations and allusions,

> Many of them are to writers from the beginning of the Renaissance to the close of the seventeenth century. A mere list of the names of some of them at once brushes aside the naïve notion, still strangely common, that, apart from classical antiquity and except for Shakespeare and Milton, the year 1660 marks something of a boundary

to Johnson's "sensibility" and knowledge. References solely to continental writers before the eighteenth century (58) include Bellarmine, Camerarius, Cardano, Castiglione, Cornaro, Cujacius, Descartes, Erasmus, Fabricius, Gassendi, Grotius, Julius Libri, Lipsius, Politian, Pontanus, Quevedo, Sannazaro, the Scaligers, and Thuanus. (*Rambler*, III: xxxii)

26. *Life of Milton*, in *Lives*, 1:143.
27. Lipking, *Ordering of the Arts*, p. 405. Vance likewise argues that "Johnson deserves a place among the more advanced historical thinkers of his age" (*Samuel Johnson and the Sense of History*, p. 138).
28. *Shakespeare*, VII:103 and 71.
29. Lipking, *Ordering of the Arts*, p. 407.
30. *Rambler*, III:157 (no. 28); IV:311 (no. 127); and III:280 (no. 52).
31. *Life*, IV:381–82. See Tankard, "'That Great Literary Projector,'" for a thorough discussion of Johnson's never-completed works. Joseph Warton, too, apparently "planned [in 1753] to unite in a volume, and publish, 'Select Epistles of Angelus Politianus, Desiderius, Erasmus [*sic*], Hugo Grotius, and others, with notes,' on a scale sufficiently extensive to embrace an history of the revival of learning" (Wooll, *Biographical Memoirs*, p. 29).
32. Weisinger discusses Restoration notions of modernity in "Study of the Revival of Learning in England from Bacon to Hallam," esp. p. 223, and he discusses Gildon in "Seventeenth-Century Reputation of the Elizabethans," p. 19.
33. See, for instance, Peacock's scheme (1821) of the ages of post-classical poetry: the iron Middle Ages, the golden Renaissance (running through Milton), the silver "long" eighteenth century (the Restoration through Gray and Collins), and finally a brass modernity, of which the Lake Poets were the most visible exemplars ("The Four Ages of Poetry," in Peacock, *Works*, VIII:16). Johnson's *now* had become Peacock's *then*.
34. McGann, "History, Herstory, Theirstory, Ourstory," p. 196.
35. Levine, *Between the Ancients and the Moderns*, p. vii.
36. Johnson, *Thoughts Concerning Falkland's Islands*, in *Political Writings*, p. 374.

1 STRUGGLING TO EMERGE FROM BARBARITY: HISTORIOGRAPHY AND THE IDEA OF THE CLASSIC

1. C. S. Lewis, *English Literature in the Sixteenth Century, Excluding Drama*, p. 56.
2. The eighteenth century made central in its conception of the revival of learning what was in fact the voice of a small minority at the time. As Mommsen notes, the idea of a dark age "attained its greatest currency in the age of the Enlightenment" ("Petrarch's Conception of the 'Dark Ages,'" p. 227). Some critics have therefore stressed not the historical rupture between the Middle Ages and the Renaissance but their continuities. The most influential twentieth-century challenge came from Haskins, who in 1927 found "the Middle Ages less dark and less static, and the Renaissance less bright and less sudden, than was once supposed" (*Renaissance of the Twelfth Century*,

p. vii). His works prompted a great many discussions of the tenability of the medieval–Renaissance divide, including Kristeller's *Renaissance Thought: The Classic, Scholastic and Humanist Strains*, pp. 92–119, and Huizinga's *Autumn of the Middle Ages*, pp. 382–96.

3. Bouwsma, *Interpretation of Renaissance Humanism*, p. 17. See also Weisinger, "Self-Awareness of the Renaissance as a Criterion of the Renaissance," and Myron P. Gilmore, *World of Humanism, 1453–1517*, p. 201.

4. Robinson provides an illuminating and entertaining discussion of the term "Middle Ages" and the various termini suggested for the age in "Medieval, the Middle Ages."

5. "Hoc enim seculum tanquam aureum, liberales disciplinas fermè iam extinctas reduxit in lucem" (letter of 1492 to Paul of Middelburg, in Ficino, *Opera Omnia*, 1:944). See also Hale, *Civilization of Europe in the Renaissance*, pp. 585–92.

6. "Quod prorsus auream fore spes est, si quot vnquam fuit aureum" (*Opus Epistolarum Des. Erasmi Roterodami*, 11:527 [epistle 566]); the translation comes from *Collected Works of Erasmus*, IV:311.

7. See Varga, *Das Schlagwort vom "finsteren Mittelalter,"* pp. 5–35, and Simone, "La Coscienza della Rinascita negli umanisti," pp. 177–83.

8. *Antibarbari*, in *Collected Works of Erasmus*, XXIII:24, 46; "in Christianam religionem conferre nitebatur," "nullam esse eruditionem . . . nisi quae sit secularis"; *Opera Omnia Desiderii Erasmi Roterodami*, 1, i, 46, 84.

9. The standard account of Petrarch's notion of history is Mommsen, "Petrarch's Conception of the 'Dark Ages' "; Mommsen dates the idea of Dark Ages to 1341. See also Ferguson, *Renaissance in Historical Thought*, p. 8; Simone, "La Coscienza della Rinascita negli umanisti"; and McLaughlin, "Humanist Concepts of Renaissance," pp. 132–34.

10. Petrarch, *On His Own Ignorance and that of Others*, p. 123.

11. "Quae corrumpuntur, privantur bono. si autem omni bono privabuntur, omnino non errunt. quaecumque sunt, bona sunt, malumque illud, quod quaerebam unde esset, non est substantia, quia, si substantia esset, bonum esset" (Augustine, *Confessions*, 7.12.18).

12. "O quantum, inquit, Poggi, haec Capitolia ab iliis distant, quae noster Maro cecinit, 'Aurea nunc, olim silvestribus horrida dumis.' Ut quidem is versus merito possit converti: 'Auream quondam, nunc squalida, spinetis vepribusque referta' " (Poggio Bracciolini, *De varietate fortunae*, IV:230).

13. "Verum enimuero quò magis superiora tempora infelicia fuere, quibus homo nemo inuentus est eruditus, eò plus his nostris gratulandum est, in quibus (si paulò amplius adnitamur) confido propediem linguam Romanam uirere plus, quàm urbem, & cum ea disciplinas omneis iri restitutum" (*De elegantiis linguae latinae*, in *Laurentii Vallae opera*, p. 4).

14. Jonson, "A Fit of Rhyme against Rhyme," lines 15–16, 26–29, in *Complete Poems*; Camden, *Remains Concerning Britain*, p. 29.

15. C. S. Lewis, *English Literature in the Sixteenth Century*, p. 20.

16. Bejczy, "Overcoming the Middle Ages," pp. 37–38.

17. "Ita non secus ipse barbaris quam illi literis infensus, adeo vt ad occursus horum frequenter aut nausearet aut incandesceret" (*Collected Works of Erasmus*, XXIII:26–27; *Opera Omnia*, I, i, 49); "rusticam illam cohortem" (*Collected Works of Erasmus*, XXIII:45; *Opera Omnia*, I, i, 70); "commentationibus optimos autores non illustrat, sed obscurat, non adornat sed contaminat... omnia confuderunt, deprauauerunt, euerterunt" (*Collected Works of Erasmus*, XXIII:44–45; *Opera Omnia*, I, i, 70); "imo adeo natos arbitrantur, vt nos quicquid est bonarum literarum dedoceant" (*Collected Works of Erasmus*, XXIII:28; *Opera Omnia*, I, i, 51).

18. Erasmus, *Education of a Christian Prince*, p. 145. Compare below: "Just as one who poisons the public fountain from which all drink deserves more than one punishment, so he is the most harmful who infects the mind of the prince with base ideas" (p. 146); "The true prince [should] be removed from the sullied opinions and desires of the common folk" (p. 150).

19. Du Bellay, *La Deffence et illustration de la langue françoyse*, p. 108; Ascham, *Scholemaster*, in *English Works*, ed. Wright, p. 260; Milton, *Complete Prose Works*, 1:519.

20. Milton, *Of Reformation*, in *Complete Prose Works*, 1:549, 524.

21. Vasari, *Lives of the Painters, Sculptors, and Architects*, 1:17–19.

22. Milton, *Complete Prose Works*, 1:566.

23. "Optimas literas, partim neglectas hactenus, partim corruptas" (Erasmus, *Opus Epistolarum*, III:527 [no. 566]). Compare Jortin's eighteenth-century portrait of Erasmus: "This worthy man spent a long and laborious life in an uniform pursuit of two points; in opposing barbarous ignorance... and in promoting useful literature, and true piety" (*Life of Erasmus*, 1:275–76).

24. "Sunt enim non minus temporum quam regionum eremi et vastitates. Tres enim tantum doctrinarum revolutiones et periodi recte numerari possunt... Neque enim causa est, ut vel Arabum vel Scholasticorum mentio fiat: qui per intermedia tempora scientias potius contriverunt numerosis tractatibus quam pondus earum auxerunt" (Bacon, *Novum Organum*, 1.78, in *Works*, 1:285–86).

25. Bacon, *Of the Advancement of Learning*, in *Works*, III:333–34.

26. Michelet, *Œuvres complètes*, VII:52, 54; Hay, *Renaissance Debate*, pp. 25–26.

27. Rogers, "Thomas Warton and the Waxing of the Middle Ages," p. 184.

28. Dryden, *Essays*, II:259, 265; Thomas Warton, *History of English Poetry*, III:409; Headley, *Select Beauties*, I:xvi; Ascham, *Scholemaster*, ed. Upton, p. iii.

29. *An Essay on Criticism*, lines 683–96, in *Poems of Alexander Pope*. See also Joseph Warton's comment on these verses: "Every custom and opinion that can degrade and deform humanity, was to be found in the times here alluded to. The most cruel tyranny, and the grossest superstition, reigned without control. Men seemed to have lost... the light of learning" (*Essay on Pope*, 1:180).

30. Oldmixon, *History of England*, p. i.

31. Winstanley, *Lives of the Most Famous English Poets*, pp. 25–26, 18; Gibbon, *Decline and Fall*, III:908; Thomas Warton, *History of English Poetry*, II:408; Collins, "An Epistle: Addrest to Sir Thomas Hanmer," lines 35–37, in *Works*.

32. *Shakespeare*, VII:81–82. Robert Anderson echoes Johnson in finding England "struggling to emerge from barbarity" (*Works of the British Poets*, II:607).

33. Johnson, "Prologue Spoken at the Opening of the Theatre in Drury-Lane, 1747," in *Poems*, p. 87.

34. Grafton, *Joseph Scaliger*, 1:25–26. See also Reynolds and Wilson, *Scribes and Scholars*, p. 120.

35. Grafton, *Joseph Scaliger*, 1:148. Jarvis comments on these surgical metaphors in *Scholars and Gentlemen*, p. 25.

36. Milton, *Of Reformation*, in *Complete Prose Works*, 1:553.

37. Wasserman, *Elizabethan Poetry in the Eighteenth Century*, p. 203.

38. Johnson, *Shakespeare*, VII:110.

39. Theobald, *Shakespeare Restored*, p. i; *Works of Shakespear*, ed. Hanmer, 1: ii; Grey, *Critical, Historical, and Explanatory Notes on Shakespeare*, 1: i; Warburton, in Smith, *Eighteenth Century Essays on Shakespeare*, p. 89. Theobald likens his textual labors to those of a physician (*Shakespeare Restored*, p. iv).

40. *Shakespeare*, VII:51–52. Ben Jonson's, by comparison, were relatively clean: Whalley points out that "a folio volume of Jonson's works was printed in his life-time, and under his own inspection" (Jonson, *Works*, ed. Peter Whalley, p. ii).

41. *Shakespeare*, VII:109–10; see also VII:106. Several modern commentators have compared Johnson's editorial practice to that of the humanists: see DeMaria, *Life of Samuel Johnson*, pp. 218–31, and Walsh, *Shakespeare, Milton, and Eighteenth-Century Literary Editing*, pp. 198–201.

42. *Shakespeare*, VII:147; *Lives*, 1:6; *Rambler*, IV:311 (no. 127). For Johnson's planned edition of Poliziano, see Boswell's *Life*, 1:89–90; Reade, *Johnsonian Gleanings*, V:100–01; Bate, *Samuel Johnson*, pp. 140–41; and DeMaria, *Life of Samuel Johnson*, p. 32. Allodoli's "Poliziano e Johnson" is a useful early survey of their relation, although its transparent Italian nationalism means it must be read with caution.

43. *Shakespeare*, VII:105.

44. *Ibid.*, VII:96.

45. Kermode, *Classic*, pp. 15–16; *Shakespeare*, VII:61.

46. P[atrick] H[ume], *Annotations on Milton's "Paradise Lost,"* in *Poetical Works of Mr. John Milton* (1695), title page. On Hume, see Erskine-Hill, "On Historical Commentary," and Walsh, "Literary Annotation and Biblical Commentary" and *Shakespeare, Milton, and Eighteenth-Century Literary Editing*, pp. 57–62. There was a tradition of scholarly commentary on Renaissance Latin scholarship: the editor of the 1738 edition of Grotius's *Rights of War and Peace* boasts that an edition came out "*cum Notis Variorum*, by which means *our Author*, within 50 Years after his Death, obtained an Honour, which was not bestow'd upon the *Ancients*, till after *many* Ages" (1: xxviii), and the 1715

editor of the same work suggests a life of Grotius allows us "to look into the Manners of *Antiquity*, and recover the Memory of *preceding* Ages" (1: i).

47. Sewell, Preface, in *Works of Shakespear*, ed. Pope, VII: vii; Anderson, *Works of the British Poets*, II:609; Haugen, "Richard Bentley," pp. 6–7. For the complicated place of classical editorial principles in Bentley's Milton, see Haugen, "Richard Bentley," pp. 275–93.

48. Ascham, *Scholemaster*, ed. Upton, p. vi; Anderson, *Works of the British Poets*, III: v, 673; IV:113, 256, 486, 527, 760.

49. Hume, *History of England*, VI:151; Thomas Warton in Milton, *Poems on Several Occasions*, p. 37.

50. See Wasserman, *Elizabethan Poetry in the Eighteenth Century*, pp. 153–91, and Curran, *Poetic Form and British Romanticism*, pp. 29–55, for the revival of the sonnet in the later eighteenth century.

51. Johnson, *Life of Cowley*, in *Lives*, 1:22. Compare Gray's "*third Italian* School, full of conceit, begun in Q: Elizabeths reign, continued under James, & Charles the first by *Donne*, Crashaw, Cleveland; carried to its height by Cowley, & ending perhaps in *Sprat*" (*Correspondence*, III:1122–24; to Thomas Warton, 15 April 1770).

52. Johnson, *Idler and Adventurer*, p. 239 (*Idler* 77); *Life of Cowley*, in *Lives*, 1:45.

53. *Miscellanies*, 1:478; Cooper, *Muses Library*, p. xii; Anderson, *Works of the British Poets*, IV:4. For a useful albeit simplistic discussion of the eighteenth-century reputation of the Metaphysical poets, see Arthur H. Nethercot, "Reputation of the 'Metaphysical Poets' during the Age of Pope" and "Reputation of the 'Metaphysical Poets' during the Age of Johnson and the 'Romantic Revival.'" On Donne in particular, see A. J. Smith, "Donne's Reputation," esp. pp. 1–9.

2 LEARNING'S TRIUMPH: HISTORICISM AND THE SPIRIT OF THE AGE

1. *Shakespeare*, VII:82. Compare Bolingbroke's fifth *Letter on the Study and Use of History*: "The truth is, nations, like men, have their infancy" (*Historical Writings*, p. 66).

2. Freedman, "Swift's Struldbruggs," p. 470, n. 16.

3. Johnson places Caxton and his contemporaries in the "infancy of learning," a phrase he often repeats: see *Idler and Adventurer*, p. 215 (*Idler* 69); *Life*, V:59; and *Shakespeare*, VII:88. As Vance notes, "To Johnson the Renaissance years saw England move from a wild, vibrant, though at times awkward and confused, adolescence to a more sophisticated and powerful, though hardly an ideal and polished, young adulthood" (*Samuel Johnson and the Sense of History*, p. 100).

4. Dryden, *Essays*, II:259.

5. Sprat, *History of the Royal Society*, p. 340; *Shakespeare*, VII:5; Thomas Warton, *History of English Poetry*, III:496; Johnson, *Observations on Macbeth*, in *Shakespeare*, VII:3.

6. Fielding, *Tom Jones*, p. 399.

7. *Shakespeare*, VII:3–4; repeated on VIII:752.

8. Stock, *Samuel Johnson and Neoclassical Dramatic Theory*, p. 142; *Shakespeare*, VII:3; Johnson, *Life of Dryden*, in *Lives*, 1:411; Lipking, "What Was It Like to Be Johnson?," p. 57, n. 21. Stock's discussion of Johnson's historicism, pp. 142–57, is the most thorough and sympathetic. Hagstrum agrees: "Johnson was as aware as any student of the literary past in his own day of the importance of historical insight for critical evaluation ... He believed that history can be of great service to criticism and that proper literary judgment can often be made only after the historian has recovered the facts upon which such judgment is based" (*Samuel Johnson's Literary Criticism*, pp. 22, 23). See also Babcock, *Genesis of Shakespeare Idolatry*, pp. 183–98, and Brownley, "Johnson and the Writing of History," p. 100.

9. Hume, "Of Refinement in the Arts," in *Essays*, p. 278; Montagu, *Essay on the Writings and Genius of Shakespear*, pp. 13–14.

10. Thomas Warton, *Observations on the Fairy Queen of Spenser*, 11:87. Warton's historicism has been often discussed. Rinaker, in "Thomas Warton and the Historical Method in Literary Criticism," argues historicism was Warton's invention; Shepard, in "Thomas Warton and the Historical Point of View in Criticism," and Miller, in "Historic Sense of Thomas Warton, Junior," provide more thorough contexts. See also Rogers, "Thomas Warton and the Waxing of the Middle Ages."

11. Marlowe, for instance, apart from brief excerpts in anthologies and editions of "The Passionate Shepherd to His Love" in 1785 and 1796, did not appear in print for the entire century: see Maclure, *Marlowe: The Critical Heritage*. Thomas Warton, one of the few who had actually read Marlowe's works, calls *Dr. Faustus* "proof of the credulous ignorance which still prevailed, and a specimen of the subjects which were then thought not improper for tragedy," but which "now only frightens children at a puppet-show in a country-town" (*History of English Poetry*, III:435, 437).

12. Johnson, "Proposals," in *Shakespeare*, VII:56; *Letters*, 1:63 (to Orrery, 9 July 1752); *Twenty of the Plays of Shakespeare*, ed. Steevens, 1:10–11; Whalley, *Enquiry into the Learning of Shakespeare*, p. iii. See also de Grazia, *Shakespeare Verbatim*, p. 112.

13. Percy, *Reliques*, 1:118; Hawkins, *Origin of the English Drama*, 1: xv, 245; *Six Old Plays*, 1: vii. Walsh discusses Capell's *School* in *Shakespeare, Milton, and Eighteenth-Century Literary Editing*, pp. 184–98.

14. Hawkins, *Life of Johnson*, in 1787 *Works*, 1:169; Ross, *Making of the English Literary Canon*, p. 241; Thomas Warton, *Observations on the Fairy Queen of Spenser*, 11:264–65. On the revaluation of such historicist research – from its dismissal as pedantry by Pope and his circle to its conquest of a place at the center of literary scholarship – see Williams, "Antiquarian Interest in Elizabethan Drama before Lamb"; Jarvis, *Scholars and Gentlemen*; and Jonathan Brody Kramnick, *Making the English Canon*, esp. pp. 84–104.

15. *Letters*, 1:81 (to Warton, 16 July 1754). Compare Todd's argument that his notes to Spenser provide "explanations arising from some attention to the

literature of the age in which Spenser lived" (*Works of Edmund Spenser*, 1: sig. A4ᵛ).

16. Sewell, quoted in Wasserman, *Elizabethan Poetry in the Eighteenth Century*, p. 13; *Shakespeare*, VII:69. Johnson's defense goes only so far: Shakespeare "sacrifices virtue to convenience," and "this fault the barbarity of his age cannot extenuate" (*Shakespeare*, VII:71).

17. Sewell, "Essay," in *Works of Shakespear*, ed. Alexander Pope, VII: ii.

18. *Shakespeare*, VII:82, 35; VIII:703; VII:49. Hanmer likewise reminds us that "he wrote for the Stage, rude and unpolished as it then was" (in Smith, *Eighteenth Century Essays on Shakespeare*, p. 86).

19. Grey, *Critical, Historical, and Explanatory Notes on Shakespeare*, 1: vii. Compare Theobald, who regrets that we must "content ourselves to be sorry for the *Levity* of the Author's *Pen*, or the *Vice* of the Times that forc'd him to bring in such *bald Witticisms*" (*Shakespeare Restored*, p. 135).

20. Whalley, *Enquiry into the Learning of Shakespeare*, p. 17. Walpole does the same in defending the apocryphal original of his *Otranto*: "Belief in every kind of prodigy was so established in those dark ages, that an author would not be faithful to the *manners* of the times who should omit all mention of them. He is not bound to believe them himself, but he must represent his actors as believing them" (*Castle of Otranto*, p. 4).

21. Cooper, *Muses Library*, pp. xi, 33; Duff, *Critical Observations*, p. 194; Johnson, Dedication to *Shakespear Illustrated*, in *Shakespeare*, VII:49. Thomas Warton agrees: see his *History of English Poetry*, III:494.

22. *Shakespeare*, VII:122, 3, 5, 82, 23.

23. *Ibid.*, VII:123; "Prologue Spoken at the Opening of the Theatre in Drury-Lane, 1747," lines 1–2, in *Poems*.

24. Whalley, *Enquiry into the Learning of Shakespeare*, p. 72. Compare Rymer: under Henry VII, "new Schemes of Navigation are devis'd, new Searches made, new Land, new Seas, another *World*, another *Indies* are found out" (*Foedera*, XII: sig. A1ᵛ–A2ʳ).

25. Thomas Warton, *History of English Poetry*, III:414, 407.

26. *Life*, III:17; Thomas Warton, *History of English Poetry*, III:491.

27. Hurd, *Moral and Political Dialogues*, in *Works*, III:236; Walpole, *Castle of Otranto*, p. 3.

28. Thomas Warton, *History of English Poetry*, III:431, 432, 423; Hume, *History of England*, III:95, 138.

29. Thomas Warton, *History of English Poetry*, III:408, 420, 432, 421. Similar phrases echo throughout the *History*: "the pedantries of a barbarous theology" (III:412); "monkish pedantry" (III:414).

30. *Ibid.*, III:421; *Observations on the Fairy Queen of Spenser*, II:106–7.

31. See Huizinga, *Men and Ideas*, p. 277.

32. Hume, *History of England*, III:81. Weisinger notes that "the text-book misconception in regard to the taking of Constantinople originates in the latter part of the seventeenth century" ("Study of the Revival of Learning in England from Bacon to Hallam," p. 228).

33. Thomas Warton, *History of English Poetry*, III:419, 408n.

34. Johnson, *Journey to the Western Islands of Scotland*, p. 15.
35. 1825 *Works*, VI:504–5.
36. *Irene*, IV.i.116–23, in *Poems*.
37. Thomas Warton, *History of English Poetry*, III:426–28.
38. "Life of Erasmus," in *Twenty Two Select Colloquies* (1725), sig. A7ᵛ.
39. Thomas Warton, *History of English Poetry*, III:417. France, it is worth noting, is often excluded in such catalogues. Italy led the pack; Spanish and Dutch humanists accounted for most of the remainder.
40. *Shakespeare*, VII:81–82.
41. Anderson, *Works of the British Poets*, I:591; Thomas Warton, *History of English Poetry*, III:421–26; Gray, *Correspondence*, III:1123–24 (to Thomas Warton, 15 April 1770); Thomas Warton, *History of English Poetry*, III:495.
42. *Life*, I:57.
43. For the edition of Poliziano, see above, chapter 1; for De Thou, see *Life*, IV:410.
44. Stephen, *Samuel Johnson*, p. 172; Houston, *Dr. Johnson*, p. 8. For a more thorough discussion of Johnson's affinities with Renaissance scholarship, see Korshin, "Johnson and the Scholars."
45. *Life*, IV:20; *Rambler*, III:198 (no. 36); *Life of A. Philips*, in *Lives*, III:317; *Rambler*, III:280 (no. 57), V:166 (no. 176), IV:125 (no. 92), III:161 (no. 29), III:157 (no. 28). On Clenardus, see Korshin, "Johnson and the Scholars," p. 52.
46. *Rambler*, III:20 (no. 4); *Life of Smith*, in *Lives*, II:19; *Idler and Adventurer*, p. 231 (*Idler* 74). The poem likening his dictionary to Scaliger's appears, with Baldwin's commentary, in *Latin and Greek Poems*, pp. 75–86; see also *Shakespeare*, VII:110, 147. The best treatment of Johnson's reading in Scaliger is Houston, *Dr. Johnson*, pp. 31–32.
47. *Voyage to Abyssinia*, p. 237 (the phrase is Johnson's, and does not appear in Lobo's original); he is likewise called "one of the greatest Men in *Europe*" by his 1715 and 1738 editors (*Rights of War and Peace*, I: iii). Gibbon calls him "a man of genius and learning, who preserved his moderation amidst the fury of contending sects" (*Decline and Fall*, I:580).
48. Grotius routinely shows up in catalogues of seventeenth-century names in many works on Johnson, but the references are nearly always in passing. The most extended treatment is DeMaria's, in *Samuel Johnson and the Life of Reading*, pp. 116–21. For Johnson's attempted reading of *De veritate religionis Christianae*, see *Miscellanies*, I:157, and Quinlan, *Samuel Johnson: A Layman's Religion*, p. 50; for his assertion that "he would change with nobody but Hugo Grotius," see Piozzi, *Thraliana*, I:377; for his support of Grotius's descendant, see *Letters*, III:39. Other relevant passages include *Life*, I:398, 454; V:89; and *Miscellanies*, II:297.
49. See, for instance, Grotius, *Rights of War and Peace*, I.iii.9 on political subordination ("The greatest confusion must follow, if under pretence of promoting good or averting evil measures, the people might struggle for the Prince's jurisdiction: a turbulent state of affairs, which no sober minded people ever

wished to experience"); 11.xxii.9 on colonization ("The title and right by discovery can apply only to countries and places, that have no owner"); and 11.xxii.12 on slavery ("There is equal injustice in the desire of reducing, by force of arms, any people to a state of servitude... Every reasonable creature ought to be left free in the choice of what may be deemed useful or prejudicial to him").

50. *Life*, 1:99, IV:524; *Rambler*, IV:214. See *Latin and Greek Poems*, p. 78, for more on Johnson's attitude toward Erasmus.

51. DeMaria suggests as much when he calls Johnson's "opposition to bloody battle" "a legacy of European humanism" (*Life of Samuel Johnson*, p. 253). On Erasmus's pacificism, see Jortin's *Life of Erasmus*, 1:47. Grotius, too, may have influenced Johnson's anti-war sentiment: see Kilbourne, "Dr. Johnson and War." The best discussion of Johnson and Erasmus is Mansfield, *Man on His Own*, pp. 93–96.

52. *Rambler*, IV:247. The most pertinent passage in *Utopia* is pp. 72–75, which provides sources and analogues for Hythlodaeus's position.

53. Grove, *History of Cardinal Wolsey*, 1:351.

54. Swift, *Gulliver's Travels*, in *Prose Works*, XI:196.

55. For the edition of Ascham published under Bennet's name, see Hazen, in *Samuel Johnson's Prefaces and Dedications*, pp. 20–21, and Brack, "Samuel Johnson Edits for the Booksellers." Ascham's reputation was great in eighteenth-century Britain; see, for instance, *Scholemaster*, ed. Upton, p. iii.

56. *Letters*, 11:48; *Prefaces and Dedications*, p. 23; *Life of Milton*, in *Lives*, 1:87; *Life of Ascham*, in 1825 *Works*, VI:517, 519.

57. *Life of Milton*, in *Lives*, 1:99, 88; *Dictionary*, s.v. *fond*, n.s. 1; *Miscellanies*, 1:159; *Life*, 1:526. See also *Life*, 1:144, 2:157, and "On School Chastisement," in 1825 *Works*, VI:467–68.

58. *Life*, 11:121, 440; *Letters*, 111:201 (to James Boswell, 27 October 1779), by way of *Life*, 111:415.

59. See Brack, "Samuel Johnson Edits for the Booksellers."

60. *Life*, 1:221–22, 308. See also Arthur Murphy, *Essay on the Life and Genius of Samuel Johnson*, in *Miscellanies*, 1:467.

61. Johnson, "Life of Browne," in 1825 *Works*, VI:485–86, 475, 499.

3 CALL BRITANNIA'S GLORIES BACK TO VIEW: TUDOR HISTORY AND HANOVERIAN HISTORIANS

1. Johnson, *Thoughts Concerning Falkland's Islands*, in *Political Writings*, p. 374.

2. Johnson, *London*, lines 21–28, in *Poems*.

3. Butterfield, for instance, rushes from the Renaissance to the nineteenth century in four pages, most of that on the Göttingen School (*Man on His Past*).

4. Smalley, for example, comments on the medieval historian's ability to "converse with Adam and Eve or Julius Caesar or Charlemagne as though they were neighbours," and contrasts it with the great development of the

Renaissance: "The humanists did not 'rediscover the past'...What they did was to discover the past *as* past" (*Historians in the Middle Ages*, pp. 192, 193).

5. Meinecke, *Historism*, p. lv.
6. Levine, *Humanism and History*, p. 74. See also pp. 99 and 155.
7. *Ibid.*, p. 192.
8. Johnson, *Idler and Adventurer*, pp. 431 (*Adventurer* 99) and 425 (*Adventurer* 95). "In nearly all the provinces of thought in the Enlightenment," writes Lovejoy, "the ruling assumption was that Reason... is the same in all men and equally possessed by all" (*The Great Chain of Being*, p. 288).
9. Barbauld, "On the Uses of History," in *Legacy for Young Ladies*, p. 121.
10. Hume, *Enquiry concerning Human Understanding*, p. 83. Hume acknowledges his debt to Renaissance historiography, admitting that his *History* was influenced by "all the best of the historians... among the moderns, such as Matchiavel, Fra paolo, Davila, Bentivoglio" (*Letters*, 1:284).
11. Sprat, *History of the Royal Society*, pp. 43–44.
12. For a discussion of Temple's planned history, see Levine, *Humanism and History*, p. 166.
13. Bolingbroke, *Historical Writings*, pp. 66, 64, 69.
14. Smollett, *Complete History of England*, 1: sig. A1ᵛ.
15. *Monsieur de Thou's History of His Own Time*, 1: sig. A1ʳ–A2ʳ.
16. *Rambler*, IV:288–89 (no. 122). On Johnson's supposed hostility to history, see Macaulay's 1831 review of Croker's Boswell: "History was, in his opinion... an old almanack: historians could, as he conceived, claim no higher dignity than that of almanack-makers; and his favourite historians were those who, like Lord Hailes, aspired to no higher dignity" (*Works*, VIII:107).
17. *Shakespeare*, VII:68. He makes the same point about his own essays in literary history: "To adjust the minute events of literary history is tedious and troublesome; it requires indeed no great force of understanding" (*Life of Dryden*, in *Lives*, 1: 368).
18. *Life of Milton*, in *Lives*, 1: 99–100.
19. He borrows a citation of Holinshed from Charlotte Lennox: see *Shakespeare*, VII:452, and cf. Sherbo, *Samuel Johnson, Editor of Shakespeare*, p. 90. He did, however, own a copy of Hall's *Union of the Noble and Illustre Families* at the time of his death. See Greene, *Samuel Johnson's Library*, p. 64.
20. Rapin, *History of England*, VI:246–47.
21. Gray, "The Bard," lines 85, 83n., and lines 51–60, in *Complete Poems*.
22. The exception is Walpole, who was at least a serious dabbler in the history of the Middle Ages. See below.
23. Mossner refers to Hume's *History* as "a popular classic within the lifetime of its author," the "work that made Hume's name familiar to all who could read" (*Life of David Hume*, p. 302).
24. Collins, "An Epistle: Addrest to Sir Thomas Hanmer," lines 77–81, in *Works*.
25. *Lives*, III:114.
26. *Shakespeare*, VII:453.

27. Grove, *History of Cardinal Wolsey*, 1:24; Rapin, *History of England*, VI:240; Lindsay, *Brief History of England*, p. 152; Gray, "The Bard," lines 93–94, in *Complete Poems*.

28. Rapin, *History of England*, VI:240, 242. Buc's *History* was first published in 1646; it was reprinted in 1719 in White Kennett's *Complete History of England*.

29. Walpole, *Historic Doubts on the Life and Reign of Richard III*, in Kendall, *Richard III: The Great Debate*, pp. 154–59.

30. Adam Smith, *Wealth of Nations*, 1:201–2, 205–6.

31. Hume, *History of England*, III:81–82. Victor Wexler notes that "The distinction between modern and medieval history, that is, between accessible, instructive history and obscure, myth-ridden history, was becoming standard historical periodization at this point" (*David Hume and the History of England*, p. 46).

32. Hume, *Letters*, 1:249 (to Andrew Millar, May 1757). He writes in another letter, "It is really the Commencement of modern History" (1:251; to William Strahan, 1757). The sentiment has not gone away: a school text of 1928, for instance, states bluntly that "with the reign of Henry VII (1485–1509) we approach the modern era" (Lunt, *History of England*, p. 309).

33. Bolingbroke, *Historical Writings*, pp. 81–83.

34. Hume, *History of England*, III:82.

35. *Shakespeare*, VIII:607.

36. Lindsay, *Brief History of England*, pp. 184–85.

37. Smollett, *Complete History of England*, II:658.

38. Hume, *History of England*, III:321.

39. Trevor-Roper, *Queen Elizabeth's First Historian*, p. 37, n. 15.

40. Birch, *Memoirs of the Reign of Queen Elizabeth*, 1:1.

41. Hume, *History of England*, IV:4; Rapin, *History of England*, IX:220.

42. Burnet, *History of the Reformation*, II:421; Johnson, *Introduction to the Political State of Great Britain*, in *Political Writings*, pp. 130, 374.

43. Swift, *Discourse of the Contests and Dissentions between the Nobles and the Commons in Athens and Rome*, p. 119; Lyttelton, *Letters from a Persian*, p. 188; Hume, *History of England*, IV:355. See also Swift's sermon of 30 January 1725–26: "In the reign of . . . Charles the Martyr, the power and prerogative of the king were much greater than they are in our times, and so had been for at least 700 years before" (*Prose Works*, IX:220).

44. Hume, *History of England*, IV:124; D'Avenant, *Essays upon Peace at Home, and War Abroad*, p. 180.

45. Gerrard, *Patriot Opposition to Walpole*, p. 151. See also Weisinger, "Seventeenth-Century Reputation of the Elizabethans," p. 15.

46. Hume, *History of England*, IV:8–9.

47. Lyttelton, *Letters from a Persian*, p. 187; D'Avenant, *Essays upon Peace and Home, and War Abroad*, p. 180. Rolt shares Lyttelton's surprise: "Rare in all ages hath been the reign of a woman, more rare the felicity of a woman in her reign, but most rare is a permanency joined with that felicity" (*Lives of the Principal Reformers*, p. 196).

48. Hume, *History of England*, IV:353, 5; Lindsay, *Brief History of England*, p. 236; Thomas Warton, *History of English Poetry*, III:493.

49. *Life*, IV:13. Such was, of course, a commonplace even in Elizabeth's day. Thomas Warton agrees with this estimation of her learning: "Every young lady of fashion was carefully instituted in classical letters: and the daughter of a duchess was taught, not only to distil strong waters, but to construe Greek. Among the learned females of high distinction, queen Elisabeth herself was the most conspicuous" (*History of English Poetry*, III:491). Hume observes that "Even the ladies of the court valued themselves on knowledge," and adduces both Elizabeth and Lady Jane Grey as examples (*History of England*, IV:385; III:402). Likewise the *Biographia Britannica* on Lady Jane Grey: "This excellent Lady . . . became wonderfully learned in the Latin and Greek tongues, reading in the latter with great ease and pleasure, the most sublime and difficult authors" (I:310). See also Rapin's *History of England*, VIII:116.

50. Thomas Warton, *History of English Poetry*, III:490; Hurd, *Moral and Political Dialogues*, in *Works*, III:209.

51. Hurd, *Moral and Political Dialogues*, in *Works*, III:274, 247–48.

52. Johnson, review of William Tytler's *Historical and Critical Enquiry*, in 1825 *Works*, VI:81; see also *Life*, I:354.

53. Quisquilius's preposterous antiquarianism in *Rambler* 182, for instance, gets some of its absurdity from his "equal veneration for the ruff of Elizabeth and the shoe of Mary of Scotland" (*Rambler*, IV:69). The word "equal" suggests that the veneration of trivial secular relics is only part of his problem: more serious is his inability to recognize the moral stakes in that dispute. For Johnson's opinion of Mary Queen of Scots, see Vance, "Johnson's Historical Reviews," pp. 75–78, and Jayne Elizabeth Lewis, "Mary Stuart's 'Fatal Box,'" esp. pp. 441–65. Lewis provides the most thorough discussion of Mary Stuart's reputation in the eighteenth century; see also O'Brien, *Narratives of Enlightenment*, pp. 114–22.

54. Rapin, *History of England*, IX:223; Smollett, *Complete History of England*, III:93, 132; Hume, *History of England*, IV:70; Hurd, *Works*, III:247–48.

55. Rapin, *History of England*, IX:225. Compare "Palæophilus Anglicanus": "She *was born* for the Glory of *England*, and *Reign'd* for an *Example* to all *succeeding Kings*" (*Conduct of Queen Elizabeth*, p. 39).

56. Addison, *Freeholder*, p. 219 (no. 41).

57. *Ibid.*, pp. 142, 144 (no. 25).

58. Bowers discusses such comparisons between Anne and Elizabeth in *Politics of Motherhood*, pp. 65–73.

59. See Gerrard, *Patriot Opposition to Walpole*, p. 153.

60. Manley, *Modest Enquiry*, pp. 16, 4, 17, 10–11.

61. Boyer, *History of the Reign of Queen Anne*, I:162; Speck, *Birth of Britain*, pp. 34–35. See also David Green, *Queen Anne*, p. 111. Anne was not the only one to use monarchical ceremonies as opportunities to draw connections between the past and present. The traditional accession anniversary service had been allowed to lapse during Charles II's reign, but James II restored

that of Elizabeth. William III used the "Gunpowder Treason" service to mark his own arrival in England. See Cuming, *History of Anglican Liturgy*, pp. 168–69.

62. Philips, "The Sixth Pastoral," lines 43–44, in *Poems*. Compare also "The Third Pastoral," lines 4–12.

63. Gay, *Poetry and Prose*, 1:90.

64. Prior, "An Ode, Humbly Inscrib'd to the Queen," lines 11–14, 21–24, in *Literary Works*.

65. Pope, *Windsor-Forest*, lines 325–28, in *Poems*.

66. Brower, *Alexander Pope: The Poetry of Allusion*, pp. 51–52.

67. Carretta observes, "Pope praises Anne by identifying her with Elizabeth, thus balancing the blame given William III. This reference to Elizabeth–Anne also would mark the return of the classical historical cycle to the immemorial Constitution" ("Anne and Elizabeth," p. 430).

68. Johnson's sincerity in recommending the country over the city has long been in question: few readers are able to reconcile such a sentiment with Johnson's famous *obiter dictum*, "When a man is tired of London, he is tired of life." Weinbrot, however, both dismisses the relevance of Johnson's sincerity and reminds us that the famous phrase comes from "the secure and settled Johnson" (*Formal Strain*, p. 168).

69. Greene, who calls *London* "a stridently political versification of the polemic stock-in-trade of the 'patriot' opposition to Walpole" (in Johnson, *Political Writings*, p. xxvi), gives the best reading of the poem as an Opposition satire, and points out the importance of the age of Elizabeth in *Politics of Samuel Johnson*, pp. 88–92.

70. *London*, lines 23–28, in *Poems*.

71. "Palæophilus Anglicanus," *Conduct of Queen Elizabeth*, p. 31.

72. Gerrard, *Patriot Opposition to Walpole*, p. 150. See also Isaac Kramnick, "Augustan Politics and English Historiography."

73. Gerrard, *Patriot Opposition to Walpole*, pp. 155–56. See also Hagstrum, *Sister Arts*, p. 258.

74. Hume, *History of England*, iv:260–71; Smollett, *Complete History of England*, iii:97.

4 THE RAGE OF REFORMATION: RELIGIOUS CONTROVERSY AND POLITICAL STABILITY

1. Strype, *Annals of the Reformation*, sig. A2^r, (a)1^r; Burnet, *History of the Reformation*, iii: sig. A2^r.

2. *Shakespeare*, vii:5; Dedication to Lindsay's *Evangelical History*, in *Prefaces and Dedications*, p. 124.

3. Stuart, *History of the Establishment of the Reformation*, p. 2.

4. Hume, *History of England*, iii:134; Smollett, *Complete History of England*, ii:599; Hume, *History of England*, iii:253.

5. Hume, *History of England*, iii:190; Strype, *Annals of the Reformation*, p. 158; *Biographia Britannica*, 1:143–44.

6. Smollett, *Complete History of England*, 11:613; Grey, *Critical, Historical, and Explanatory Notes on Shakespeare*, 11:90; James Thomson, *Summer*, lines 1488–90, in *Complete Poetical Works*; Hume, *History of England*, 111:222.

7. Hume, *History of England*, 111:435.

8. Oldmixon, *Critical History*, 1:114; Oldmixon, *History of England*, p. 293; Hume, *History of England*, 111:407; Smollett, *Complete History of England*, 11:688, 708. Compare Gilbert Stuart, who refers to Mary as "that furious bigot" (*History of the Establishment of the Reformation*, p. 77), and Rapin, who writes of "the excessive Bigotry of Queen *Mary*" (*History of England*, VIII:215).

9. *Acts and Monuments* was remarkably popular throughout the century. Its first appearance after 1700 was in an abridged edition illustrated with copperplates, "revised and corrected by an impartial hand," in 1732, often reprinted. Another abridged illustrated edition appeared in 1746, after which came a two-volume version "rendered into modern English" in 1747–48. In 1761, another set of selections appeared in Edinburgh, and in 1784 Alexander Hogg published *The New and Complete Book of Martyrs*, with a second edition in the next year, a third in 1790, an expanded two-volume New York edition in 1794, and a new London edition "embellished with near 300 elegant engravings" in 1795 and again in 1800. In 1795 came *The New Book of Martyrs in Quarto*, also with illustrations.

10. Hume, *History of England*, 111:436. His catalogue is entirely conventional; see, for instance, Rapin's *History of England*, VIII:182–83, 196, 212–13.

11. Smollett, *Complete History of England*, 11:699.

12. Anderson, *Life of Sackville*, in *Works of the British Poets*, 1:651.

13. Johnson, *Journey to the Western Islands of Scotland*, p. 159; *Life*, 11:105; Johnson, *Sermons*, p. 76. Boswell never knew what to make of Johnson's declaration that he was "no great enemy to the Roman Catholick religion": see *Life*, 1:465; 11:103–4, 150; 111:407; IV:288–89; and V:71. Johnson does, however, criticize monastical institutions for their disengagement from the world (*Rambler*, V:290 [no. 203]), and recounts at least one story of Catholic persecution when he refers to "Anne Askew, one of the first sufferers for the Protestant Religion, who in the time of Henry VIII was tortured in the Tower" (*Life of Sheffield*, in *Lives*, 11:171).

14. Swift, *Tale of a Tub*, pp. 136–38.

15. Johnson, *Journey to the Western Islands of Scotland*, pp. 122, 6; *Life*, V:61; Johnson, *Journey to the Western Islands of Scotland*, p. 6.

16. Hawkins, *Life of Samuel Johnson*, in 1787 *Works*, 1:474; Smollett, *Complete History of England*, 111:144; *Biographia Britannica*, 1:311; Stuart, *History of the Establishment of the Reformation*, pp. 114–19, 86.

17. Lockman, *New History of England*, p. 142.

18. Hooker, *Laws*, 1:300 (IV.viii.3).

19. Strype, *Annals of the Reformation*, p. 568.

20. Swift, *Prose Works*, IX:172; Lindsay, *Brief History of England*, p. 227.

21. Rapin, *History of England*, VIII:20–21; Strype, *Annals of the Reformation*, p. 41, marginal note.

22. Hume, *History of England*, III:243.
23. Pope, "The First Satire of the Second Book of Horace," line 66, in *Poems*; Mansfield, *Phoenix of His Age*, pp. 264–65.
24. Rolt, *Lives of the Principal Reformers*, p. 47. He adds: "He lived somewhat like a Papist; but died more like a Protestant" (p. 48).
25. Jortin, *Life of Erasmus*, 1:21; cf. 1:52–53, 60–63, 71–72. Jortin follows Jean Le Clerc in this; his *Life* amounts to an augmented translation of Le Clerc's earlier biography of Erasmus.
26. *Twenty Two Select Colloquies*, sig. A2ᵛ. Zwingli, Oecolampadius, and Bucer were other Continental reformers the English were pleased to adopt; Rolt notes that "Zuinglius conducted the reformation in Switzerland with as much progress as Luther conducted that in Saxony; though he carried himself with more moderation and prudence" (*Lives of the Principal Reformers*, p. 54), and that both "Zuinglius and Oecolampadius were more esteemed by the learned men of their time, than any other of the reformers; because they had more moderation" (p. 58). Bucer is "the Moderate Reformer" (p. 87). Burnet too praises Bucer: "He was a very learned, judicious, pious, and moderate Person . . . *Melancthon* and he . . . may be ranked a-part by themselves" (*History of the Reformation*, II:164).
27. Landa, in Swift, *Prose Works*, IX:119; Burke, "On a Motion for Leave to Bring a Bill to Repeal and Alter Certain Acts Respecting Religious Opinions" (i.e., "Speech on the Petition of the Unitarians"), in *Works*, VI:115; Middleton, *Dissertation on the Power of the Church*, p. 21. Compare Lindsay's *Brief History of England*, sig. a4ᵛ.
28. Hume, *History of England*, IV:124, 70; Manley, *Modest Enquiry*, pp. 10–11.
29. Hooker, *Faithful Abridgment*, sig. A3ʳ, A2ʳ⁻ᵛ, A1ᵛ.
30. "Gibson," *Memoirs of Queen Anne*, pp. 1–3.
31. *Protestant Memorial*, pp. 8–9.
32. Dickens provides useful historical background in *English Reformation*, p. 78.
33. Pope, *An Essay on Man*, III.305, in *Poems*; Smollett, *Complete History of England*, II:658; Hume, *History of England*, III:366, 224.
34. Grotius, *Truth of the Christian Religion*, sig. a2ᵛ–a3ʳ. Compare Oldmixon, *Critical History*, 1:140. Compare Swift: "Men should consider, that raising Difficulties concerning the Mysteries in Religion, cannot make them more wise, learned, or virtuous; better Neighbours, or Friends, or more serviceable to their Country" (*Prose Works*, IX:166–67).
35. Burnet, *Exposition of the Thirty-nine Articles*, pp. iii–iv. For things indifferent, see pp. vii–x. See also his *History of the Reformation*, III:305–6.
36. Hooker, *Faithful Abridgment*, sig. A2ʳ.
37. Locke, *Epistola de tolerantia*, p. 102:

Dices: Anne igitur negabis, quae ab omnibus conceditur, magistratui in res adiaphoras potestatem, quae si auferatur, nulla restabit legum ferendarum materia? . . . Si quid ex usu reipublicae non fuerit, utcunque sit res indifferens, non potest ilico lege sanciri. Res utcunque sua natura indifferentes extra magistratus jurisdictionem positae sunt, cum in ecclesiam et cultum divinum transferuntur, quia illo in usu nullam habent cum rebus civilibus connectionem.

38. Hooker, *Laws*, 1:245 (III.x.7); 1:29 (Preface 6.1).
39. Hudson, *Samuel Johnson and Eighteenth-Century Thought*, p. 215.
40. See Kaminski, *Early Career of Samuel Johnson*, pp. 67–76; McAdam, "Johnson's Lives of Sarpi, Blake, and Drake"; and Chapple, "Samuel Johnson's *Proposals for Printing the History of the Council of Trent* [1738]."
41. *Letters*, 1:156. See Tankard, " 'That Great Literary Projector.' "
42. See Osborn, "Johnson on the Sanctity of an Author's Text," p. 929.
43. Hawkins was the first to reckon Johnson's debts to sixteenth- and seventeenth-century divines: see his *Life of Johnson*, in 1787 *Works*, 1:271, 463, 504, 542. For more modern assessments, see Hagstrum and Gray, in Johnson, *Sermons*, pp. xlv–xlvi; Chapin, *Religious Thought of Samuel Johnson*, p. 70; and Quinlan, *Samuel Johnson: A Layman's Religion*, pp. 154–57. My own essay, "Johnson and Hooker on Civil and Ecclesiastical Polity," is forthcoming in *The Review of English Studies*.
44. Johnson, *Sermons*, p. 77.
45. *Life of Milton*, in *Lives*, 1:155; *Life*, V:71, 391; II:187.
46. DeMaria sees in Johnson "an acknowledgment that civil government depends on moral and religious government to such an extent that politics cannot satisfactorily be pursued apart from theology. This connection is most explicit in Hooker" ("Politics of Johnson's *Dictionary*," p. 69).
47. *Life*, II:126.
48. Hooker, *Laws*, 1:140 (I.xvi.6). See also Hooker's argument that "better it was . . . that sometime an erroneous sentence should prevaile . . . then that strifes should have respit to growe, and not come speedily unto some ende" (*Laws*, 1:31 [Preface 6.3]).
49. *Life of Milton*, in *Lives*, 1:114; Hooker, *Laws*, 1:56 (I.i.1).
50. *Life*, IV:426.
51. Hawkins, *Life of Johnson*, in 1787 *Works*, 1:463, 163; Johnson, "Life of Browne," in 1825 *Works*, VI:497; *Sermons*, p. 30; *Life*, II:124; Hooker, *Laws*, 1:85 (I.viii.5); *Laws*, 1:59 (I.ii.2); Chambers, *Course of Lectures*, 1:84. Compare Swift: "It would be well, if People would not lay so much Weight on their own Reason in Matters of Religion, as to think every thing impossible and absurd which they cannot conceive . . . The *Reason* of every particular Man is weak and wavering" (*Prose Works*, IX:166).
52. *Life*, II:254.
53. *Ibid.*, 1:405; 1825 *Works*, VI:502.
54. *Life of Milton*, in *Lives*, 1:108.
55. Johnson, Introduction to the *Harleian Miscellany* (i.e., "An Essay on the Origin and Importance of Small Tracts and Fugitive Pieces"), in *Prefaces and Dedications*, p. 57; *Life*, II:249; Swift, *Prose Works*, IX:151. See also Swift's sermon of 30 January 1725–26: "If [a man's] religion be different from that of his country, and the government think fit to tolerate it . . . he ought to be fully satisfied, and give no offence, by writing or discourse, to the worship established" (*Prose Works*, IX:227).
56. Strype, *Annals of the Reformation*, p. 582.

57. *Dictionary*, s.v. *confessor, orthodoxly*, and *soundly*. Johnson refers to Bacon's "*Advice of Villiers.*"
58. *Life*, 11:150–51. Johnson likewise tells Boswell,

> "Predestination was a part of the clamour of the times, so it is mentioned in our articles, but with as little positiveness as could be." BOSWELL. "Is it necessary, Sir, to believe all the thirty-nine articles?" JOHNSON. "Why, Sir, that is a question which has been much agitated. Some have thought it necessary that they should all be believed; others have considered them to be only articles of peace, that is to say, you are not to preach against them." (*Life*, 11:104)

5 THE GROUND-WORK OF STILE: LANGUAGE AND NATIONAL IDENTITY

1. *Dictionary*, 1: sig. C2^r.
2. *Ibid.*, 1: sig. C1^r.
3. McAdam briefly notes their relationship in "Inkhorn Words Before Dr. Johnson," p. 205.
4. Davie, *Purity of Diction in English Verse*, p. 30.
5. Aristotle, *Ars Rhetorica*, 3.2.1–3; Horace, *Serm.* 2.1, in *Opera*; Cicero, *De Oratore*, 1.144, 2.153, in *Rhetorica*; Quintilian, *Institutionis oratoriae*, 1.5.5 and 12.10.10–39. See also Croll, " 'Attic Prose' in the Seventeenth Century," in *Style, Rhetoric, and Rhythm*, p. 85 and n., and Scott, *Controversies over the Imitation of Cicero*, 1:3–9.
6. Dante, *De Vulgari Eloquentia*, 1.xvii.3 ("Magistratu quidem sublimatum videtur, cum de tot rudibus Latinorum vocabulis, de tot perplexis constructionibus, de tot defectivis prolationibus, de tot rusticanis accentibus"), in *Opere Minori*, 11:132.
7. Ascham, *Scholemaster*, in *English Works*, ed. Wright, pp. 185, 265; Campion, *Art of English Poesie*, in *Works*, p. 293.
8. Vives, *De causis corruptarum artium*, 2.5 ("qui eam primi mendaciis corruperint, et cur?," p. 310) and 2.2 ("eo tempore, quum a populo peti poterat usus certissimus magister sermonis, ut Quintiliani tempore, etiam Tullii, et usus prave loquentium plerumque analogia refellebatur," p. 274); Scaliger, *Poetices*, 5.2 ("ita in Poete pectus multa sese insinuant: non omnia sunt admittenda," p. 214).
9. Edward Phillips, *New World of English Words*, sig. b3^r.
10. For Erasmus's attitudes toward Ciceronianism, see Scott, *Controversies over the Imitation of Cicero*, 1:24–41; the Introduction to *Ciceronianus*, in *Collected Works of Erasmus*, XXVIII:324–41; Margaret Mann Phillips, "Erasmus and the Classics," pp. 22–25; and D. F. S. Thomson, "Latinity of Erasmus," pp. 121–24.
11. Dolet, *Dialogus de imitatione Ciceroniana*, pp. 54–55; Camerarius, ed. of the *Tusculan Disputations*, cited in Scott, *Controversies over the Imitation of Cicero*, 1:103. Scott's is still the standard account in English of Renaissance Ciceronianism; see also Kristeller, *Renaissance Thought*, p. 143, n. 17. The first study of

Ciceronian imitation appeared in the eighteenth century: Jean Lévesque de Burigny's *Sur la querelle qui s'eleva dans le* XVIe *siècle au suject de l'estime qui était due à Cicéron.*

12. Terence, *Eunuchus*, Prologue, 41, in *Comoediae.* In this spirit, see the full title of Robert Estienne's *Dictionarium, seu latinae linguae thesaurus, non singulas modo dictiones contenens, sed integros quoque latine et loquendi et scribendi formulas, ex Catone, Cicerone, Plinio, Avunculo, Terentio, Varrone, Livio, Plinio Secundo, Virgilio, Caesare, Columella, Plauto, Martiale.*

13. Croll writes, "The defect of the Anti-Ciceronian movement before 1575 was its failure to offer a program of literary imitation in exchange for the one that it attacked... For it was not until it had learned to suggest other models for imitation in place of Cicero and Isocrates... that the Anti-Ciceronian movement became a positive force" (*Style, Rhetoric, and Rhythm*, p. 145).

14. Cortesi, cited in Scott, *Controversies over the Imitation of Cicero*, 1:19; *Ciceronianus*, in *Collected Works of Erasmus*, XXVIII:390. For such statements, the anonymous translator of the 1725 *Colloquies* calls Erasmus "one of the chief *Restorers* of the Purity of the *Latin* Tongue on this side the *Alpes*" (sig. A3^r).

15. C. S. Lewis, *English Literature in the Sixteenth Century*, p. 21.

16. For Johnson's knowledge of Renaissance linguistic theory, see DeMaria, *Life of Samuel Johnson*, p. 103, and Korshin, "Johnson and the Renaissance Dictionary."

17. *Rambler*, V:318–19 (no. 208).

18. Sprat, *History of the Royal Society*, pp. 112, 413; Evelyn, letters to Samuel Pepys (1689) and Sir Peter Wyche (1665), in Spingarn, *Critical Essays of the Seventeenth Century*, 11:328 and 311. See also Williamson, *Senecan Amble*, pp. 301–6.

19. Sprat, *History of the Royal Society*, p. 113. Pellisson-Fontanier too has linguistic purity in mind when he discusses the founding of the Academie Françoise: Richelieu "a eû un si grand succez de cette institution, qu'il a vû la langue Françoise abondamment purifiée" (*Histoire de l'Academie Françoise*, pp. 4–5).

20. Swift, *Proposal for Correcting, Improving and Ascertaining the English Tongue*, in *Prose Works*, IV:6, 10; Defoe, *True-Born Englishman*, p. 12.

21. Campbell, *Philosophy of Rhetoric*, pp. 170, 172–75, 177. Compare Blair: "Purity, is the use of such words, and such constructions, as belong to the idiom of the Language which we speak; in opposition to words and phrases that are imported from other Languages, or that are obsolete, or new-coined, or used without proper authority" (*Lectures on Rhetoric and Belles Lettres*, 1:236). For a discussion of Campbell's influence, see Stern, "Concept of Linguistic Purity," p. 48.

22. Stern, "Concept of Linguistic Purity," p. 95.

23. Ascham, *English Works*, ed. Wright, p. 286; Dryden, "Defence of the Epilogue," in *Works*, XI:204–5; Swift, *Prose Works*, IV:9–10.

24. Pope, *Essay on Criticism*, line 483, in *Poems*. Compare Benjamin Martin: "Addison, Pope, and Foster, may appear to our posterity in the same light as Chaucer, Spencer, and Shakespear do to us; whose language is now grown old and obsolete; read by very few, and understood by antiquarians only" (*Institutions of Language*, p. 111).

25. Swift, *Prose Works*, II:174; IV:8–9.
26. Swift, *Prose Works*, IV:10; Chesterfield, letter to *The World*, in Boulton, *Johnson: The Critical Heritage*, pp. 96–97; Chesterfield, *Letters*, V:2097. See also Stein, "Sorting Out the Variants," pp. 1–17.
27. *Dictionary*, I: sig. C2^r; *Idler and Adventurer*, p. 197 (*Idler* 63); Preface to Shakespeare, in *Shakespeare*, VII:60.
28. *Dictionary*, I: sig. C3^r. Johnson's practice does not always bear out the principles in the Preface. His excoriation of words as "barbarous" (forty-nine in the first edition) is perhaps lower than the Preface would lead us to expect, but still shows that he can sometimes hear the barbarians at the gates. Thirty-five usage notes and fourteen etymologies call words or usages "barbarous," "barbaric," "barbarism," "used by barbarians," and so on. The *Dictionary* suggests, and the OED confirms, that *barbarous* (pertaining to verbal solecisms) and *barbaric* (vicious, savage, uncivilized) had not yet gone their separate ways in the eighteenth century. See also Thomas B. Gilmore, "Johnson's Attitude toward French Influence on the English Language."
29. Hedrick, "Fixing the Language," p. 426. Hedrick, though, overstates Johnson's linguistic authoritarianism and paternalism in passages like this: "Johnson sees etymons... in the way that Filmer sees fathers – as 'natural magistrates.' Any attempt to coin words... without a proper patent or birthright is barbarous, impious, and treasonable, for to know the past is to obey the law... Etymology has an implicitly patriarchal character" (pp. 426–27).
30. McLaughlin argues that Bembo is the first to "impos[e] the humanist Latin model of Golden Age–Decline–Revival" on vernacular literature (*Literary Imitation in the Italian Renaissance*, pp. 262–74).
31. The Preface "A Lettori" reads: "Abbiamo stimato necessario di ricorrere all' autorità di quegli scrittori, che vissero, quando questo idioma principalmente fiorì, che fù da' tempi di Dante, o uer poco prima, sino ad alcuni anni, dopo la morte del Boccaccio." Writers later than 1400, he complains, "corruppero non piccola parte della purità del sauellare di quel bon secolo" (sig. a3^v).
32. *Dictionnaire françois*, title page and sig. **^{r}.
33. Donawerth, *Shakespeare and the Sixteenth-Century Study of Language*, p. 34.
34. *Dictionary*, I: sig. D1^r.
35. Camden, *Remains Concerning Britain*, p. 23; Edward Phillips, *New World of English Words*, sig. b3^v.
36. Cited in Sledd and Kolb, *Dr. Johnson's "Dictionary,"* p. 14.
37. Starnes and Noyes, *English Dictionary from Cawdrey to Johnson*, pp. 7–8.
38. Camden, *Remains Concerning Britain*, pp. 25, 27; Edward Phillips, *New World of English Words*, sig. c1^v, b4^v. Compare Martin: "We are now arrived at the Basis and Foundation of the English Tongue, I mean, the Teutonic Language" (*Institutions of Language*, p. 74).
39. "Gothic vigor" has a significance beyond the history of the language. See Gerrard, *Patriot Opposition to Walpole*, chapter 5, and Barrell, *English Literature in History*, pp. 121–22, for discussions of some of the political uses of Britain's Saxon past.

40. *Dictionary*, 1: sig. C3^v, b1^r, b1^v. See also Stern, "Concept of Linguistic Purity," pp. 28–29, on Webster and Priestley.
41. *Letters*, 1:197 (10 June 1761).
42. *Dictionary*, 1: sig. C3^v.
43. Swift, *Prose Works*, IV:12.
44. Segar, "Dictionary Making in the Early Eighteenth Century," p. 210; Spence, *Observations*, 1:170–71.
45. Swift, *Prose Works*, IV:10.
46. Hawkins, *Life*, in 1787 *Works*, 1:96–97; *Life*, 1:219.
47. *Rambler*, V:319 (no. 208). Gwin J. and Ruth A. Kolb, on the other hand, argue Johnson's use of Renaissance authors in the *Dictionary* is not so extensive as the Preface would lead one to believe: see "Selection and Use of the Illustrative Quotations in Dr. Johnson's *Dictionary*," p. 67.
48. Edward Phillips, *New World of English Words*, sig. c2^v; Dryden, Preface to *All for Love*, in *Works*, XIII:18; Edward Howard, "Criticism and Censure," in *Poems, and Essays*, p. 24; Swift, *Prose Works*, IV:9–10; Hurd, *Works*, III:210–11.
49. *Idler and Adventurer*, p. 197 (*Idler* 63); *Dictionary*, 1: sig. D1^r.
50. *Idler and Adventurer*, p. 198 (*Idler* 63).
51. *Dictionary*, 1: sig. C1^r.
52. The words beginning with *na-* make a convenient sample: they are not distorted by the inclusiveness Johnson abandoned after the first few letters of the alphabet, and include no prefixes such as *electro-* or *micro-* which, being associated with seventeenth-century scientific developments, would skew the results. The five words, with the *OED*'s date of first appearance, are *nab* (1686), *naptaking* (unattested, but perhaps too obvious a compound to warrant inclusion), *nationalness* (1681), *navigableness* (1720), and *nauseously* (1668). Note that none of the five is Gallic. *Naulage* is not an *OED* headword, but appears in a quotation from 1580 (s.v. *freight*). *Nauseous*, from Greek, is attested in the Renaissance: only the adverbial form is a late development. *Nationalness* and *navigableness* are latinate, but their root words have Renaissance English pedigrees, and only the forms with the Saxon *-ness* are unknown before the Restoration. Johnson also includes several obsolete words (such as *narrable*, *nasicornous*, *nathless*, and *naturity*) attested only before 1660 – many from Spenser and Browne.
53. Camden, *Remains Concerning Britain*, p. 32. See also Swift's *Proposal*: "Our Language, between two and three hundred Years ago, seems to have had a greater Mixture with the *French* than at present" (*Prose Works*, IV:7). Barber considers the years from 1580 to 1660 – exactly the period in which Johnson sees the "pure sources" – as the "peak period" of Latin imports (*English Language*, p. 177).
54. "Proposals," in *Shakespeare*, VII:53. Compare, however, his note on *Coriolanus*, that "Many French words were mingled in the time of Elizabeth with our language, which have since been ejected" (VIII:820).
55. Tacitus, *Agricola* 21, "qui modo linguam Romanam abnuebant," in *Opera minora*.

56. DeMaria, *Johnson's "Dictionary" and the Language of Learning*, pp. 214–15.

57. Preface, in *Shakespeare*, VII:70; *Dictionary*, 1: sig. C1ᵛ, C2ʳ; *Life*, IV:315; *Shakespeare*, VIII:996; VII:105.

58. *Works of Mr. Edmund Spenser*, ed. Hughes, 1: xci. Hughes's practice did not always follow this declaration; Todd complains that "The text of Spenser has been reduced to modern orthography by Hughes. Yet he professed to follow, *for the most part* ... the old spelling" (*Works of Spenser*, ed. Todd, 1: sig. A3ᵛ). The critique is fair. Compare Hughes's work, however, to Donne's *Poems on Several Occasions* of 1719, which sometimes resorts to old spelling – "Goe, and catch a faling starre" – but just as often regularizes the orthography. The intention here seems to be quaint archaizing, not painstaking transcription of old spelling.

59. Ritson, *English Anthology*, 1: ii; Richardson, *Explanatory Notes and Remarks*, p. cxxxviii; Capell, *Prolusions*, p. ii.

60. Starnes and Noyes, *English Dictionary from Cawdrey to Johnson*, p. 126; Anderson, *Works of the British Poets*, 11:591–603; Walsh, "Eighteenth-Century Editing, 'Appropriation,' and Interpretation," p. 137. Walsh discusses Capell's *Notes and Various Readings to Shakespeare* (1779–83) in *Shakespeare, Milton, and Eighteenth-Century Literary Editing*, pp. 180–97. Jonathan Brody Kramnick writes of the new attention to historically specific forms of the language:

The recovery of older English literature crystallizes a series of oppositions inherited from Addison, Pope and elsewhere: original/translation, difficulty/ease, ancient/modern, literate/illiterate. [Thomas] Warton's novelty is to suggest that in each case the first term's having given way to the second is the condition of degraded taste and indolent readers. Literacy is a scholarly facility with languages. (*Making the English Canon*, p. 143)

61. *Rambler*, V:319 (no. 208); *Idler and Adventurer*, pp. 282, 283 (*Idler* 91).

62. Camden, *Remains Concerning Britain*, pp. 27, 30.

63. Cited in Baugh, *History of the English Language*, p. 261.

64. Daniel, *Defence of Rhyme*, in Smith, *Elizabethan Critical Essays*, 11:384. See also Moore, *Tudor–Stuart Views on the Growth, Status, and Destiny of the English Language*, esp. pp. 15–27 and 45–79.

65. Sewell, Preface, in *Works of Shakespear*, ed. Pope (1725), VII: xii.

66. Chambers, *Cyclopædia*, 1: xx–xxi; see also Sledd and Kolb, *Dr. Johnson's "Dictionary,"* p. 23.

67. Cited in Stern, "Concept of Linguistic Purity," p. 32.

68. Campbell, *Philosophy of Rhetoric*, p. 173.

69. Blount, *Glossographia*, sig. A5ʳ.

70. Edward Phillips, *New World of English Words*, sig. b3ᵛ; "Advertisement" (n.p.).

71. *Idler and Adventurer*, p. 284 (*Idler* 91); Halifax, *Works*, 1:237.

72. Cannon, *Samuel Johnson and the Politics of Hanoverian England*, p. 237; Sledd and Kolb, *Dr. Johnson's "Dictionary,"* p. 25. See also Weinbrot, "Samuel Johnson's *Plan* and *Preface* to the *Dictionary*," pp. 88–89.

73. *Le Grand dictionnaire*, sig. *2ᵛ.

74. Camden, *Remains Concerning Britain*, p. 31; Edward Phillips, *New World of English Words*, sig. c4ʳ; Chesterfield, letter to *The World*, in Boulton, *Johnson: The Critical Heritage*, pp. 96–97; *Idler and Adventurer*, p. 283 (*Idler* 91); *Dictionary*, 1: sig. C3ᵛ; *Letters*, 1:81 (to Thomas Warton, 16 July 1754).

75. Nagashima, *Johnson the Philologist*, p. 75; DeMaria, *Johnson's "Dictionary" and the Language of Learning*, p. 111; Johnson, *London*, lines 26–28, in *Poems*.

76. Cannon, *Samuel Johnson and the Politics of Hanoverian England*, p. 216; Kohn, *Idea of Nationalism*, p. 3.

77. Colley, *Britons*, pp. 5–6.

78. Camden, *Remains Concerning Britain*, p. 23.

79. Colley, *Britons*, p. 90.

80. Barrell, *English Literature in History*, pp. 152, 155.

6 STUDIED BARBARITY: JONSON, SPENSER, AND THE IDEA OF PROGRESS

1. *Spectator*, III:572 (no. 419).

2. Thomas Warton, *History of English Poetry*, 1: v. Eighteenth-century notions of linguistic progress are treated at length in chapter 5, above, and discussed by Jonathan Brody Kramnick, *Making the English Canon*, pp. 43–53.

3. *Shakespeare*, VII:5.

4. Cooper, *Muses Library*, p. 1; Hayward, *British Muse*, title page; Dryden, "Epilogue to the Second Part of *Granada*," lines 25–26, in *Works*, XIII:201; "Defence of the Epilogue," in *Works*, XI:210; Gildon, *Life of Mr. Thomas Betterton*, p. 174.

5. *Dictionary*, sig. F2ʳ; Pope, *Windsor-Forest*, lines 291–92 and n., in *Poems*. See also Patricia Thomson, *Wyatt: The Critical Heritage*.

6. Spence, *Observations*, p. 184; Dryden, *Essay of Dramatick Poesy*, in *Works*, XVII:21; Shadwell, *Humorists*, epilogue, p. 79.

7. Edward Phillips, *Theatrum Poetarum*, p. 19; Jonson, *Works*, ed. Whalley, 1: iv; Anderson, *Works of the British Poets*, IV:523, 529.

8. Johnson, "Drury-Lane Prologue," lines 9–16, in *Poems*.

9. Gerald Eales Bentley analyzes more than 3,000 seventeenth-century allusions and discovers that "The last decade of the century is the only one in which more Shakespeare than Jonson allusions have been found" (*Shakespeare and Jonson*, p. 57). See also Noyes, *Ben Jonson on the English Stage*, pp. 3–38, and Craig, *Ben Jonson: The Critical Heritage*, pp. 20–23.

10. Whalley, *Enquiry into the Learning of Shakespeare*, p. 18; Collins, "An Epistle: Addrest to Sir Thomas Hanmer," lines 55–56, in *Works*.

11. Spence, *Observations*, p.180; Winstanley, *Lives of the Most Famous English Poets*, pp. 42–43. In his imitation of Horace's *Epistle* II.i, Pope calls him "Beastly Skelton." Thomas Warton is similarly blunt in his notes: "Skelton bad" (Fairer, "Origins of Warton's *History of English Poetry*," p. 52). See also Edwards, *Skelton: The Critical Heritage*.

12. Wasserman, *Elizabethan Poetry in the Eighteenth Century*, p. 92; Henson, "*Fictions of Romantick Chivalry*," p. 39.
13. *Life of Hughes*, in *Lives*, 11:162. In fact thirty-five years elapsed between Hughes's first and second editions.
14. Hurd, *Letters on Chivalry and Romance*, in *Works*, IV:239.
15. Addison, "An Account of the Greatest English Poets," lines 23–24, in *Miscellaneous Works*, 1:32.
16. See Tucker, "Spenser's Eighteenth-Century Readers."
17. See Weinberg, *History of Literary Criticism in the Italian Renaissance*, pp. 954–1073, and Javitch, *Proclaiming a Classic*.
18. Thomas Warton, *Observations on the Fairy Queen of Spenser*, 1:4. On Spenser's imitation of Ariosto, see 1:17, 198–228, and on Hughes, 1: lxi–lxii.
19. Rymer, "Preface to Rapin," in Spingarn, *Critical Essays of the Seventeenth Century*, 11:167–68; Dryden, Dedication of the *Aeneis*, in *Works*, V:276; *Works of Mr. Edmund Spenser*, ed. Hughes, 1: lix; Sidney, *Defence of Poetry* (1787), sig. a2^r.
20. Rymer, "Preface to Rapin," in Spingarn, *Critical Essays of the Seventeenth Century*, 11:168. Spenserian allegory is examined by Hughes, Spence (in *Polymetis*, reprinted as *A Dissertation on the Defects of Spenser's Allegory* in Todd's variorum Spenser edition), Warton (in both the *Observations on the Fairy Queen* and the *History of English Poetry*), and John Bell (*Poets of Great Britain*, XV: xix–xl).
21. Temple, *Upon Poetry*, in Cummings, *Spenser: The Critical Heritage*, p. 222; Addison, "An Account of the Greatest English Poets," lines 25–26, in *Miscellaneous Works*, 1:32; *Spectator*, 111:336 (no. 357).
22. Rymer, "Preface to Rapin," in Spingarn, *Critical Essays of the Seventeenth Century*, 11:168; Thomas Warton, *Observations on the Fairy Queen of Spenser*, 1:113.
23. *An Epistle to a Friend Concerning Poetry*, in Cummings, *Spenser: The Critical Heritage*, p. 310.
24. Pope, Preface to the *Pastorals*, in *Poems*, p. 122.
25. *Works of Mr. Edmund Spenser*, 1: xcv.
26. Wasserman, *Elizabethan Poetry in the Eighteenth Century*, p. 94; *Works of Mr. Edmund Spenser*, 1: lviii–lix; Cibber, *Lives of the Poets of Great Britain*, 1:99.
27. *Works of Mr. Edmund Spenser*, 1: lxi, lxiii; Addison, "An Account of the Greatest English Poets," lines 18–19, in *Miscellaneous Works*, 1:32. Cf. Hurd, *Works*, IV:147–48, which echoes Hughes.
28. Thomas Warton, *Observations on the Fairy Queen of Spenser*, 1:12; *Works of Mr. Edmund Spenser*, 1: lxii, xciii.
29. Dryden, *A Discourse Concerning the Original and Progress of Satire*, in *Works*, IV:14.
30. Dryden, *Works*, V:323; *Works of Mr. Edmund Spenser*, 1: lxi.
31. Thomas Warton, *Observations on the Fairy Queen of Spenser*, 1:1–2. See also 1:122: "It is indeed surprising on the whole, that Spenser should execute a poem of uncommon length, with so much spirit and ease, laden as he was with so many shackles."
32. Radcliffe, *Edmund Spenser: A Reception History*, p. 56.

33. *Works of Mr. Edmund Spenser*, 1: xlvi. Hurd uses a similar botanical metaphor: "This *Gothic* method of design in poetry may be, in some sort, illustrated by what is called the *Gothic* method of design in gardening" (*Works*, IV:300–301). See also Radcliffe, *Edmund Spenser: A Reception History*, p. 45.

34. Rymer, "Preface to Rapin," in Spingarn, *Critical Essays of the Seventeenth Century*, II:142.

35. *Works of Mr. Edmund Spenser*, 1: lx–lxi. Cf. Hurd: "When an architect examines a *Gothic* structure by Grecian rules, he finds nothing but deformity. But the *Gothic* structure has its own rules, by which when it comes to be examined, it is seen to have its merit, as well as the Grecian" (*Works*, IV:296).

36. Weinbrot stresses the importance of an irregular native tradition in the development of an eighteenth-century canon: "The English can be successfully correct when they wish; they generally do not so wish because, grâce à dieu, they are not French" ("Twentieth-Century Scholarship and the Eighteenth-Century Canon," p. 411).

37. Pope, "The Preface of the Editor to the *Works of Shakespear*," in *Prose Works*, II:16, 25–26.

38. *Life*, 1:49; Henson, "*Fictions of Romantick Chivalry*," p. 19; Hawkins, *Life*, in 1787 *Works*, 1:96–97; Watkins, *Johnson and English Poetry before 1660*, pp. 66–67.

39. See *Letters*, 1:7–8 (to Gilbert Repington, May 1735), and the discussion in Reade, *Johnsonian Gleanings*, V:27–28, 213–29. Reade identifies "Spenser's Works 3 vol." as the *Works* of 1679. A six-volume *Works*, probably by Hughes (either the first edition of 1715 or the second of 1750), appears as lot 268 in Fleeman, *Sale Catalogue of Samuel Johnson's Library*, p. 36.

40. Hannah More writes that the king "enjoined him to add Spencer to his Lives of the Poets . . . He promised to think of it, but said the booksellers had not included him in their list of the poets" (in *Miscellanies*, II:192). Cf. Boswell's *Life*, IV:410, and Tyers, in *Miscellanies*, II:372–73.

41. *Life*, IV:381–82.

42. Among the most thorough treatments of eighteenth-century Spenserianism are Frushell, *Edmund Spenser in the Early Eighteenth Century*; Radcliffe, *Edmund Spenser: A Reception History*, pp. 21–82; Kucich, *Keats, Shelley, and Romantic Spenserianism*, pp. 11–64; Gerrard, *Patriot Opposition to Walpole*, pp. 166–84; and Jonathan Brody Kramnick, *Making the English Canon*, pp. 137–89. See also Wasserman, *Elizabethan Poetry in the Eighteenth Century*, pp. 92–152; Johnston, *Enchanted Ground*, pp. 43–46, 61–74, 100–19; and Tucker, "Spenser's Eighteenth-Century Readers and the Question of Unity in *The Faerie Queene*." Cummings, *Spenser: The Critical Heritage*, discusses the first two decades of the eighteenth century. Johnson's own interest in the Renaissance generally and Spenser in particular is discussed in Watkins, *Johnson and English Poetry before 1660*, pp. 66–69; Henson, "*Fictions of Romantick Chivalry*," esp. pp. 19–22, 31–49; Radcliffe, *Edmund Spenser: A Reception History*, pp. 76–78; and Turnage, "Samuel Johnson's Criticism of the Works of Edmund Spenser."

43. *Lives*, III:251.

44. *Shakespeare*, VII:82.
45. *Rambler*, III:20 (no. 4); *Shakespeare*, VII:61–62.
46. *Dictionary*, I: sig. C1ʳ; *Idler and Adventurer*, p. 282 (*Idler* 91); *Dictionary*, I: sig. C1ʳ; *Plan*, in 1825 *Works*, V:20; *Dictionary*, I: sig. C1ʳ. Turnage counts 2,878 quotations in the entire *Dictionary* ("Samuel Johnson's Criticism of the Works of Edmund Spenser, " p. 559). By Lewis Freed's count, Spenser appears 1,546 times in the first volume of the *Dictionary*, compared with Shakespeare's 8,694, Dryden's 5,627, Milton's 2,733, and Pope's 2,108. See Wimsatt, *Philosophic Words*, p. 34 n.
47. *Rambler*, III:203 (no. 37).
48. *Ibid.*, IV:122 (no. 92).
49. *Faerie Queene* II.xii.85, in *Works of Edmund Spenser: A Variorum Edition*.
50. Preface to Shakespeare, in *Shakespeare*, VII:79. Compare Thomas Warton's estimation of Spenser: "It is true, that his romantic materials claim great liberties; but no materials exclude order and perspicuity" (*Observations on the Fairy Queen of Spenser*, II:268).
51. *Life of Milton*, in *Lives*, 1:175; *Life*, 1:49; *Life of Milton*, in *Lives*, 1:194. See also Henson, "*Fictions of Romantick Chivalry*," esp. pp. 19–22.
52. *Life of Milton*, *Life of Cowley*, and *Life of Dryden*, in *Lives*, 1:185–86, 51, 436–37; McIntosh, *Choice of Life*, p. 104.
53. *Rambler*, IV:285 (no. 121).
54. McIntosh, *Choice of Life*, p. 105.
55. See the Introduction to *Vision of Theodore*, in *Rasselas and Other Tales*, pp. 182–88.
56. *Life*, II:238.
57. *Rambler*, IV:149–50.
58. *Ibid.*, IV:182 (no. 102).
59. *Rasselas and Other Tales*, pp. 204, 205, 211.
60. Pope, *An Essay on Poetry*, line 483, in *Poems*; Cibber, *Lives of the Poets of Great Britain*, 1:19–20; *Works of Mr. Edmund Spenser*, I: xxv–xxvi. See also Cooper: "I can't read [Langland's] Work, without lamenting the Unhappiness of a fluctuating Language, that buries even Genius itself in its Ruins: 'Tis raising Edifices of Sand, that every Breath of Time defaces" (*Muses Library*, p. 7).
61. Addison, "An Account of the Greatest English Poets," lines 11–16, in *Miscellaneous Works*.
62. *Letters*, 1:81 (to Thomas Warton, 16 July 1754).
63. *Life of Hughes*, in *Lives*, II:162.
64. *Dictionary*, I: sig. C2ʳ, C1ᵛ, C2ʳ.
65. *Ibid.*, I: sig. C1ʳ, G2ᵛ.
66. *Life of Denham*, in *Lives*, 1:75; *Life of Prior*, in *Lives*, II:208; *Life of Dryden*, in *Lives*, 1:420–21; *Plan*, in 1825 *Works*, V:18.
67. *Works of Mr. Edmund Spenser*, I: cxv–cxl.
68. The counts are unavoidably approximate: Hughes, for instance, catalogues unfamiliar spellings, which Johnson regularizes, and Johnson sometimes rejects Hughes's improper or imprecise definitions. Some of the counts seem

skewed, as when Johnson adduces more than one Spenserian quotation for certain words. The counts of quotations by source (below) are also approximate, as some quotations resist identification. Quotations from Spenser make up a large part of the material added to the fourth edition (1773): see Reddick, *Making of Johnson's Dictionary*, pp. 95–96.

69. Compare these figures with Turnage, who examined 2,878 quotations from Spenser: *The Faerie Queene*, 53 percent; *The Shepheardes Calender*, 6 percent; *Mother Hubberds Tale*, 4 percent; *A View of the Present State of Ireland*, 18 percent; other works, 20 percent ("Samuel Johnson's Criticism of the Works of Edmund Spenser," p. 559). The most significant differences are *The Shepheardes Calender* (18 percent in my count *versus* 6 percent in hers) and *A View* (my 2 percent *versus* her 18 percent). My sample draws especially on obsolete words, to illustrate which Johnson naturally drew more heavily on the pastorals and less heavily on the prose.

70. The lone quotations from the third book (s.v. *paragon*, from III.x.35) and the fourth (s.v. *to tine*, from IV.xi.36) are copied from Hughes's glossary. Only the quotation from the sixth book (s.v. *aghast*, from VI.xi.22) resists explanation. A plausible deduction is that Johnson had only the first two books at hand as he prepared the quotations, although only one pre-1755 text – Birch's three-volume *Faerie Queene* (1751) – was routinely bound so as to separate the first two books from the rest. It is likely that Johnson either used this edition, or that he simply examined only the first two books when he prepared the *Dictionary*. Of course copies of other editions may have been differently bound, and since Johnson regularizes the orthography and often misquotes the text of the original, it is impossible to identify the edition he used on the basis of the quotations. See Wurtsbaugh, *Two Centuries of Spenserian Scholarship*, p. 64.

71. Such words include *pionings, star-read, to tine, ventail, umbriere, unwist*, etc. See also McCue, "Sam. Johnson's Word-Hoard," p. 44.

72. *Rambler*, IV:286 (no. 121); "Lines Written in Ridicule of Thomas Warton's Poems," line 6, in *Poems*; *Life of Prior*, in *Lives*, II:204. Venturo discusses Johnson's parodies of his friends' archaisms in *Johnson the Poet*, pp. 190–99.

73. *Rambler*, IV:280, 285 (no. 121); *Life of Cowley*, in *Lives*, I:59; *Rambler*, III:202–3 (no. 37).

74. *Life of Dryden*, in *Lives*, I:468.

75. *Rambler*, IV:285–86 (no. 121).

76. *Ibid.*, IV:285 (no. 121).

77. *Life of Pope*, in *Lives*, III:14.

78. *Shakespeare*, VII:61; *Life of Milton*, in *Lives*, I:163; Hume, *History of England*, IV:386.

79. *Shakespeare*, VII:62.

80. Jonathan Brody Kramnick picks up on Johnson's distaste for Spenserian diction, referring to his "studied barbarism [*sic*]," but overextends Johnson's critique to cover Spenserianism in general: "Spenserianism [for Johnson]

is just nostalgia, a relation to the past shorn of any vital connection to the present" (*Making the English Canon*, p. 198).

81. *Shakespeare*, VII:62. Compare the Preface: "Whatever advantages he might once derive from personal allusions, local customs, or temporary opinions, have for many years been lost" (*Shakespeare*, VII:61). See also Thomas Warton: "Thy powerful hand has broke the Gothic chain, / And brought my bosom back to truth again; / To truth by no peculiar taste confined, / Whose universal pattern strikes mankind; / To truth, whose bold and unresisted aim / Checks frail caprice, and Fashion's fickle claim" ("Verses on Reynolds's Window," lines 63–68, in *Three Wartons*).

7 THE LAST AGE: RENAISSANCE LOST

1. Sanderson, XXXVI *Sermons*, p. 490.
2. Dryden, "Defence of the Epilogue," in *Works*, XI:203; Etherege, *The Man of Mode*, I.i, in *Plays*.
3. Rymer, *Tragedies of the Last Age Consider'd*, title page; Villiers, *General Key to the Writings of the Poets of the Last Age*, p. iv.
4. Richardson, *Explanatory Notes and Remarks*, p. lxxxvi.
5. Dryden, "The Secular Masque," lines 90–91, in *Poems and Fables*, p. 839; Prologue to *Aureng-Zebe*, lines 21–22, in *Works*, XII:159; Peacock, "The Four Ages of Poetry," in *Works*, VIII:16.
6. Lauder, *Milton's Use and Imitation of the Moderns*, sig. b2^r–b3^v; Cooper, *Muses Library*, p. xii; Gray, *Correspondence*, III:1124 (to Thomas Warton, 15 April 1770).
7. Haugen discusses Bentley's conjectural emendations to *Paradise Lost* and relates them to his classical editions in "Richard Bentley," chapter 6, esp. pp. 276–77.
8. Although Becket's *Concordance to Shakespeare* appeared in 1787, the first concordance of Pope's works appeared in 1875. A nine-volume self-consciously "classicizing" edition of Pope was rushed into print not long after Pope's death by Warburton in 1751, but more serious editorial treatment had to await Gilbert Wakefield's incomplete 1794 edition and Joseph Warton's edition of 1797. Warton's variorum Dryden was left incomplete at his death, to be revised and published by his son in 1811. There was no concordance to Dryden's verse until 1957.
9. Levine, *Between the Ancients and the Moderns*, p. 63; Ferry, *Milton and the Miltonic Dryden*, p. 21.
10. Dupré de Saint-Maur, *State of Innocence and Fall of Man* (1745). A second edition appeared ten years later. Other early translations are catalogued in the 1753 edition of the *Prose Works*, including Thomas Power's Latin translation of *Paradise Lost* (1691), Michael Bold's Latin version of the first book (1702), Trap's Latin *Paradise Lost* (1741), William Dobson's Latin translation of the first six books (1750), an anonymous Dutch translation from Haarlem (1728),

an Italian version by Paolo Rolli (1736), and a planned but never completed Greek version by Richard Dawes (1736).

11. Marsden notes a similar situation in Shakespeare scholarship: editors of the middle eighteenth century "indicate a growing concern for preserving the words of Shakespeare as they were written," while "The Restoration solution...was to rewrite his text rather than to emend or annotate it." In either case, "publishing Shakespeare's works was no longer as simple as reprinting an easily comprehensible near contemporary" (*Re-Imagined Text*, p. 68). See also Walsh, "Eighteenth-Century Editing, 'Appropriation,' and Interpretation."

12. *Adventurer* 101 (23 October 1753), cited in Shawcross, *Milton: The Critical Heritage*, 11:226; Thomas Warton, in Milton, *Poems upon Several Occasions*, p. xxiv; *Life*, 1:301; *Life of Milton*, in *Lives*, 1:87; *Shakespeare*, VII:56, 207. Arthur Sherbo notes that "Milton is quoted or alluded to in Johnson's notes [to Shakespeare] far more often (31 times) than any other writer" (*Samuel Johnson, Editor of Shakespeare*, p. 24).

13. See Knoppers, *Historicizing Milton*, pp. 4–8.

14. Sensabaugh points out that "many Whigs...considered Milton a main source of their strength and shaped their political principles in accordance with those expressed in his program for man and society" (*That Grand Whig, Milton*, p. 3). See also Lipking, *Ordering of the Arts*, p. 329, and Wittreich, *Romantics on Milton*, pp. 11–12.

15. Winstanley, *Lives of the Most Famous English Poets*, p. 195; Anderson, *Works of the British Poets*, VII:762; note to "On Time," in Milton, *Poems on Several Occasions*, p. 296 n. (the first edition reads, "The poet should be distinguished from the puritan"); "Upon Bentley's Emendation of Milton," in Shawcross, *Milton: The Critical Heritage*, 11:198. Reddick summarizes the "particular problems" posed by Milton: "Milton represented two different and powerful figures: (1) the great English poet, author of the great English epic...and (2) the Puritan rebel republican, outspoken supporter for Cromwell and for the execution of the king" (*Making of Johnson's Dictionary*, p. 129).

16. *Milton, Essay upon Divorcement* (London, 1715).

17. Milton, *Areopagitica* (1738), with other editions in 1772, 1791 ("Dedicated to the Rt. Hon. Charles James Fox, the friend of truth and liberty"), and 1792; *A Manifesto of the Lord Protector* (1738); *Complete Collection of the Historical, Political, and Miscellaneous Works of John Milton* (1738).

18. *Works of John Milton, Historical, Political, and Miscellaneous* (1753).

19. Richardson, *Explanatory Notes and Remarks*, p. xiv; Milton, *Poems upon Several Occasions*, p. xi; Sidney, *Defence of Poetry*, ed. Van Dorsten, p. 61; Anderson, *Works of the British Poets*, V: iv.

20. Johnson, *Life of Milton*, in *Lives*, 1:134, 110; Dedication to Kennedy's *Chronology*, in *Prefaces and Dedications*, p. 76. Boswell applies the same logic to Johnson himself: "His literary career appears to have been almost totally suspended in the years 1745 and 1746, those years which were marked by a civil war in Great-Britain" (*Life*, 1:176). He ignores the *Observations on Macbeth* and the

Plan for the *Dictionary*, written at that time, and so has given rise to much ill-informed speculation on Johnson's involvement in the 'Forty-five.

21. Dobson, *Making of the National Poet*, p. 219. The most extensive account of Garrick's festival is Deelman, *The Great Shakespeare Jubilee*; Dobson, however, provides a more interesting account of its implications. See esp. pp. 214–27.

22. Flannagan, "Puckish or Perverse?," pp. 147–48. See also Tomarken, *History of the Commentary on Selected Writings of Samuel Johnson*, pp. 119–45, and Wittreich, *Romantics on Milton*, esp. pp. 10–11. A definitive account of Johnson's opinion of Milton has yet to be written. His distaste for *Lycidas* and his unfortunate involvement with Lauder have turned him into Milton's arch-enemy, and even today some think Milton needs defending from Johnson's attacks. Vereen Bell mentions Johnson's "open hostility toward Milton," finding him a "hardheaded rationalist...clearly out of his element in judging Milton" ("Johnson's Milton Criticism in Context," pp. 127, 132). Brink attempts a corrective in "Johnson and Milton."

23. Cited in *Life of Milton*, in *Lives*, 1:84, n. 1.

24. Blackburne, *Remarks on Johnson's Life of Milton*, pp. vi, 127–28, 148.

25. Nath (in "Johnson Agonistes and Milton's *Samson*"), Jain (in "Echoes of Milton in Johnson's *Irene*"), and Ogden (in "Johnson Borrowing from Milton") have identified Miltonic sources and analogues for Johnson's writings. Redford considers at greater length Milton's influence on Johnson in "Defying Our Master."

26. *Life*, 11:239; *Life of Milton*, in *Lives*, 1:154, 170.

27. Fussell, *Samuel Johnson and the Life of Writing*, p. 52.

28. *Life of Milton*, in *Lives*, 1:140, 102, 116.

29. *Ibid.*, 1:156–57.

30. *Dictionary*, 1: sig. B2^v. Only a few quotations from *Of Education* appear. Reddick observes Johnson's avoidance of Milton's prose in the *Dictionary*, especially the fourth edition: "The Puritan Milton was viewed as a dangerous political influence whose presence and authority were to be resisted... Johnson almost never quoted from Milton's prose works" (*Making of Johnson's Dictionary*, pp. 129–30). See also DeMaria, "Politics of Johnson's *Dictionary*," p. 70.

31. *Life of Milton*, in *Lives*, 1:101; *Life*, 1:227.

32. Hagstrum, *Samuel Johnson's Literary Criticism*, p. 39.

33. *Rambler*, 1v:383 (no. 140). By Coleridge's day, the transformation was complete and Johnson's criticism was simply impertinent: "These divine Poets, Homer, Eschylus, and the two Compeers, Dante, Shakespeare, Spencer, Milton, who deserve to have Critics, χριταί, are placed above Criticism in the vulgar sense" (in Wittreich, *Romantics on Milton*, p. 254).

34. Piozzi's *Anecdotes*, in *Miscellanies*, 1:487.

35. *Spectator*, 11:587 (no. 279); Dennis, *Critical Works*, 11:221–22; Collins, "Ode on the Poetical Character," lines 55–58, in *Works*.

36. *Life of Milton*, in *Lives*, 1:177.

37. Gray, "The Progress of Poetry," line 98, in *Complete Poems*.

38. Marsden discusses eighteenth-century interpretations of Shakespeare as sublime in *Re-Imagined Text*, pp. 114–20.

39. *Paradise Lost*, 2.799–801; 6.339–40.

40. Collins, "Ode to Fear," lines 64–65; "An Ode on the Popular Superstitions of the Highlands of Scotland," lines 177–78; "A Song from Shakespear's Cymbeline," lines 5–6; "Song: The Sentiments Borrowed from Shakespeare," lines 5 and 9; "An Epistle: Addrest to Sir Thomas Hanmer," lines 47–50, in *Works*; *Shakespeare*, VII:52–53.

41. Joseph Warton, *Essay on Pope*, 1:7; Anderson, *Works of the British Poets*, IV:529.

42. Dryden, "Lines on Milton," in *Works*. See also Johnson's Latin translation in *Latin and Greek Poems*, p. 23.

43. *Life of Dryden*, in *Lives*, 1:447–48; *Spectator*, III:564; Pope, *Poems*, VII:12; *Spectator*, II:587 (no. 279).

44. Shawcross, *Milton: The Critical Heritage*, 1:98.

45. Gray, "The Progress of Poetry," lines 111–13 and note, in *Complete Poems*; Collins, "An Epistle: Addrest to Sir Thomas Hanmer," lines 67–68, in *Works*; Lauder, *Milton's Use and Imitation of the Ancients*, p. 163; Joseph Warton, *Essay on Pope*, 1: iv.

46. On Warton's role in the development of a new aesthetic, see Robert Griffin, *Wordsworth's Pope*, pp. 28–45, and Pittock, *The Ascendancy of Taste*, pp. 122–66.

47. *Life of Pope*, in *Lives*, III:251, 223.

48. Joseph Warton, *Essay on Pope*, II:480–81.

49. See especially Robert Griffin, *Wordsworth's Pope*, pp. 24–63.

50. Rowe, *Tragedy of Jane Shore*, sig. A3ᵛ; Collins, "Ode to Fear," lines 68–69; "Ode on the Poetical Character," lines 71–76; "An Epistle: Addrest to Sir Thomas Hanmer," lines 47–48, 52–54, in *Works*.

51. Joseph Warton, *Essay on Pope*, 1:29–30. To some degree this anxiety was international, for Voltaire lamented that "*Milton* is the last in *Europe* who wrote an *Epick* Poem" (*Essay upon the Civil Wars of France*, p. 102).

52. Dryden, Dedication to the *Aeneis*, in *Works*, V:267; *Life of Milton*, in *Lives*, 1:170; *Life*, V:35.

53. See, for instance, Christopher Hill: "Milton's was the last great epic, the last major attempt at a totally integrated world view. It was followed by the half-century of the mock epic, a confession of defeat. Better poets like Dryden and Pope translated the great traditional epics: this was defeat too" (*Some Intellectual Consequences of the English Revolution*, p. 83).

54. *Life of Pope*, in *Lives*, III:188.

55. *Life of Blackmore*, in *Lives*, II:242.

56. *Rambler*, IV:87.

57. Young, *Conjectures on Original Composition*, p. 17.

58. Dustin Griffin, *Regaining Paradise*, pp. 2, 232.

59. In Shawcross, *Milton: The Critical Heritage*, 1:82.

60. "Rhapsody to Milton," in Whaley, *Collection of Original Poems and Translations*, pp. 182–86.

61. Young, *Conjectures on Original Composition*, p. 9.

62. *Life of Milton*, in *Lives*, 1:194.

63. Dryden, *Essay of Dramatic Poesy*, in *Works*, XVII:73.

64. *Ciceronianus*, in *Collected Works of Erasmus*, XXVIII:377.

65. Thomas Warton, *History of English Poetry*, III:500; *Observations on the Fairy Queen*, II:111; Joseph Warton, *Essay on Pope*, 1:334.

66. Pope, "The First Epistle of the Second Book of Horace Imitated," lines 272–73, in *Poems*.

67. Hurd, *Works*, IV:350; Ramsay, *The Ever Green*, in Durham, *Critical Essays of the Eighteenth Century*, pp. 399–400.

68. *Life*, IV:305; *Life of Milton*, in *Lives*, 1:177; *Idler and Adventurer*, p. 196; *Life of Cowley*, in *Lives*, 1:20–21.

69. *Life of Prior*, in *Lives*, II:208; *Life of Waller*, in *Lives*, 1:294. The phrase is repeated from an earlier *Life*: Cowley "is never pathetick, and rarely sublime, but always either ingenious or learned, either acute or profound" (*Life of Cowley*, in *Lives*, 1:56).

70. Goldsmith, *Citizen of the World*, letter XL, in *Collected Works*, II:172–73.

71. Curran, *Poetic Form and British Romanticism*, p. 22; Headley, *Select Beauties*, 1: xiv–xvi.

72. *Letters of John Keats*, p. 96 (to John Hamilton Reynolds, 3 February 1818).

73. Dryden, "To My Dear Friend Mr. Congreve," lines 5–14, in *Works*. Johnson notes a similar concern even in Milton himself, who fears "that his book is to be written in 'an age too late' for heroick poesy" (*Life of Milton*, in *Lives*, 1:137).

74. Joseph Warton, "The Enthusiast; or, The Lover of Nature," in *Three Wartons*.

Bibliography

Addison, Joseph. *The Miscellaneous Works of Joseph Addison*. Ed. A. C. Guthkelch. 2 vols. London: G. Bell, 1914.

The Freeholder. Ed. James Leheny. Oxford: Clarendon Press, 1979.

Allodoli, Ettore. "Poliziano e Johnson." *La Rinascita* 5, no. 27 (Sept. 1942): 459–71.

Anderson, Robert, ed. *The Works of the British Poets, with Prefaces, Biographical and Critical*. 13 vols. Edinburgh, 1792–95.

Anglicanus, Palæophilus [pseud.]. *The Conduct of Queen Elizabeth, towards the Neighbouring Nations, and Particularly Spain; Compared with that of James I in View of the Late and Present Behaviour of Great Britain*. London, 1729.

Aristotle. *Ars rhetorica*. Ed. W. D. Ross. Oxford: Clarendon Press, 1959.

Ascham, Roger. *The Scholemaster: Shewing a Plain and Perfect Way of Teaching the Learned Language*. Ed. James Upton. 3rd edn. London, 1729.

The English Works of Roger Ascham. Ed. James Bennet [i.e. Samuel Johnson?]. London, 1761.

English Works. Ed. William Aldis Wright. Cambridge: Cambridge University Press, 1904.

Augustine. *Confessions*. Ed. James J. O'Donnell. 3 vols. Oxford: Clarendon Press, 1992.

Babcock, Robert Witbeck. *The Genesis of Shakespeare Idolatry, 1766–1799: A Study in English Criticism of the Late Eighteenth Century*. Chapel Hill: University of North Carolina Press, 1931.

Bacon, Francis. *The Works of Francis Bacon*. Ed. James Spedding, Robert Leslie Ellis, and Douglas Denton Heath. 15 vols. Boston: Brown and Taggard, 1860–64.

Barbauld, Anna Letitia. *Legacy for Young Ladies*. London, 1826.

Barber, Charles. *The English Language: A Historical Introduction*. Cambridge: Cambridge University Press, 1993.

Barrell, John. *English Literature in History, 1730–80: An Equal, Wide Survey*. London: Hutchinson, 1983.

Bate, Walter Jackson. *The Burden of the Past and the English Poet*. New York: Norton, 1972.

Samuel Johnson. London: Chatto & Windus, 1978.

Baugh, Albert C. *A History of the English Language*. 2nd edn. New York: Appleton-Century-Crofts, 1957.

Becket, Andrew. *A Concordance to Shakespeare: Suited to All the Editions, in which the Distinguished and Parallel Passages in the Plays of that Justly Admired Writer Are Methodically Arranged*. London, 1787.

Bejczy, István. "Overcoming the Middle Ages: Historical Reasoning in Erasmus' *Antibarbarian Writings*." *Erasmus of Rotterdam Society Yearbook* 16 (1996): 34–53.

Bell, John, ed. *The Poets of Great Britain Complete from Chaucer to Churchill*. 109 vols. London, 1777–87.

Bell, Vereen M. "Johnson's Milton Criticism in Context." *English Studies* 49 (1968): 127–32.

Benjamin, Walter. *Illuminationen*. Frankfurt am Main: Suhrkamp Verlag, 1961.

Bentley, Gerald Eades. *Shakespeare and Jonson: Their Reputations in the Seventeenth Century Compared*. Chicago: University of Chicago Press, 1945.

Biographia Britannica. 6 vols. in 7. London, 1747–66.

Birch, Thomas. *Memoirs of the Reign of Queen Elizabeth, from the Year 1581 till Her Death*. 2 vols. London, 1754.

Blackburne, Francis. *Remarks on Johnson's Life of Milton, to Which Are Added Milton's Tractate of Education and Areopagitica*. London, 1780.

Blair, Hugh. *Lectures on Rhetoric and Belles Lettres*. 2nd edn. 3 vols. London, 1785.

Blount, Thomas. *Glossographia*. London, 1656.

Blumenberg, Hans. *The Legitimacy of the Modern Age*. Trans. Robert M. Wallace. Cambridge, MA: MIT Press, 1983.

Bodin, Jean. *Method for the Easy Comprehension of History*. Trans. Beatrice Reynolds. New York: Columbia University Press, 1945.

Bolingbroke, Henry St. John, Viscount. *Historical Writings*. Ed. Isaac Kramnick. Chicago: University of Chicago Press, 1972.

Boswell, James. *The Life of Samuel Johnson, LL.D.* Ed. G. B. Hill, rev. L. F. Powell. 6 vols. Oxford: Clarendon Press, 1934–64.

Boulton, James T. *Johnson: The Critical Heritage*. New York: Barnes & Noble, 1971.

Bouwsma, William J. *The Interpretation of Renaissance Humanism*. Washington, DC: Service Center for Teachers of History, 1959.

Bowers, Toni. *The Politics of Motherhood: British Writing and Culture 1680–1760*. Cambridge: Cambridge University Press, 1996.

Boyer, Abel. *The History of the Reign of Queen Anne, Digested into Annals*. 11 vols. London, 1703–13.

Bracciolini, Poggio. *De varietate fortunae*. In *Codice Topografico della Città di Roma*, ed. Roberto Valentini and Giuseppe Zucchetti. 4 vols. Rome: Istituto Palazzo Borromini, 1953.

Brack, O M, Jr. "Samuel Johnson Edits for the Booksellers: Sir Thomas Browne's 'Christian Morals' (1756) and 'The English Works of Roger Ascham' (1761)." *Library Chronicle of the University of Texas* 21, no. 3 (1991): 12–39.

Brink, J. R. "Johnson and Milton." *SEL* 20 (1980): 493–503.

Brower, Reuben A. *Alexander Pope: The Poetry of Allusion*. Oxford: Clarendon Press, 1959.

Brown, Marshall. "Periods and Resistances." *Modern Language Quarterly* 62, no. 4 (Dec. 2001): 309–16.

Browne, Thomas. *Christian Morals*. Ed. John Jeffery and Samuel Johnson. London, 1756.

Brownley, Martine Watson. "Johnson and the Writing of History." In *Johnson after Two Hundred Years*, ed. Paul J. Korshin, pp. 97–109. Philadelphia: University of Pennsylvania Press, 1986.

Burckhardt, Jacob. *The Civilization of the Renaissance in Italy: An Essay*. Trans. S. G. C. Middlemore. London: Phaidon Press, 1951.

Bürger, Peter. "On Literary History." *Poetics* 14 (1985): 199–207.

Burigny, Jean Lévesque de. *Sur la querelle qui s'eleva dans le XVIe siècle au suject de l'estime qui était due à Cicéron*. Paris, 1756.

Burke, Edmund. *The Works of the Right Honourable Edmund Burke*. 8 vols. London, 1854–89.

Burnet, Gilbert. *The History of the Reformation of the Church of England*. 3 vols. London, 1681–1753.

An Exposition of the Thirty-nine Articles of the Church of England. London, 1699.

Bush, Douglas. *The Renaissance and English Humanism*. 2nd edn. Toronto: University of Toronto Press, 1956.

Butterfield, Herbert. *Man on His Past: The Study of the History of Historical Scholarship*. Cambridge: Cambridge University Press, 1955.

Camden, William. *Remains Concerning Britain*. Ed. R. D. Dunn. Toronto: University of Toronto Press, 1984.

Campbell, George. *The Philosophy of Rhetoric*. Ed. Lloyd F. Bitzer. Carbondale: Southern Illinois University Press, 1963.

Campion, Thomas. *The Works of Thomas Campion*. Ed. Walter R. Davis. New York: Norton, 1970.

Cannon, John. *Samuel Johnson and the Politics of Hanoverian England*. Oxford: Clarendon Press, 1994.

Capell, Edward. *Prolusions; or, Select Pieces of Antient Poetry, Compil'd with Great Care from their Several Originals, and Offer'd to the Publick as Specimens of the Integrity that Should Be Found in the Editions of Worthy Authors*. London, 1760.

Notes and Various Readings to Shakespeare. 3 vols. London, 1779–83.

Carretta, Vincent. "Anne and Elizabeth: The Poet as Historian in *Windsor Forest*." *Studies in English Literature, 1500–1900* 21 (1981): 425–37.

Cellarius, Christophorus. *Historia Vniversalis breviter ac prespicue exposita, in antiquam, et medii aevi ac nouam divisa*. 7th edn. Jena, 1727.

Historia nova, hoc est XVI et XVII saeculorum. Jena, 1727.

Chambers, Ephraim. *Cyclopædia; or, An Universal Dictionary of Arts and Sciences*. 2nd edn. 2 vols. London, 1738.

Chambers, Sir Robert. *A Course of Lectures on the English Law, Delivered at the University of Oxford 1767–1773*. Ed. Thomas M. Curley. 2 vols. Madison: University of Wisconsin Press, 1986.

Chandler, James. *England in 1819: The Politics of Literary Culture and the Case of Romantic Historicism*. Chicago: University of Chicago Press, 1998.

Chapin, Chester F. *The Religious Thought of Samuel Johnson*. Ann Arbor: University of Michigan Press, 1968.

Chapple, J. A. V. "Samuel Johnson's *Proposals for Printing the History of the Council of Trent* [1738]." *The Bulletin of the John Rylands Library* 45 (1963): 340–69.

Chesterfield, Philip Dormer Stanhope, Fourth Earl of. *The Letters of Philip Dormer Stanhope, Fourth Earl of Chesterfield*. Ed. Bonamy Dobree. 6 vols. London: Eyre & Spottiswoode, 1932.

Cibber, Theophilus [i.e. Robert Shiels]. *The Lives of the Poets of Great Britain and Ireland, to the Time of Dean Swift*. 5 vols. London, 1753.

Cicero. *Rhetorica*. Ed. A. S. Wilkins. 2 vols. Oxford: Clarendon Press, 1902–03.

Clarendon, Edward Hyde, Earl of. *The History of the Rebellion and Civil Wars in England*. Ed. W. Dunn Macray. Oxford: Clarendon Press, 1992.

Colley, Linda. *Britons: Forging the Nation, 1707–1837*. New Haven: Yale University Press, 1992.

Collingwood, R. G. *The Idea of History*. Ed. Jan van der Dussen. Rev. edn. Oxford: Clarendon Press, 1993.

Collins, William. *The Works of William Collins*. Ed. Richard Wendorf and Charles Ryskamp. Oxford: Clarendon Press, 1979.

Cooper, Elizabeth. *The Muses Library; or, A Series of English Poetry . . . Being a General Collection of All the Old Valuable Poetry Extant*. London, 1738.

Craig, D. H., ed. *Ben Jonson: The Critical Heritage, 1599–1798*. London: Routledge, 1990.

Croce, Benedetto. *Theory and History of Historiography*. Trans. Douglas Ainslie. London: George G. Harrap & Co., 1921.

Croll, Morris W. *Style, Rhetoric, and Rhythm: Essays by Morris W. Croll*. Ed. J. Max Patrick and Robert O. Evans. Princeton: Princeton University Press, 1966.

Cuming, G. J. *A History of Anglican Liturgy*. London: Macmillan, 1969.

Cummings, Robert M., ed. *Spenser: The Critical Heritage*. London: Routledge & Kegan Paul, 1971.

Curran, Stuart. *Poetic Form and British Romanticism*. New York: Oxford University Press, 1986.

Daniel, Samuel. *The Poetical Works of Mr. Samuel Daniel, Author of the English History*. 2 vols. London, 1718.

Dante. *Opere Minori*. Ed. Pier Vincenzo Mengaldo *et al*. 2 vols. Milan: Ricciardi, 1979.

D'Avenant, Charles. *Essays upon Peace at Home, and War Abroad*. 2nd edn. London, 1704.

Davie, Donald. *Purity of Diction in English Verse*. 2nd edn. London: Routledge & Kegan Paul, 1967.

Davies, Horton. *Worship and Theology in England*. 5 vols. Princeton: Princeton University Press, 1961–75.

Davies, Sir John. *The Poetical Works of Sir John Davies*. London, 1773.

Deelman, Christian. *The Great Shakespeare Jubilee*. New York: Viking, 1964.

Defoe, Daniel. *The True-Born Englishman: A Satyr*. London, 1720.

De Grazia, Margreta. *Shakespeare Verbatim: The Reproduction of Authenticity and the 1790 Apparatus*. Oxford: Clarendon Press, 1991.

DeMaria, Robert, Jr. *Johnson's "Dictionary" and the Language of Learning*. Chapel Hill: University of North Carolina Press, 1986.

"The Politics of Johnson's *Dictionary*." *PMLA* 104 (1989): 64–74.

"Johnson's *Dictionary* and the 'Teutonick' Roots of the English Language." In *Language and Civilization: A Concerted Profusion of Essays and Studies in Honor of Otto Hietsch*, ed. Claudia Blank and Patrick Selim Huck, 2 vols., 1:20–36. Frankfurt: Peter Lang, 1992.

The Life of Samuel Johnson: A Critical Biography. Oxford: Blackwell, 1993.

Samuel Johnson and the Life of Reading. Baltimore: Johns Hopkins University Press, 1997.

Dennis, John. *The Critical Works of John Dennis*. Ed. Edward Niles Hooker. 2 vols. Baltimore: Johns Hopkins University Press, 1939–43.

Dickens, A. G. *The English Reformation*. 2nd edn. London: Batsford, 1989.

Dobson, Michael. *The Making of the National Poet: Shakespeare, Adaptation, and Authorship, 1660–1769*. Oxford: Clarendon Press, 1992.

Dolet, Etienne. *Stephani Doleti dialogus, de imitatione Ciceroniana, aduersus Desiderium Erasmum Roterodamum, pro Christophoro Longolio*. Lyons, 1535.

Donawerth, Jane. *Shakespeare and the Sixteenth-Century Study of Language*. Urbana: University of Illinois Press, 1983.

Donne, John. *Poems on Several Occasions*. London, 1719.

Dryden, John. *Essays of John Dryden*. Ed. W. P. Ker. 2 vols. Oxford: Clarendon Press, 1900.

The Works of John Dryden. Ed. Edward Niles Hooker and H. T. Swedenborg, Jr. 20 vols. Berkeley and Los Angeles: University of California Press, 1956–.

The Poems and Fables of John Dryden. Ed. James Kinsley. London: Oxford University Press, 1962.

Du Bellay, Joachim. *La Deffence et illustration de la langue françoyse*. Ed. Henri Chamard. Paris: M. Didier, 1948.

Duff, William. *Critical Observations on the Writings of the Most Celebrated Original Geniuses in Poetry*. London, 1770.

Dupré de Saint-Maur, Nicolas-François. *The State of Innocence and Fall of Man, Described in Milton's Paradise Lost, Render'd into Prose*. Trans. "a gentleman of Oxford" [i.e. George Green Smith]. London, 1745.

Durham, Willard Higley, ed. *Critical Essays of the Eighteenth Century, 1700–1725*. 2nd edn. New York: Russell & Russell, 1961.

Edwards, A. S. G., ed. *Skelton: The Critical Heritage*. London: Routledge & Kegan Paul, 1981.

Erasmus, Desiderius. *Twenty Two Select Colloquies out of Erasmus Roterodamus: Pleasantly Representing Several Superstitious Levities that Were Crept into the Church of Rome in His Days*. London, 1725.

Opus Epistolarum Des. Erasmi Roterodami. Ed. P. S. Allen. 12 vols. Oxford: Clarendon Press, 1906–58.

The Education of a Christian Prince. Trans. Lester K. Born. New York: Columbia University Press, 1936.

Opera Omnia Desiderii Erasmi Roterodami. Ed. J. H. Waszink *et al*. Amsterdam: North-Holland, 1969–.

The Collected Works of Erasmus. 46 vols. to date. Toronto: University of Toronto Press, 1974–.

Erskine-Hill, Howard. "On Historical Commentary: The Example of Milton and Dryden." In *Presenting Poetry: Composition, Publication, Reception*, ed. Howard Erskine-Hill and Richard A. McCabe, pp. 52–74. Cambridge: Cambridge University Press, 1995.

Estienne, Robert. *Dictionarium, seu latinae linguae thesaurus, non singulas modo dictiones contenens, sed integros quoque latine et loquendi et scribendi formulas, ex Catone, Cicerone, Plinio, Avunculo, Terentio, Varrone, Livio, Plinio Secundo, Virgilio, Caesare, Columella, Plauto, Martiale*. Paris, 1536.

Etherege, George. *The Plays of George Etherege*. Ed. Michael Cordner. Cambridge: Cambridge University Press, 1982.

Evelyn John. *The Diary of John Evelyn*. Ed. E. S. de Beer. 6 vols. Oxford: Clarendon Press, 1955.

Fairer, David. "The Origins of Warton's *History of English Poetry*." *Review of English Studies* 32 (1981): 37–63.

Falco, Giorgio. *La Polemica sul medio evo*. Ed. Fulvio Tessitore. New edn. Naples: Guida, 1974.

Ferguson, Wallace K. *The Renaissance in Historical Thought: Five Centuries of Interpretation*. Cambridge, MA: Houghton Mifflin, 1948.

Ferry, Anne. *Milton and the Miltonic Dryden*. Cambridge, MA: Harvard University Press, 1968.

Ficino, Marsilio. *Opera Omnia*. 2 vols. Basel, 1576.

Fielding, Henry. *The History of Tom Jones, a Foundling*. Ed. Martin Battestin. Middletown, CT: Wesleyan University Press, 1975.

Flannagan, Roy. "Bate's *Samuel Johnson* and Johnson's *Life of Milton*: Puckish or Perverse? A Review Article." *Milton Quarterly* 12 (1978): 147–48.

Fleeman, J. D., ed. *The Sale Catalogue of Samuel Johnson's Library: A Facsimile Edition*. Victoria: University of Victoria Press, 1975.

Foxe, John. *The Book of Martyrs: Containing an Account of the Sufferings and Death of the Protestants in the Reign of Queen Mary the First, Illustrated with Copper-Plates*. London, 1732; 2nd edn., 1741; 3rd edn., 1761; 4th edn., 1776; 5th edn., 1784.

A Select History of the Lives and Sufferings of the Principal English Protestant Martyrs. London, 1746.

The Book of Martyrs . . . Extracted from the Three Large Volumes of . . . Mr. John Fox, and Divers Other Books . . . and Now Rendered into Modern English. Ed. Thomas Mason. London, 1747–48.

The History of the Ten Persecutions in the Primitive Church . . . Extracted from the Martyrology of Mr. John Fox. Edinburgh, 1761.

The New and Complete Book of Martyrs; or, An Universal History of Martyrdom: Being Fox's Book of Martyrs, Revised and Corrected . . . by Paul Wright . . . Embellished with . . . Uncommonly High-Finished Copper-Plates. London, 1784; 2nd edn., 1785; 3rd edn., 1790; 4th edn., 2 vols., 1794; 5th edn., 1800.

Fox's Original and Complete Book of Martyrs . . . Now Carefully Revised, Corrected, and Improved, by a Minister of the Gospel . . . Embellished with near 300 Elegant Engravings. London, 1795.

New Book of Martyrs in Quarto, with Engravings from Original Designs. Ed. J. S. Jordan. London, 1795.

Freed, Lewis M. "The Sources of Johnson's *Dictionary.*" PhD diss., Cornell University, 1939.

Freedman, William. "Swift's Struldbruggs, Progress, and the Analogy of History." *Studies in English Literature, 1500–1900* 35 (1995): 457–72.

Frushell, Richard C. "Spenser and the Eighteenth-Century Schools." *Spenser Studies* 7 (1986): 175–98.

Edmund Spenser in the Early Eighteenth Century: Education, Imitation, and the Making of a Literary Model. Pittsburgh: Duquesne University Press, 1999.

Frye, Northrop. *Anatomy of Criticism: Four Essays.* Princeton: Princeton University Press, 1957.

Furetière, Antoine. *Dictionaire universel, contenant generalement tous les mots françois.* 2 vols. The Hague, 1690.

Fussell, Paul. *Samuel Johnson and the Life of Writing.* New York: Harcourt Brace Jovanovich, 1971.

Gay, John. *Poetry and Prose.* Ed. Vinton A. Dearing. 2 vols. Oxford: Clarendon Press, 1974.

Gerrard, Christine. *The Patriot Opposition to Walpole: Politics, Poetry, and National Myth, 1725–1742.* Oxford: Clarendon Press, 1994.

Gibbon, Edward. *The History of the Decline and Fall of the Roman Empire.* Ed. David Womersley. 3 vols. London: Allen Lane, The Penguin Press, 1994.

Gibson [pseud.]. *Memoirs of Queen Anne: Being a Compleat Supplement to the History of Her Reign, wherein the Transactions of the Last Four Years Are Fully Related.* London, 1729.

Gildon, Charles. *The Life of Mr. Thomas Betterton.* London, 1710.

Gilmore, Myron P. *The World of Humanism, 1453–1517.* New York: Harper, 1952.

Gilmore, Thomas B., Jr. "Johnson's Attitudes toward French Influence on the English Language." *Modern Philology* 78 (1981): 243–60.

Goldsmith, Oliver. *Collected Works.* Ed. Arthur Friedman. 5 vols. Oxford: Clarendon Press, 1966.

Grafton, Anthony. *Joseph Scaliger: A Study in the History of Classical Scholarship.* 2 vols. Oxford: Clarendon Press, 1983–93.

Le Grand dictionnaire de l'Académie françoise. 2nd edn. Paris, 1695.

Gray, James. *Johnson's Sermons: A Study.* Oxford: Clarendon Press, 1972.

Gray, Thomas. *Correspondence of Thomas Gray.* Ed. Paget Toynbee and Leonard Whibley. 3 vols. Oxford: Clarendon Press, 1935.

The Complete Poems of Thomas Gray: English, Latin and Greek. Ed. H. W. Starr and J. R. Hendrickson. Oxford: Clarendon Press, 1966.

Green, David. *Queen Anne.* New York: Scribner, 1970.

Green, William M. "Augustine on the Teaching of History." *Publications in Classical Philology* 12, no. 18 (1944): 315–32.

Greene, Donald J. *Samuel Johnson's Library: An Annotated Guide.* Victoria: University of Victoria Press, 1975.

The Politics of Samuel Johnson. 2nd edn. Athens: University of Georgia Press, 1990.

Grey, Zachary. *Critical, Historical, and Explanatory Notes on Shakespeare, with Emendations of the Text and Metre.* 2 vols. London, 1754.

Griffin, Dustin. *Regaining Paradise: Milton and the Eighteenth Century.* Cambridge: Cambridge University Press, 1986.

Griffin, Robert J. *Wordsworth's Pope: A Study in Literary Historiography.* Cambridge: Cambridge University Press, 1995.

"The Age of 'The Age of' Is Over: Johnson and New Versions of the Late Eighteenth Century." *Modern Language Quarterly* 62, no. 4 (Dec. 2001): 377–91.

Grotius, Hugo. *H. Grotius of the Rights of War and Peace.* 3 vols. London, 1715.

The Rights of War and Peace, in Three Books. London, 1738.

The Rights of War and Peace, Including the Law of Nature and of Nations. Trans. A. C. Campbell. London: M. W. Dunne, 1901.

The Truth of the Christian Religion. 4th edn. London, 1743.

Grove, Joseph. *The History of the Life and Times of Cardinal Wolsey, Prime Minister to King Henry VIII.* 4 vols. London, 1742–44.

Hagstrum, Jean. *Samuel Johnson's Literary Criticism.* Minneapolis: University of Minnesota Press, 1952.

The Sister Arts: The Tradition of Literary Pictorialism and English Poetry from Dryden to Gray. Chicago: University of Chicago Press, 1958.

Hale, John. *The Civilization of Europe in the Renaissance.* New York: Atheneum, 1994.

Halifax, George Savile, Marquis of. *The Works of George Savile, Marquis of Halifax.* Ed. Mark N. Brown. 3 vols. Oxford: Clarendon Press, 1989.

Haskins, Charles Homer. *The Renaissance of the Twelfth Century.* Cambridge, MA: Harvard University Press, 1927.

Haugen, Kristine Louise. "Richard Bentley: Scholarship and Criticism in Eighteenth-Century England." PhD diss., Princeton University, 2001.

Hawkins, Thomas. *The Origin of the English Drama: Illustrated in Its Various Species, viz., Mystery, Morality, Tragedy, and Comedy, by Specimens from Our Earliest Writers.* 3 vols. Oxford, 1773.

Hay, Dennis. *The Renaissance Debate.* New York: Holt, Rinehart and Winston, 1965.

Hayward, Thomas. *The British Muse; or, A Collection of Thoughts Moral, Natural, and Sublime, of Our English Poets Who Flourished in the Sixteenth and Seventeenth Centuries.* 3 vols. London, 1738.

Hazlitt, William. *The Collected Works of William Hazlitt*. Ed. A. R. Waller and Arnold Glover. 12 vols. London: Dent, 1902–04.

Headley, Henry. *Select Beauties of Ancient English Poetry*. 2 vols. London, 1787.

Hedrick, Elizabeth. "Fixing the Language: Johnson, Chesterfield, and *The Plan of a Dictionary*." *ELH* 55 (1988): 421–42.

Henson, Eithne. *"The Fictions of Romantick Chivalry": Samuel Johnson and Romance*. Rutherford, NJ: Fairleigh Dickinson University Press, 1992.

Hill, Christopher. *Some Intellectual Consequences of the English Revolution*. Madison: University of Wisconsin Press, 1980.

Hill, G. B., ed. *Johnsonian Miscellanies*. 2 vols. Oxford: Clarendon Press, 1897.

The History of the Life and Reign of Queen Elizabeth. 2 vols. London, 1740.

Hollis, Christopher. *Dr. Johnson*. London: Golancz, 1928.

Hooker, Richard. *A Faithful Abridgment of the Works of That Learned and Judicious Divine, Richard Hooker*. London, 1705.

— *Of the Laws of Ecclesiastical Polity*. In the Folger Library Edition of the Works of Richard Hooker. Ed. W. Speed Hill *et al.* 7 vols. in 8. Cambridge, MA: Harvard University Press; Binghamton, NY: Medieval & Renaissance Texts & Studies, 1977–93.

Horace. *Opera*. Ed. Edward C. Wickham. Oxford: Clarendon Press, 1901.

Houston, Percy Hazen. *Dr. Johnson: A Study in Eighteenth-Century Humanism*. Cambridge, MA: Harvard University Press, 1923.

Howard, Edward. *Poems, and Essays: With a Paraphrase of Cicero Laelius, or, Of Friendship*. London, 1674.

Howard, W. *A Paraphrase in Verse, on Part of the First Book of Milton's Paradise Lost*. London, 1738.

Hudson, Nicholas. *Samuel Johnson and Eighteenth-Century Thought*. Oxford: Clarendon Press, 1988.

Huizinga, Johan. *Men and Ideas: History, the Middle Ages, the Renaissance: Essays*. Trans. James S. Holmes and Hans van Marle. New York: Meridian Books, 1959.

— *The Autumn of the Middle Ages*. Trans. Rodney J. Payton and Ulrich Mammitzsch. Chicago: University of Chicago Press, 1996.

Hume, David. *The Letters of David Hume*. Ed. J. Y. T. Greig. 2 vols. Oxford: Clarendon Press, 1932.

— *Essays Moral, Political and Literary*. Oxford: Oxford University Press, 1963.

— *The Enquiries concerning Human Understanding and concerning the Principles of Morals*. Ed. L. A. Selby-Bigge, rev. P. H. Nidditch. 3rd edn. Oxford: Clarendon Press, 1975.

— *The History of England from the Invasion of Julius Caesar to the Revolution in 1688*. 6 vols. Indianapolis: Liberty Fund, 1983.

Hurd, Richard. *The Works of Richard Hurd*. 8 vols. London, 1811.

Jackson, Andrew. *Paradise Lost: A Poem, Attempted in Rhime*. London, 1740 [i.e. 1739].

Jackson, H. J. "Johnson and Burton: The *Anatomy of Melancholy* and the *Dictionary of the English Language*." *English Studies in Canada* 5 (1979): 36–48.

Jackson, William. *Lycidas: A Musical Entertainment*. London, 1767.

Jain, Nalini. "Echoes of Milton in Johnson's *Irene.*" *American Notes & Queries* 24 (1986): 134–36.

Japp, Uwe. *Beziehungssinn: Ein Konzept der Literaturgeschichte*. Frankfurt am Main: Europäische Verlagsanstalt, 1980.

Jarvis, Simon. *Scholars and Gentlemen: Shakespearian Textual Criticism and Representations of Scholarly Labour, 1725–1765*. Oxford: Clarendon Press, 1995.

Javitch, Daniel. *Proclaiming a Classic: The Canonization of "Orlando Furioso."* Princeton: Princeton University Press, 1991.

Johnson, Samuel. *A Dictionary of the English Language*. 2 vols. London, 1755.

The Works of Samuel Johnson. Ed. Sir John Hawkins. 11 vols. London, 1787.

The Works of Samuel Johnson. 11 vols. Oxford, 1825.

Lives of the English Poets. Ed. G. B. Hill. 3 vols. Oxford: Clarendon Press, 1905.

Samuel Johnson's Prefaces and Dedications. Ed. Allen T. Hazen. New Haven: Yale University Press, 1937.

Diaries, Prayers, and Annals. Ed. E. L. McAdam, Jr. Vol. 1 of the Yale Edition of the *Works of Samuel Johnson*. New Haven: Yale University Press, 1958.

The Idler and the Adventurer. Ed. W. J. Bate, John M. Bullitt, and L. F. Powell. Vol. 11 of the Yale Edition of the *Works of Samuel Johnson*. New Haven: Yale University Press, 1963.

The Rambler. Ed. Walter Jackson Bate and Albrecht B. Strauss. Vols. 111–v of the Yale Edition of the *Works of Samuel Johnson*. New Haven: Yale University Press, 1969.

Poems. Ed. E. L. McAdam, Jr. Vol. v1 of the Yale Edition of the *Works of Samuel Johnson*. New Haven: Yale University Press, 1964.

Johnson on Shakespeare. Ed. Arthur Sherbo. Vols. v11 and v111 of the Yale Edition of the *Works of Samuel Johnson*. New Haven: Yale University Press, 1968.

A Journey to the Western Islands of Scotland. Ed. Mary Lascelles. Vol. 1x of the Yale Edition of the *Works of Samuel Johnson*. New Haven: Yale University Press, 1971.

Political Writings. Ed. Donald J. Greene. Vol. x of the Yale Edition of the *Works of Samuel Johnson*. New Haven: Yale University Press, 1977.

Sermons. Ed. Jean Hagstrum and James Gray. Vol. x1v of the Yale Edition of the *Works of Samuel Johnson*. New Haven: Yale University Press, 1978.

A Voyage to Abyssinia. Ed. Joel Gold. Vol. xv of the Yale Edition of the *Works of Samuel Johnson*. New Haven: Yale University Press, 1985.

Rasselas and Other Tales. Ed. Gwin J. Kolb. Vol. xv1 of the Yale Edition of the *Works of Samuel Johnson*. New Haven: Yale University Press, 1990.

The Letters of Samuel Johnson. Ed. Bruce Redford. 5 vols. Princeton: Princeton University Press, 1992–94.

The Latin and Greek Poems of Samuel Johnson: Text, Translation and Commentary. Ed. Barry Baldwin. London: Duckworth, 1995.

A Dictionary of the English Language on CD-ROM: The First and Fourth Editions. Ed. Anne McDermott. Cambridge: Cambridge University Press, 1996.

Johnston, Arthur. *Enchanted Ground: The Study of Medieval Romance in the Eighteenth Century*. London: Athlone Press, 1964.

Jonson, Ben. *The Works*. Ed. Peter Whalley. 7 vols. London, 1756.

   The Complete Poems. Ed. George Parfitt. New Haven and London: Yale University Press, 1975.

Jortin, John. *The Life of Erasmus*. 2 vols. London, 1758–60.

Kaminski, Thomas. *The Early Career of Samuel Johnson*. New York: Oxford University Press, 1987.

Keats, John. *The Letters of John Keats*. Ed. Maurice Buxton Forman. 3rd edn. London: Oxford University Press, 1947.

Kemp, Anthony. *The Estrangement of the Past: A Study in the Origins of Modern Historical Consciousness*. Oxford: Oxford University Press, 1991.

Kendall, Paul Murray, ed. *Richard III: The Great Debate: Sir Thomas More's "History of King Richard III," Horace Walpole's "Historic Doubts on the Life and Reign of King Richard III."* New York: W. W. Norton, 1965.

Kermode, Frank. *The Classic: Literary Images of Permanence and Change*. Revised edn. Cambridge, MA: Harvard University Press, 1983.

Kerrigan, William, and Gordon Braden. *The Idea of the Renaissance*. Baltimore: Johns Hopkins University Press, 1989.

Kilbourne, H. R. "Dr. Johnson and War." *ELH* 12 (June 1945): 130–43.

Knoppers, Laura Lunger. *Historicizing Milton: Spectacle, Power, and Poetry in Restoration England*. Athens: University of Georgia Press, 1994.

Kohn, Hans. *The Idea of Nationalism: A Study in Its Origins and Background*. New York: Macmillan, 1944.

Kolb, Gwin J., and Ruth A. Kolb. "The Selection and Use of the Illustrative Quotations in Dr. Johnson's *Dictionary*." In *New Aspects of Lexicography: Literary Criticism, Intellectual History, and Social Change*, ed. Howard D. Weinbrot, pp. 61–72. Carbondale: Southern Illinois University Press, 1972.

Korshin, Paul J. "Johnson and the Renaissance Dictionary." *Journal of the History of Ideas* 35 (1974): 300–12.

   "Johnson and the Scholars." In *Samuel Johnson: New Critical Essays*, ed. Isobel Grundy, pp. 51–69. London: Vision, 1984.

Kramnick, Isaac. "Augustan Politics and English Historiography: The Debate on the English Past, 1730–35." *History and Theory* 8 (1967): 33–56.

Kramnick, Jonathan Brody. *Making the English Canon: Print Capitalism and the Cultural Past, 1700–1770*. Cambridge: Cambridge University Press, 1998.

Kristeller, Paul Oskar. *Renaissance Thought: The Classic, Scholastic and Humanist Strains*. New York: Harper & Row, 1961.

Kucich, Greg. *Keats, Shelley, and Romantic Spenserianism*. University Park: Pennsylvania State University Press, 1991.

Lauder, William. *An Essay on Milton's Use and Imitation of the Moderns, in His Paradise Lost*. London, 1750.

Lévi-Strauss, Claude. *The Savage Mind*. Chicago: University of Chicago Press, 1966.

Levine, Joseph M. *Humanism and History: Studies in the Development of Modern British Historiography*. Ithaca: Cornell University Press, 1987.

Between the Ancients and the Moderns: Baroque Culture in Restoration England. New Haven: Yale University Press, 1999.

Lewis, C. S. *English Literature in the Sixteenth Century, Excluding Drama*. New York: Oxford University Press, 1954.

Lewis, Jayne Elizabeth. "Mary Stuart's 'Fatal Box': Sentimental History and the Revival of the Casket Letters Controversy." *The Age of Johnson: A Scholarly Annual* 7 (1996): 427–73.

The Life and Glorious Reign of Queen Elizabeth. London, 1708.

Lillo, George. *The Dramatic Works of George Lillo*. Ed. James L. Steffensen. Oxford: Clarendon Press, 1993.

L[indsay], J. *A Brief History of England, Both in Church and State; by Way of Question and Answer*. London, 1748.

Lipking, Lawrence. *The Ordering of the Arts in Eighteenth-Century England*. Princeton: Princeton University Press, 1970.

"What Was It Like to Be Johnson?" *The Age of Johnson: A Scholarly Annual* 1 (1987): 35–57.

Locke, John. *Epistola de tolerantia: A Letter on Toleration*. Ed. Raymond Klibansky; trans. J. W. Gough. Oxford: Clarendon Press, 1968.

Lockman, John. *A New History of England, by Question and Answer*. London, 1734.

Lovejoy, Arthur O. *The Great Chain of Being: A Study of the History of an Idea*. Cambridge, MA: Harvard University Press, 1936.

Lunt, W. E. *History of England*. New York: Harper, 1928.

Lyttelton, George, Baron Lyttelton. *Letters from a Persian in England, to His Friend at Ispahan*. 3rd edn. London, 1735.

McAdam, E. L., Jr. "Johnson's Lives of Sarpi, Blake, and Drake." *PMLA* 58 (1943): 466–76.

Dr. Johnson and the English Law. Syracuse: Syracuse University Press, 1951.

"Inkhorn Words Before Dr. Johnson." In *Eighteenth-Century Studies in Honor of Donald F. Hyde*, ed. W. H. Bond, pp. 187–206. New York: Grolier Club, 1970.

McCue, George S. "Sam. Johnson's Word-Hoard." *MLN* 63 (1948): 43–45.

McGann, Jerome. "History, Herstory, Theirstory, Ourstory." In *Theoretical Issues in Literary History*, ed. David Perkins, pp. 196–205. Cambridge, MA: Harvard University Press, 1991.

McIntosh, Carey. *The Choice of Life: Samuel Johnson and the World of Fiction*. New Haven: Yale University Press, 1973.

McLaughlin, Martin L. "Humanist Concepts of Renaissance and Middle Ages in the Tre- and Quattrocento." *Renaissance Studies* 2, no. 2 (1988): 131–42.

Literary Imitation in the Italian Renaissance: The Theory and Practice of Literary Imitation in Italy from Dante to Bembo. Oxford: Clarendon Press, 1995.

Macaulay, Thomas Babington, 1st Baron. *The Works of Lord Macaulay*, 12 vols. London: Longmans, Green, 1898.

Maclure, Millar, ed. *Marlowe: The Critical Heritage, 1588–1896*. London: Routledge & Kegan Paul, 1979.

Manley, Delarivier. *A Modest Enquiry into the Reasons of the Joy Expressed by a Certain Sett of People, upon the Spreading of a Report of Her Majesty's Death*. London, 1714.

Mansfield, Bruce. *The Phoenix of His Age: Interpretations of Erasmus c. 1550–1750*. Toronto: University of Toronto Press, 1979.

Man on His Own: Interpretations of Erasmus c. 1750–1920. Toronto: University of Toronto Press, 1992.

Marsden, Jean I. *The Re-Imagined Text: Shakespeare, Adaptation, and Eighteenth-Century Literary Theory*. Lexington: University Press of Kentucky, 1995.

Martin, Benjamin. *Institutions of Language: Containing a Physico-grammatical Essay on the Propriety and Rationale of the English Tongue*. London, 1748.

Meinecke, Friedrich. *Historism: The Rise of a New Historical Outlook*. Trans. J. E. Anderson. London: Routledge & Kegan Paul, 1972.

Michelet, Jules. *Œuvres Complètes*. Ed. Paul Viallaneix. 21 vols. Paris: Flammarion, 1971–.

Middleton, Patrick. *A Dissertation upon the Power of the Church; in a Middle Way*. London, 1733.

Miller, Frances Schouler. "The Historic Sense of Thomas Warton, Junior." *ELH* 5 (1938): 71–92.

Milton, John. *Poetical Works of Mr. John Milton*. London, 1695.

A Complete Collection of the Historical, Political, and Miscellaneous Works of John Milton, Both English and Latin. Ed. John Toland. 3 vols. Amsterdam [i.e. London], 1698.

An Essay upon Divorcement; Writ for the Good of Both Sexes. London, 1715.

Considerations touching the Likeliest Means of Removing Hirelings out of the Church. London, 1717; 2nd edn., London, 1723; 3rd edn., Newcastle-upon-Tyne, 1732; 4th edn., Edinburgh and London, 1756; "3rd edn." [i.e. 5th edn.], London, 1743; 6th edn., London, 1787; 7th edn., Edinburgh, 1797.

Comus, a Mask: Now Adapted to the Stage, as Alter'd from Milton's Mask at Ludlow-Castle. Adapted by John Dalton. 2nd edn. London, 1735.

Areopagitica: A Speech of Mr. John Milton, for the Liberty of Unlicens'd Printing, to the Parliament of England. Preface by James Thomson. London, 1738.

A Complete Collection of the Historical, Political, and Miscellaneous Works of John Milton. Ed. Thomas Birch. 2 vols. London, 1738.

A Manifesto of the Lord Protector . . . wherein Is Shewn the Reasonableness of the Cause of this Republic against the Depredations of the Spaniards. London, 1738.

The Tractate of Education. Glasgow, 1746.

Paradise Lost. Ed. Thomas Newton. 2 vols. London, 1749.

An Essay of Education. London, 1751.

A Tractate of Education. Berwick-upon-Tweed, 1753.

The Works of John Milton, Historical, Political, and Miscellaneous. Ed. Thomas Birch, rev. Richard Baron. 2 vols. London, 1753.

Eikonoklastes. Ed. and enlarged by Richard Baron. London, 1756; 2nd edn., 1770.

An Old Looking-glass for the Laity and Clergy of All Denominations, Who Either Give or Receive Money under Pretence of the Gospel: Being Considerations touching the Likeliest Means to Remove Hirelings out of the Church of Christ. Philadelphia, 1770.

The First Six Books of Milton's Paradise Lost, Rendered into Grammatical Construction. Ed. James Buchanan. Edinburgh, 1773.

The Tenure of Kings and Magistrates. Dublin, 1784.

A Treatise of Civil Power in Ecclesiastical Causes. London, 1790.

A Ready and Easy Way to Establish a Free Commonwealth. London, 1791.

Poems upon Several Occasions. Ed. Thomas Warton. 2nd edn. London, 1791.

The Complete Prose Works of John Milton. Ed. Douglas Bush *et al.* 8 vols. in 10. New Haven: Yale University Press, 1953–82.

Mommsen, Theodor E. "Petrarch's Conception of the 'Dark Ages.' " *Speculum* 17 (1942): 226–42.

Montagu, Elizabeth. *An Essay on the Writings and Genius of Shakespear, Compared with the Greek and French Dramatic Poets*. London, 1796.

Moore, J. L. *Tudor–Stuart Views on the Growth, Status, and Destiny of the English Language*. Halle a.S.: M. Niemeyer, 1910.

More, Thomas. *Utopia*. Ed. Edward Surtz, S.J., and J. H. Hexter. Vol. IV of the *Complete Works of St. Thomas More*. New Haven: Yale University Press, 1965.

Mossner, Ernest Campbell. *The Life of David Hume*. 2nd edn. Oxford: Clarendon Press, 1980.

Nagashima, Daisuke. *Johnson the Philologist*. Osaka: Intercultural Research Institute, 1988.

Nath, Prem. "Johnson Agonistes and Milton's *Samson*." *American Notes & Queries* 20 (1982): 69–70.

Nauert, Charles G., Jr. *Humanism and the Culture of Renaissance Europe*. Cambridge: Cambridge University Press, 1995.

Nethercot, Arthur H. "The Reputation of the 'Metaphysical Poets' during the Age of Pope." *Philological Quarterly* 4 (1925): 161–79.

"The Repuation of the 'Metaphysical Poets' during the Age of Johnson and the 'Romantic Revival.' " *Studies in Philology* 22 (1925): 81–132.

Nichols, John, ed. *Progresses and Public Processions of Queen Elizabeth*. 3 vols. London, 1788–1821.

Illustrations of the Literary History of the Eighteenth Century. 8 vols. London, 1817–58.

Noyes, Gertrude E. "The Critical Reception of Johnson's *Dictionary* in the Latter Eighteenth Century." *Modern Philology* 52 (1955): 175–91.

Noyes, Robert Gale. *Ben Jonson on the English Stage, 1660–1776*. Cambridge, MA: Harvard University Press, 1935.

O'Brien, Karen. *Narratives of Enlightenment: Cosmopolitan History from Voltaire to Gibbon*. Cambridge: Cambridge University Press, 1997.

Ogden, James. "A Johnson Borrowing from Milton." *Notes & Queries* 39 (1992): 482.

Oldmixon, John. *The Critical History of England Ecclesiastical and Civil*. 2 vols. London, 1724.

The History of England During the Reigns of Henry VIII. Edward VI. Queen Mary. Queen Elizabeth. Including the History of the Reformation of the Churches of England and Scotland. London, 1739.

Osborn, James M. "Johnson on the Sanctity of an Author's Text." *PMLA* 50 (1935): 928–29.

Parker, G. F. *Johnson's Shakespeare*. Oxford: Clarendon Press, 1989.

Pater, Walter. *The Renaissance: Studies in Art and Poetry*. Ed. Donald L. Hill. Berkeley: University of California Press, 1980.

Peacock, Thomas Love. *The Works of Thomas Love Peacock*. Ed. H. F. B. Brett-Smith and C. E. Jones. 10 vols. London: Constable, 1924.

Pellisson-Fontanier, Paul. *Histoire de l'Academie françoise*. New edn. Amsterdam, 1717.

Percy, Thomas. *Reliques of Ancient English Poetry*. 3 vols. London, 1765.

Petrarca, Francesco. *On His Own Ignorance and that of Others*. In *The Renaissance Philosophy of Man*, ed. Ernst Cassirer, Paul Oskar Kristeller, and John Herman Randall, Jr., pp. 47–133. Chicago: University of Chicago Press, 1948.

Philips, Ambrose. *The Poems of Ambrose Philips*. Ed. M. G. Segar. Oxford: Basil Blackwell, 1937.

Phillips, Edward. *The New World of English Words; or, A General Dictionary*. London, 1658.

   Theatrum Poetarum; or, A Compleat Collection of the Poets. London, 1675.

Phillips, Margaret Mann. "Erasmus and the Classics." In *Erasmus*, ed. T. A. Dorey, pp. 1–30. London: Routledge & Kegan Paul, 1970.

Piozzi, Hester Lynch. *Thraliana: The Diary of Mrs. Hester Lynch Thrale (Later Mrs. Piozzi), 1776–1809*. Ed. Katherine C. Balderston. 2 vols. Oxford: Clarendon Press, 1942.

Pittock, Joan. *The Ascendancy of Taste: The Achievement of Joseph and Thomas Warton*. London: Routledge & Kegan Paul, 1973.

Pope, Alexander. *The Twickenham Edition of the Poems of Alexander Pope*. Ed. John Butt *et al*. 11 vols. in 12. New Haven: Yale University Press, 1939–69.

   The Prose Works of Alexander Pope. Vol. 11. Ed. Rosemary Cowler. Hamden, CT: Archon Books, 1986.

Prior, Matthew. *The Literary Works of Matthew Prior*. Ed. H. Bunker Wright and Monroe K. Spears. 2 vols. Oxford: Clarendon Press, 1959.

A Protestant Memorial for the Seventeenth of November: Being the Inauguration-Day of Queen Elizabeth. London, 1713.

Quinlan, Maurice James. *Samuel Johnson: A Layman's Religion*. Madison: University of Wisconsin Press, 1964.

Quintilian. *Institutionis oratoriae libri duodecim*. Ed. M. Winterbottom. 2 vols. Oxford: Clarendon Press, 1970.

Radcliffe, David Hall. *Edmund Spenser: A Reception History*. Columbia, SC: Camden House, 1996.

Rapin-Thoyras, Paul de. *The History of England*. Trans. Nicholas Tindal. 15 vols. London, 1726–31.

Reade, Aleyn Lyell, ed. *Johnsonian Gleanings*. 11 vols. London: Francis, 1909–52.

Reddick, Allen. *The Making of Johnson's Dictionary, 1746–1773*. 2nd edn. Cambridge: Cambridge University Press, 1996.

Redford, Bruce. "Defying Our Master: The Appropriation of Milton in Johnson's Political Tracts." *Studies in Eighteenth-Century Culture* 20 (1990): 81–91.

Reynolds, L. D., and N. G. Wilson. *Scribes and Scholars: A Guide to the Transmission of Greek and Latin Literature*. 3rd edn. Oxford: Clarendon Press, 1991.

Richardson, Jonathan, father and son. *Explanatory Notes and Remarks on Milton's Paradise Lost*. London, 1734.

Richelet, Pierre. *Dictionnaire françois, contenant les mots et les choses, plusieurs nouvelles remarques sur la langue françoise*. Geneva, 1680.

Ridley, Glocester. *The Life of Dr. Nicholas Ridley, Sometime Bishop of London: Shewing the Plan and Progress of the Reformation*. London, 1763.

Rinaker, Clarissa. "Thomas Warton and the Historical Method in Literary Criticism." *PMLA* 30 (1915): 79–109.

Ritson, Joseph. *The English Anthology*. 3 vols. London, 1793–94.

Robinson, Fred C. "Medieval, the Middle Ages." *Speculum* 59 (1984): 745–56.

Rogers, Pat. "Thomas Warton and the Waxing of the Middle Ages." In *Medieval Literature and Antiquities: Studies in Honour of Basil Cottle*, ed. Myra Stokes and T. L. Burton, pp. 175–86. Cambridge: D. S. Brewer, 1987.

Rolt, Richard. *The Lives of the Principal Reformers, Both Englishmen and Foreigners, comprehending the General History of the Reformation*. London, 1759.

Ross, Trevor. *The Making of the English Literary Canon: From the Middle Ages to the Late Eighteenth Century*. Montreal and Kingston: McGill-Queen's University Press, 1998.

Rowe, Nicholas. *The Tragedy of Jane Shore*. London, 1714.

Ruffhead, Owen. *The Life of Alexander Pope, Esq*. London, 1769.

Rupp, Gordon. *Religion in England, 1688–1791*. Oxford: Clarendon Press, 1986.

Rymer, Thomas. *The Tragedies of the Last Age Consider'd and Examin'd by the Practice of the Ancients*. London, 1678.

    Foedera, conventiones, literae, et cujuscunque generis acta publica: inter reges Angliae, et alios quosvis imperatores, reges, pontifices, principes, vel communitates: ab ineunte saeculo duo-decimo, viz. ab anno 1101, ad nostra usque tempora habita aut tractata. 20 vols. London, 1704–35.

Sanderson, Robert. XXXVI *Sermons*. 8th edn. London, 1689.

Scaliger, Julius Caesar. *Poetices libri septem*. Lyons, 1561.

Schmidt, Siegfried J. "On Writing Histories of Literature: Some Remarks from a Constructivist Point of View." *Poetics* 14 (1985): 279–301.

Scott, Izora. *Controversies over the Imitation of Cicero as a Model for Style and Some Phases of their Influence on the Schools of the Renaissance*. 2 vols. in 1. New York: Columbia University Teachers College, 1910.

Segar, Mary. "Dictionary Making in the Early Eighteenth Century." *Review of English Studies* 7 (1931): 210–13.

Sensabaugh, George. *That Grand Whig, Milton*. Stanford: Stanford University Press, 1952.

Shadwell, Thomas. *The Humorists*. London, 1671.

Shakespeare, William. *The Works of Shakespear*. 7 vols. Ed. Alexander Pope. London, 1725.

    The Works of Shakespear. Ed. Thomas Hanmer. 6 vols. Oxford, 1744.

The Works of William Shakespeare. Ed. Samuel Johnson. 8 vols. London, 1765.

Twenty of the Plays of Shakespeare, Being the Whole Number Printed in Quarto during His Life-Time, or Before the Restoration. 4 vols. London, 1766.

Shawcross, John T., ed. *Milton: The Critical Heritage.* 2 vols. London: Routledge & Kegan Paul, 1970–72.

Shepard, Odell. "Thomas Warton and the Historical Point of View in Criticism." *JEGP* 16 (1917): 153–63.

Sherbo, Arthur. *Samuel Johnson, Editor of Shakespeare.* Urbana: University of Illinois Press, 1956.

Sidney, Sir Philip. *Sir Philip Sydney's Defence of Poetry.* London, 1787.

A Defence of Poetry. Ed. Jan Van Dorsten. Oxford: Oxford University Press, 1966.

Simone, Franco. "La Coscienza della Rinascita negli umanisti." *La Rinascita* 2 (1939): 383–71; 3 (1940): 163–86.

Six Old Plays, on which Shakspeare Founded His Measure for Measure, Comedy of Errors, Taming the Shrew, King John, K. Henry IV. and K. Henry V., King Lear. Ed. John Nichols and George Steevens. 2 vols. London, 1779.

Sledd, James H., and Gwin J. Kolb. *Dr. Johnson's "Dictionary": Essays in the Biography of a Book.* Chicago: University of Chicago Press, 1955.

Smalley, Beryl. *Historians in the Middle Ages.* New York: Charles Scribner's Sons, 1974.

Smith, A. J. "Donne's Reputation." in *John Donne: Essays in Celebration,* ed. A. J. Smith, pp. 1–27. London: Methuen, 1972.

Smith, Adam. *An Inquiry into the Nature and Causes of the Wealth of Nations.* Ed. Edwin Cannan. 2nd edn. 2 vols. in 1. Chicago: University of Chicago Press, 1976.

Smith, D. Nichol, ed. *Shakespeare in the Eighteenth Century.* Oxford: Clarendon Press, 1928.

Eighteenth Century Essays on Shakespeare. 2nd edn. Oxford: Clarendon Press, 1963.

Smith, George Green. *A New Version of the Paradise Lost; or, Milton Paraphrased.* Oxford, 1756.

Smith, Gregory, ed. *Elizabethan Critical Essays.* 2 vols. Oxford: Clarendon Press, 1904.

Smollett, Tobias. *A Complete History of England: Deduced from the Descent of Julius Caesar, to the Treaty of Aix La Chapelle, 1748.* 4 vols. London, 1757–58.

Speck, W. A. *The Birth of Britain: A New Nation, 1700–1710.* Oxford: Blackwell, 1994.

The Spectator. Ed. Donald F. Bond. 5 vols. Oxford: Clarendon Press, 1965.

Spence, Joseph. *Observations, Anecdotes, and Characters of Books and Men Collected from Conversation.* Ed. James M. Osborn. 2 vols. Oxford: Clarendon Press, 1966.

Spenser, Edmund. *The Works of Mr. Edmund Spenser.* Ed. John Hughes. 6 vols. London, 1715.

The Faerie Queene by Edmund Spenser, with an Exact Collation of the Two Original Editions. Ed. T. Birch. 3 vols. London, 1751.

The Works of Edmund Spenser. Ed. Henry John Todd. 8 vols. London, 1805.

The Works of Edmund Spenser: A Variorum Edition. Ed. Edwin Greenlaw, Charles Grosvenor Osgood, and Frederick Morgan Padelford. 11 vols. Baltimore: Johns Hopkins University Press, 1932–57.

Spingarn, J. E., ed. *Critical Essays of the Seventeenth Century*. 3 vols. Oxford: Clarendon Press, 1908–9.

Sprat, Thomas. *History of the Royal Society*. Ed. Jackson I. Cope and Harold Whitmore Jones. St. Louis: Washington University Press, 1958.

Starnes, DeWitt T., and Gertrude E. Noyes. *The English Dictionary from Cawdrey to Johnson, 1604–1755*. 2nd edn. Amsterdam and Philadelphia: J. Benjamin, 1991.

Stein, Dieter. "Sorting Out the Variants: Standardization and Social Factors in the English Language 1600–1800." In *Towards a Standard English, 1600–1800*, ed. Dieter Stein and Ingrid Tieken-Boon van Ostade, pp. 1–17. Berlin: Mouton de Gruyter, 1994.

Stephen, Leslie. *Samuel Johnson*. New York: Harper, 1900.

Stern, Henry Raymond. "The Concept of Linguistic Purity in England from 1700 to the Present." PhD diss., Northwestern University, 1968.

Stillingfleet, Benjamin. *Paradise Lost: An Oratorio*. London, 1760.

Stock, R. D. *Samuel Johnson and Neoclassical Dramatic Theory: The Intellectual Context of the "Preface to Shakespeare."* Lincoln: University of Nebraska Press, 1973.

Stromberg, Roland N. *Religious Liberalism in Eighteenth-Century England*. London: Oxford University Press, 1954.

Strype, John. *Annals of the Reformation and Establishment of Religion . . . during the First Twelve Years of Queen Elizabeth's Happy Reign*. London, 1709.

Stuart, Gilbert. *The History of the Establishment of the Reformation of Religion in Scotland*. London and Edinburgh, 1780.

Surrey, Henry Howard, Earl of. *Poems of Henry Howard, Earl of Surrey, Who Flourish'd in the Reign of Henry the Eighth; Printed from a Correct Copy, with the Poems of Sir Thomas Wiat*. Ed. George Sewell [?]. London, 1717.

Swift, Jonathan. *The Prose Works of Jonathan Swift*. Ed. Herbert Davis. 14 vols. Oxford: Basil Blackwell, 1939–68.

A Tale of a Tub, to Which Is Added the Battle of the Books and the Mechanical Operation of the Spirit. Ed. A. C. Guthkelch and D. Nichol Smith. 2nd edn. Oxford: Clarendon Press, 1958.

A Discourse of the Contests and Dissentions between the Nobles and the Commons in Athens and Rome. Ed. Frank H. Ellis. Oxford: Clarendon Press, 1967.

Tacitus. *Opera minora*. Ed. Henry Furneaux and J. G. C. Anderson. Oxford: Clarendon Press, 1939.

Tankard, Paul. " 'That Great Literary Projector': Samuel Johnson's *Designs*, or Catalogue of Projected Works." *The Age of Johnson: A Scholarly Annual* 13 (2002): 103–80.

Terence. *Comoediae*. Ed. Robert Kauer and Wallace M. Lindsay. Oxford: Clarendon Press, 1958.

Theobald, Lewis. *Shakespeare Restored*. London, 1726.

Thomson, D. F. S. "The Latinity of Erasmus." In *Erasmus*, ed. T. A. Dorey, pp. 115–37. London: Routledge & Kegan Paul, 1970.

Thomson, James. *The Complete Poetical Works of James Thomson*. Ed. J. Logie Robertson. London: Oxford University Press, 1908.

Thomson, Patricia, ed. *Wyatt: The Critical Heritage*. London: Routledge & Kegan Paul, 1974.

Thou, Jacques-Auguste de. *Monsieur de Thou's History of His Own Time*. Trans. Bernard Wilson. 2 vols. London, 1729–30.

Tomarken, Edward. *A History of the Commentary on Selected Writings of Samuel Johnson*. Columbia, SC: Camden House, 1994.

Trevor-Roper, Hugh. *Queen Elizabeth's First Historian: William Camden and the Beginnings of English "Civil History."* London: Cape, 1971.

Tucker, Herbert F., Jr. "Spenser's Eighteenth-Century Readers and the Question of Unity in *The Faerie Queene*." *University of Toronto Quarterly* 46 (1977): 322–41.

Turnage, Maxine. "Samuel Johnson's Criticism of the Works of Edmund Spenser." *Studies in English Literature, 1500–1900* 10 (1970): 557–67.

"Upon Bentley's Emendation of Milton." *Student; or, The Oxford and Cambridge Monthly Miscellany* 2 (1751): 58.

Valla, Lorenzo. *Laurentii Vallae opera*. Basel, 1540.

Vance, John A. *Samuel Johnson and the Sense of History*. Athens: University of Georgia Press, 1984.

"Johnson's Historical Reviews." In *Fresh Reflections on Samuel Johnson: Essays in Criticism*, ed. Prem Nath, pp. 63–84. Troy, NY: Whitston, 1987.

Varga, Lucie. *Das Schlagwort vom "finsteren Mittelalter."* Aalen: Scientia Verlag, 1978.

Vasari, Giorgio. *Lives of the Painters, Sculptors, and Architects*. Trans. A. B. Hinds. 4 vols. London: J. M. Dent, 1963.

Venturo, David. *Johnson the Poet: The Poetic Career of Samuel Johnson*. Newark: University of Delaware Press, 1999.

Vickers, Brian, ed. *Shakespeare: The Critical Heritage*. 6 vols. London: Routledge & Kegan Paul, 1974–81.

Villiers, George, Second Duke of Buckingham. *A General Key to the Writings of the Poets of the Last Age*. London, 1723.

Vives, Juan Luis. *Über die Gründe des Verfalls der Künste / De causis corruptarum artium: Lateinisch-deutsche Ausgabe*. Ed. Emilio Hidalgo-Serna. München: Wilhelm Fink Verlag, 1990.

Vocabolario degli Accademici della Crusca. Venice, 1612.

Vogler, Thomas. "Romanticism and Literary Periods." *New German Critique* 38 (1986): 131–60.

Voltaire. *An Essay upon the Civil Wars of France*. London, 1727.

Wake, William. *William Wake's Gallican Correspondence and Related Documents, 1716–1731*. Ed. Leonard Adams. 7 vols. New York: Peter Lang, 1988–93.

Walpole, Horace. *The Castle of Otranto: A Gothic Story*. Ed. W. S. Lewis. London: Oxford University Press, 1964.

Walsh, Marcus. "Literary Annotation and Biblical Commentary: The Case of Patrick Hume's *Annotations* on *Paradise Lost.*" *Milton Quarterly* 22 (1988): 109–14.

Shakespeare, Milton, and Eighteenth-Century Literary Editing: The Beginnings of Interpretative Scholarship. Cambridge: Cambridge University Press, 1997.

"Eighteenth-Century Editing, 'Appropriation,' and Interpretation," *Shakespeare Survey* 51 (1998): 125–39.

Warton, Joseph. *An Essay on the Writings and Genius of Pope.* 2 vols. London, 1756–62.

Warton, Thomas. *Observations on the Fairy Queen of Spenser.* 2nd edn. 2 vols. London, 1762.

The History of English Poetry. 4 vols. London, 1775–81.

The Correspondence of Thomas Warton. Ed. David Fairer. Athens: University of Georgia Press, 1995.

Warton, Thomas, the Elder, Joseph Warton, and Thomas Warton the Younger. *The Three Wartons: A Choice of Their Verse.* Ed. Eric Partridge. London: Scholartis Press, 1927.

Wasserman, Earl R. *Elizabethan Poetry in the Eighteenth Century.* Urbana: University of Illinois Press, 1947.

Watkins, W. B. C. *Johnson and English Poetry before 1660.* Princeton: Princeton University Press, 1936.

Weinberg, Bernard. *A History of Literary Criticism in the Italian Renaissance.* Chicago: University of Chicago Press, 1961.

Weinbrot, Howard D. *The Formal Strain: Studies in Augustan Imitation and Satire.* Chicago: University of Chicago Press, 1969.

"Samuel Johnson's *Plan* and *Preface* to the *Dictionary*: The Growth of a Lexicographer's Mind." In *New Aspects of Lexicography: Literary Criticism, Intellectual History, and Social Change,* ed. Howard D. Weinbrot, pp. 73–94. Carbondale: Southern Illinois University Press, 1972.

"Twentieth-Century Scholarship and the Eighteenth-Century Canon." *Modern Language Quarterly* 61, no. 2 (June 2000): 395–414.

Weisinger, Herbert. "The Self-Awareness of the Renaissance as a Criterion of the Renaissance." *Papers of the Michigan Academy* 39 (1944): 561–67.

"The Seventeenth-Century Reputation of the Elizabethans." *Modern Language Quarterly* 6, no. 1 (March 1945): 13–20.

"The Study of the Revival of Learning in England from Bacon to Hallam." *Philological Quarterly* 25, no. 3 (July 1946): 221–47.

Wellek, René. "Periods and Movements in Literary History." In *English Institute Annual 1940,* pp. 73–93. New York: Columbia University Press, 1941.

The Rise of English Literary History. Chapel Hill: University of North Carolina Press, 1941.

Wexler, Victor G. *David Hume and the History of England.* Philadelphia: American Philosophical Society, 1979.

Whaley, John, ed. *A Collection of Original Poems and Translations.* London, 1745.

Whalley, Peter. *An Enquiry into the Learning of Shakespeare, with Remarks on Several Passages of His Plays, in a Conversation between Eugenius and Neander.* London, 1748.

Williams, Robert D. "Antiquarian Interest in Elizabethan Drama before Lamb." *PMLA* 53, no. 2 (June 1938): 434–44.

Williamson, George. *The Senecan Amble: A Study in Prose Form from Bacon to Collier*. Chicago: University of Chicago Press, 1951.

Wimsatt, W. K. *Philosophic Words: A Study of Style and Meaning in the "Rambler" and "Dictionary" of Samuel Johnson*. New Haven: Yale University Press, 1948.

Winstanley, William. *The Lives of the Most Famous English Poets; or, The Honour of Parnassus*. London, 1687.

Wittreich, Joseph Anthony, Jr., ed. *The Romantics on Milton: Formal Essays and Critical Asides*. Cleveland: Case Western Reserve University Press, 1970.

Wooll, John. *Biographical Memoirs of the Late Rev. Joseph Warton*. London, 1806.

Wurtsbaugh, Jewel. *Two Centuries of Spenserian Scholarship (1609–1805)*. Baltimore: Johns Hopkins University Press, 1936.

Young, Edward. *Conjectures on Original Composition: In a Letter to the Author of Sir Charles Grandison*. London, 1759.

Index